From 1874 to 1890, the company or theater of Georg II, duke of Saxe-Meiningen, toured Europe, giving over 2,500 performances that revolutionized the nineteenth-century European theater. Under the personal supervision of Georg, the Meiningen troupe introduced radical innovations in theater staging and ensemble playing, revived forgotten works and presented new ones, and delighted audiences with their historically accurate settings and costumes, most designed by Georg himself.

This study focuses on two of the many aspects of Georg's activity in the theater: the forces that shaped his ideas of theatrical art and the way he attempted to transfer those ideas to the theater. It examines, in his own words and drawings as much as possible, what he thought a drama should be like on stage and exactly what he did that made him, thirty years before Stanislavski, the first modern stage director.

Much of the book is derived from Georg's letters, only recently opened to scholars, and from the Meiningen State Archive, subsequently closed to the public. The book contains some 30 illustrations, most from Georg's own hand, of set and costume designs and blocking methods.

THE THEATER DUKE

The Theater Duke

GEORG II OF SAXE-MEININGEN
AND THE GERMAN STAGE

ANN MARIE KOLLER

STANFORD UNIVERSITY PRESS 1984
STANFORD, CALIFORNIA

SOURCES OF ILLUSTRATIONS
1-6, 8-13 (jester), 14-19, 21, 23-28, Meiningen Museum; 7, Karl Grube, *Die Meininger* (Berlin, 1904); 13 (Molière), Theatermuseum, Cologne; 20, Victoria and Albert Museum, London; 22, *Die Gartenlaube*, 1879; 29, *Pester-Lloyd*, 1888

Published with the assistance of the
Andrew W. Mellon Foundation

STANFORD UNIVERSITY PRESS, STANFORD, CALIFORNIA
© 1984 by the Board of Trustees of the Leland Stanford Junior University
Printed in the United States of America
ISBN 0-8047-1196-8   LC 82-42911

To the memory of
LEE SIMONSON,
artist, scholar, set designer,
and teacher, who introduced
me to the Theater Duke

𝕴n the third quarter of the nineteenth century, the company of the court theater of Georg II, duke of Saxe-Meiningen, toured Europe, playing in great cities and small, for seventeen consecutive years. These performances, 2,591 in all, revolutionized the concept of theater staging and earned for Georg the title "the first modern director" and the sobriquet "the Theater Duke." Much has been written about the Meininger, as his company came to be called, but little about the education and training that shaped the duke's views of art, or about how he expressed these views in his direction of the Meininger.

It was long thought that Georg, influenced by the work of Charles Kean in England, wished merely to translate a historical picture onto the stage. Nothing could have been farther from his goal. It is evident that to earn the praise of such disparate theater men as J. T. Grein, William Poel, Henry Irving, and Frank Benson, and to put his stamp on the work of other reformers like André Antoine and Constantin Stanislavski, he must have done more than put splendid pictures on the stage. That is not to say that all his innovations were healthy for the well-being of the theater, for, imitated by less able men, they led to an excess that tarnished the reputation of the Meininger.

In this study I have chosen to inquire into two of the many aspects of Georg's activity in the theater: to look at those forces that shaped his ideas of theatrical art and to describe in detail the way he attempted to transfer those ideas—and ideals—to the theater. In other words, to examine, in his own words as much as possible, what he thought a drama should look like on stage and exactly what he did that made him the first modern director. Other aspects of Georg's long and richly varied life and of his reign are not part of this story. The tours from 1874 to 1890, which deserve a history of their own, are represented here primarily as a chronicle of the productions given during those years. My comments on them are confined to details that point up some aspect of the duke's method.

Besides the collection of the duke's papers in the archives of the East German State Library, there are three great collections of material specifically related to the Meininger, much of it unstudied. One is the Carl Niessen Collection in the Theater Museum at the University of Cologne, which includes the papers of Max and Gotthold Brückner, the painters who made most of the Meininger sets; the duke's letters of instruction to them, often accompanied by sketches; and photographs. A second collection is in the Meiningen State Archive, where I was allowed to work in the 1960's, but which has since been closed to the public. There is a wealth of letters, photographs, designs, accounts, bills, and contracts in that institution, all waiting to be investigated. The third important collection—and very impressive it is—is in the Meiningen Theater Museum. The unsorted mounds of books, papers, and photographs that I saw when I first visited the museum in 1961 have been transformed into a researcher's delight, thanks to the efforts of Rolf-Dieter Meissner, director of the Meiningen Museum, and Volker Reissland, director of the Theater Museum. Housed in the Castle Elisabethenburg, the Meiningen Museum includes one floor of rooms that the duke and his family occupied. The paintings, furniture, and accessories are from their time; the duke's workroom is as he left it. The Great Hall, where the court theater first performed in the 1770's, is now the Theater Museum. In the anteroom are displayed posters, photographs, costumes, maps, and the like. The Great Hall itself is hung with some of the Brückners' original backdrops—one is from the very early *Hamlet*—and the set for *Wallensteins Lager* is on permanent display at the far end. The splendid ceiling and floors have been restored. At the time of my last visit, the old chapel was being converted into a music room, something that would certainly have pleased the duke. The Landestheater, in the city proper, has a number of restored backdrops used during the tours.

The state libraries of Munich and Vienna have Meininger holdings, and there is an abundance of research materials on theaters contemporary with Georg's in the London Theatre Museum. In the Colindale Newspaper Repository of the British Museum, I found reviews from foreign newspapers that are no longer available in their countries of origin. Both the State Library of Moscow and the State Library of Leningrad have many materials on the Meininger, and both were generous in furnishing copies; much of this material remains to be translated into one of the Western languages.

One of the pleasures of working on a project of this sort is the company we keep while doing so. For providing otherwise unobtainable materials, I thank Director Rolf-Dieter Meissner of the Meiningen Museum; Professors Barry V. Daniels (Kent, Ohio), Roswitha Flatz (Cologne), Herbert A. Frenzel (Berlin), Kirsten Gram Holmström (Stockholm), Dieter Hoffmeier (East Berlin), Ute Kösser (Leipzig), Ingeborg Krengel-Strudthoff (Berlin), and Jörn Langsted (Aarhus); dramaturge Hans Melde (Meiningen Landestheater); International Theatre Institute officers Elizabeth Burdick (New York) and Irene Geysi and staff (East Berlin); and librarians Dr. Peter Frank and staff (Stanford University), Danny Friedman (Victoria and Albert Theatre Museum), Leslie Getz (Getz Dance Library), and Dr. Hans-Erich Teitge and staff (East German State Library).

For their encouragement and good advice: Phyllis Hartnoll, Antony Hippisley-Coxe, Stanley Kauffmann, Ingrid Keller, and Birdie Rainsford; in Meiningen, Alfred Büchner and Erna Susi Trautvetter, and in Schleswig, Hartmut Gerstenhauer. For editorial assistance: Jim Armistead, Leanne Grega, Chip Haven, Robert Lyhne, and Anthony and Margaret Simmons. For reading and criticizing my manuscript: Professors Wendell Cole, William Melnitz, and Robert Sarlós. For preparation of charts and photographs: Robert Johnson and Donald Myers. For financial grants: John Borden and Michael Simmons. And finally, for the use of unpublished research: Heinz Isterheil, former intendant of the Meiningen Landestheater, and Volker Reissland, director of the Meiningen Theater Museum. Had they not been so generous in allowing me to draw on their own studies, this book could not have been written.

A.M.K.

CONTENTS

THE THEATER DUKE

INTRODUCTION

On an April day in 1874, Eduard Fritze, a loyal subject of His Serene Highness Georg II, duke of Saxe-Meiningen, Hildburghausen, and Saalfeld, paused to look at the notices posted on an advertising column in Berlin. His eye was immediately caught by a poster announcing the first of a series of performances to be given the following month by the Meiningen court theater. He read the details with astonishment—and with heartfelt anguish. He saw his provincial homeland making itself ridiculous by offering its theatricals to the capital city; and he could already picture the condescending smiles of his Berlin acquaintances.[1]

If any Berliners had even thought about it, they would have agreed. A guest appearance was a familiar event, but the guest had always been a star, not an entire company with its own scenery, properties, costumes, and orchestra. What could a tiny, provincial court theater contribute to the cultural life of a people who had already seen the finest in staging and acting? Within the past decade, Prussia had achieved preeminence among the German lands; and Berlin, just four years after the founding of the Empire, had suddenly grown large and supremely conscious of its importance as the capital of the new nation.

Despite his misgivings, on the evening of May 1 Fritze found his way to the Friedrich-Wilhelmstädtisches Theater to see the troupe's first performance. They were giving Shakespeare's *Julius Caesar*. He saw with satisfaction that the theater was filled to the last place, but he knew that complimentary tickets had been generously distributed to members of the press and to other influential people. This was not the usual theater audience. Distinguished and reserved, it seemed to be made up entirely of critics.

I

The play began. The first two acts were politely applauded; everyone seemed satisfied. Then came the third act. "The audience became all eyes, all ears, all breathless suspense! The viewers in the balcony and the loges leaned farther and farther over the railings. Then came the scene with Mark Antony! It was a masterpiece of individual and ensemble working together effectively, something not yet seen on the German stage. When at the end of Act III the Roman citizen Cinna cried out in a bitter voice, 'Rend him! Tear him to pieces! Everything to the torch!,' and the curtain fell swiftly, there arose a storm of applause unlike any the theater had seen or heard before.* Everyone jumped from his seat, shouting triumphantly and exultingly. Again and again actors were recalled with thunderous bravos! The applause would not subside." [2]

Julius Caesar was the first of forty-seven performances in Berlin that changed the direction of the German stage and pointed it unswervingly toward modern theater practice. Some twenty years later, the literary historian Berthold Litzmann commented, in a lecture to students at Bonn University:

The impression made by the first appearance of the Meininger on May 1, 1874— they gave *Julius Caesar*—is difficult to describe. . . . You yourselves cannot know from your own experience what took place in a production of a drama by Shakespeare, Schiller, or Goethe on the German stage before the appearance of the Meininger; therefore, you can hardly imagine how that company affected us in those days. Everything they brought was effectively a new creation. One of the most worn-out pieces of the classical repertoire, *Die Räuber*, which so strongly bore the stamp of the Sturm und Drang period on its language and on its whole world of ideas that it was no longer expected to make any impression on modern audiences—yes, even that, as it was first given by the Meininger, seemed like a première. What Schiller, that most gifted poet of the modern stage—for Shakespeare created his dramas for a different kind of stage—imagined in the development of his mass scenes was first truly expressed one hundred years later. And that constitutes the permanent contribution and merit of the Meininger: they have set the poet again on the throne, they have made him master of the stage, and they have put the art of the actor again in its rightful place as an attendant art. [3]

Litzmann's words give some inkling of the extent of Georg of Meiningen's reforms, but in order to understand his work, we must first under-

---

* By the time Fritze wrote this article, 50 years may have confused his memory, for the poet Cinna does not speak these words in Shakespeare's play; a Roman citizen says them of him. But Georg did make such changes in his acting versions of Shakespeare. We will see another notable example in the discussion of the *Merchant of Venice*, where words are put into Shylock's mouth that are spoken by others in the original. For staging purposes on the road, Georg also often condensed the number of acts and scenes to avoid shifting locales.

stand the artistic conditions in the German theater before the Meininger appeared. In the 1870's, Germany had no national theater, nothing, certainly, comparable to Drury Lane or Covent Garden, much less the Comédie Française. In fact, for years there had been two "theaters" in Germany: the public, usually municipal, theater (Stadttheater) and the court theater (Hoftheater). Great cities like Hamburg, Leipzig, Frankfurt am Main, Cologne, and Breslau possessed large, often magnificent, theaters administered directly by city officials. Other public theaters fell into two groups, those belonging to a city and managed by someone appointed by the city, and those belonging to a city or a private party that were leased to individuals for their own undertakings.

By the end of the eighteenth century, most of the court theaters in Germany, once merely protected and supported by the ruling princes for their own amusement, had been taken over entirely by their noble patrons.[4] The ruler or his surrogate, usually the court chamberlain, made all the appointments, determined the salaries of the theater personnel, and paid their pensions. The theater manager (the intendant) was usually drawn from court circles: officers, aristocrats with artistic pretensions, noble lovers of leading actresses, and in one case, at the Vienna Burgtheater, the court theater of the Habsburgs, the so-called Head Officer of the Kitchens. Sometimes, in a progressive court, an actor was chosen, as was Ernst von Possart in Munich. Occasionally, a famous writer was selected to add prestige to the theater, as was Friedrich von Bodenstedt in Meiningen. These intendants sought out the best actors, the leading dramaturges, the most outstanding orchestra leaders and stage directors. Since few of them knew anything about dramatic art, they depended on agents, unless the ruler himself took a hand. Occasionally, they made a lucky selection, and if they were wise enough to relinquish control of the stage and its work to people who knew their craft, the theater might flower, but rarely was this the case.

That the court theater did not become entirely the plaything of the court was more than the result of lucky chance and destiny. There were aristocrats of conviction and taste, like Prince Kaunitz in Vienna and Baron von Dahlberg in Mannheim; writers like Gotthold Lessing in Hamburg and Goethe in Weimar; scholars like Johann Christoph Gottsched and Joseph von Sonnenfels; and not least, the great actors of the early times.[5] And there were the August Ifflands, August Klingemanns, Heinrich Marrs, Karl Immermanns, and Eduard Devrients, too, fanatical reformers all. Yet it remained to the ruling prince to seal the fate of the court theater with his means, his interest, and his character.

When Georg II became the duke of Meiningen in 1866, the state of the theater in the German-speaking countries was at a low point. In the revolutionary period of 1848 and the following years of reaction there had been a break with the old classical theater traditions. Friedrich Hebbel was the last representative of the great German drama, and after him—with the possible exception of Otto Ludwig—came no dramatist strong enough to forge a new theater. The breach between the literary theorists, who decried the deterioration of the drama, and the theater managers, who were forced to fill their stages with whatever paid at the box office, seemed unbridgeable. In the 1850's and 1860's, only a few isolated managers—Heinrich Laube in Vienna, Franz Dingelstedt in Weimar, and Eduard Devrient in Karlsruhe—made a serious effort to distinguish their stages. Elsewhere, the presentation of the spoken drama was mediocre at best, and sometimes ridiculous.

The repertoire was trivialized to meet the demand of an increasingly uneducated audience. Anything to entice a public seeking light entertainment was reckoned good enough: French comedies, pastiches, farces, or extravaganzas so expensive that they had to reuse their decorations year after year.[6] The instability of the repertoire made the educated public mistrustful, then increasingly indifferent, before it abandoned the theater entirely to a less discriminating audience. On February 26, 1876, Josef Kainz, who was just beginning his acting career in Marburg, wrote his parents, "This is terrible! Not a single classical piece anymore. Nothing but operettas, farces, comedies! I detest learning them."[7] Joseph Schreyvogel's prophecy had come to pass: "The theater of a nation must be based on classical works if it is to be worthy of its destiny. Without a repertoire of such works, we shall have neither a tragic nor a comic stage, nor a public which knows how to understand them, nor actors who know how to play in them."[8]

Since no worthwhile contemporary drama was being written, it might be asked why the classics were not resorted to. Germany had a great storehouse of native drama, plays by Lessing, Goethe, Schiller, and Kleist, as well as translations of Shakespeare, Molière, and Calderón. Most of the world's great drama had appeared in Germany, often in distinguished translations; but the theater-going public had little training in understanding such literature. And, more practically, few theater managers knew their business well enough to engage directors who could do more than push one poorly prepared production after the other on stage. In 1867, in the course of six months, one of Germany's leading court theaters, with a staff of eighty including the opera chorus, presented sixteen productions new to the cast and director, including four grand operas, and gave new productions of six plays that had been done earlier, including two grand operas. Such a program was common. Dress rehearsals were unknown; the most important person on the stage was the prompter.[9]

The actor had little time for training; he hardly had time to learn his lines. That actors could perform at all under these conditions was due to the *Fach*, or stock-character system, borrowed from the commedia dell'arte. Although the system was never a law in the theater, it was a universal and binding custom, often written into contracts.[10] An actor was engaged according to his category, and all the roles that by custom belonged to that category were his if they were in his repertoire. These were precisely defined in first and second categories, which were represented on all stages.

The roles in the first category were the First Hero, the Youthful Hero, the Heroic Father, the Young Character Actor, the Young Comic, and the Bon Vivant. The corresponding feminine roles were the First Heroine, the First Sentimental, the Heroic Mother, the Comic Old Lady, the Innocent Naïve, and the Soubrette. This basic group made up the personnel of all nineteenth-century German theaters, large and small; but the roles were not necessarily divided the same way in all companies. For example, in some theaters the Shy Lover might be played by the Young Hero, in others by the Fop. Every theater had a role book listing the categories at use there and the roles assigned to the first categories.[11]

Actors engaged in the second category held no exclusive right to any role and were almost always required to take part in the chorus of the opera and to appear in any crowd scenes. Among these secondary actors, the most important were the First and Second "Chargen," who usually played the roles in which emotion was exaggerated or carried to excess. Frequently these roles, although not always large or leading, were decisive in the drama. Shylock in *The Merchant of Venice* was a Chargen role.

When an actor finished the season, appraised his velvet, and packed his paints, he compiled a list of all the roles he had studied, had played, and could play the following season. This list he submitted with his other qualifications to an agent, who then applied to theaters; or the actor might represent (or misrepresent) himself with such a list. This was his "repertoire," and if he was engaged for the first category, he had the right to play all the roles in that category and in his repertoire. The great temptation for an actor was to lay claim to all the roles in a category whether he had mastered them or not. This was a dangerous practice, for if a director had to substitute a piece at the last moment, the actor was supposed to be ready to play any role he claimed in his repertoire.

This system was to the advantage of the engaged actors, who clung to their rights; and such rights were scrupulously respected by theaters. The disadvantage to the drama is obvious and can be assessed by observing only one category, that of the Sentimental. A tender voice, a soulful glance, were enough, says Eduard von Winterstein, to destine a young actress for this category, which included such important roles as Luise in Schiller's *Kabale und Liebe*, Gretchen in Goethe's *Faust*, and, as one might guess, Shakespeare's Juliet and Ophelia. Even a gifted actress would find it difficult to excel in these greatly different roles, but there was not a young actress engaged in this category who would not have stood on her rights to play them. They were in her category, so they were hers.

When the Sentimental grew too old to play Juliet or Gretchen, she changed to the category Heroine, with predictably laughable results.[12] The grand duke in *Der Prinz von Homburg* calls Natalie "little daughter," "sweet child" and "little niece," but the "sweet child" was usually a middle-aged and often stoutish woman. When Don Carlos whispered ecstatically to an Eboli old enough to be his mother, "sweet soulful maiden," the effect was ridiculous.[13] Lessing's twenty-one-year-old Minna von Barnhelm was in this category, and there was not a Heroine on the German stage who would allow this part to slip from her hands. "Is it any wonder," asks Winterstein, "that no one cared to see this piece, and it was given only to schoolchildren?" When an actress became too old even to attempt the Heroine category, she would be reborn, albeit reluctantly, as the Heroic Mother.

With Fach book in hand, even the most inept director had no difficulty in casting a play. He merely determined the traditionally assigned roles and chose those actors who had been engaged for the categories into which they fell. Suitability was rarely a consideration; time and custom had decided everything. The director did his part if he saw to it that the actor entered and left at the right time, stood on the right part of the stage, knew his lines reasonably well, and was not a nuisance. It would not have occurred to the average director to try to influence the action in any way. Even if he had had an idea for a new way to stage a scene, he would not have had time to work it out. And "if the director had had the effrontery, not to say the impudence, to try to give any actor of the first category any advice on how to play his role, it would probably have led to blows."[14] Few directors had the skill or the spirit to maintain discipline on the stage, and rehearsals became scenes of carelessness, capriciousness, quarrelsomeness, and selfishness. Any young actor with the temerity to introduce a new interpretation of a role would almost certainly have been driven from the stage by his colleagues, reproached for holding up the rehearsal, and accused of "arrogance," the one characteristic no actor could forgive in another.[15]

Since the rehearsal was the only place where a young actor could get practical instruction, few actors had much training. Even the court theaters, most of which fostered the art of acting for its own sake, and many of which had brilliant individual actors, rarely produced an ensemble. That drama was made up of an interplay of many characters, and that a small role might add to the effectiveness of the whole production, does not seem to have occurred to the average management. This was especially true of the public theaters, where the personnel changed from year to year. Even supposing an actor had learned to speak, he was not apt to have learned to listen and to react to the words of his colleagues. Each actor was absorbed in his own performance—and intent on defending it against any and all interference.

The formal, elevated style of speaking of the Weimar school had by now deteriorated into mere declamation; yet many actors continued to use it, although their colleagues on stage may have learned a more natural manner. Each actor repeated the roles of his repertoire with no thought of accommodating the style of another actor. Everyone played for himself. "Whoever could scream the loudest, roll his eyes the most violently, and almost pull the wings from their hinges—he was the greatest actor." [16]

Monologues were not rehearsed. That "wasted the time" of the other actors. Actors "indicated" what they were going to do; that is, cues were given, but no actual words were spoken except on the night of the performance. Nor did actors rehearse in the full spirit or feeling of their roles. [17] If a part called for great passion or stormy emotion, the actor showed he realized this by opening his mouth very wide as he spoke in his ordinary voice. So much was left to the inspiration of the evening that only a public lacking in education and taste could have accepted the results. Such were the practices on the better, so-called well-managed stages. The situation in the small theaters was much worse, as can be seen from the accounts of actors who started their careers there. [18]

The setting of the dramas was no better. In contrast to the elaborate productions of the opera, operetta, circus, and variety—for which the best artistic talents of the time were employed—the scenery and technical effects for the spoken drama were shameful. Most scenes, interior and exterior, were played in wings with a backdrop painted in perspective. Usually cast off from the property room of the opera, the sets were general enough to be used for every play in any period: "the woods," "the park," "the old German city." Furniture was painted on walls, flowers on bushes, storms on clear skies, bottles on shop windows. Few sets were designed for a particular drama; and when, on rare occasion, a backdrop was commissioned, it was usually a beautiful picture with little relation to the action on stage.

7

The scene was seldom narrowed; actors were dwarfed by the size of the stage; and since they had to move in a painted perspective, they dared not move upstage, lest they tower over trees or declaim into second-story windows. Little use was made of levels, elevations, or step units; doors rarely opened, windows almost never. The German theater at that time did not consider itself an agency of illusion. In a performance at the Berlin Königliches Schauspielhaus, the "first theater" of Germany, the ghost of Hamlet's father crossed the stage in front of the footlights, allowing his "incorporeal" body to block the audience's view of Horatio and Marcellus. The shade's subsequent descent to the underworld was accomplished by much grinding and scraping of the trap. Well, "maybe not at the Schauspielhaus—everything was well oiled there—but everywhere else." [19]

On May 8, 1874, the same week Berlin saw the first appearance of the Meininger, the internationally celebrated actor Ernesto Rossi appeared as Othello at the Victoria-Theater. The magazine *Die Gegenwart*'s review of the production was blistering:

Without doubt Rossi is one of the greatest living tragedians. The company that serves as his counterfoil certainly does not contribute to the elevation of his art, but it does not detract much either. It is a shame, however, that the accoutrement on which the Victoria-Theater prides itself—not without some right—is in the case of the Italian star so unpardonably wretched. A Venetian street in Othello's day with gas lanterns and an inn sign on which the viewer can read through his opera glasses BEER SOLD HERE, an interior in Cyprus with dark red armchairs like those we are used to seeing in the waiting room of a little-employed dentist in a small town, Desdemona's bedroom with an alcove so drafty that the dirty red curtains had to be held together by a stagehand so they would not flutter—well, all that goes beyond being funny. [20]

Costuming was in no less sorry a state. Early in the century Count von Brühl, intendant of the Berlin Königliches Schauspielhaus, had attempted a small reform, introducing costumes that were historical in cut, tasteful in color, and in other ways attractive. Unfortunately, they were not particular to the characters who would wear them—young or old, rich or poor—and the actors resisted the change on finding themselves the object of laughter as they all appeared on the same stage in garments identical in cut, design, and color. So long as actresses had to provide their own costumes—which was the case until the end of the century—there could be little regulation of the garments they wore. Only the most dedicated artist would choose a costume to fit her role rather than to enhance her appearance. So like everything else in the theater of the spoken word, the costumes became traditional: "the knight's costume," "the Spanish costume," "the rococo," and so on. As the saying went, "Before Christ, naked legs [naturally, in knitted tights; no actor would have appeared on stage with bare legs]; after Christ, knight's boots." [21]

Actors almost never rehearsed in costume; often the actor did not see what he was to wear until the evening of the performance. Paul Heyse, dramatist and novelist, remembered a performance he had seen in Berlin:

> I still recall from my youth a performance of *Götz* at the Königliches Schauspielhaus in which the first scene took place in front of an inn. There was a small, brown-painted table with skinny legs standing in the middle of the stage. In the background was a shabby forest drop, on the left a projecting inn, on the right a few meager tree wings. At the table, in glassy tin armor, sat the Knight Götz; opposite him was Brother Martin, dressed in a new brown habit. Nothing was reminiscent of the past, for even in the case of the costumes, it was easy to see that only a superficial attempt had been made to fit them to the different stations. Above all, they were clean and fresh as befitted the Königliches Schauspielhaus. I remember, too, seeing in *Nathan der Weise* the Knight Templar in his freshly laundered cloak on the corner of which had been painted a small brown spot as a symbol that he had just rescued a maiden from a burning house. [22]

The general decadence of the drama and the lamentable conditions on most stages worked to the advantage of one group in the theater, those actors whose dramatic talents or personalities made them stars. The Fach system, with its assurance that every actor in the first category had a firm hold on all roles in his repertoire, led to role monopoly. Especially in the court theaters, where there was little turnover in personnel, an actor could gradually gather to himself all the effective parts and discourage the engagement of possible rivals. [23]

From role monopoly it was only a step to the star system, where leading actors took as their personal property, not only lines and parts, but whole plays. Dramas were rewritten to give the star the best lines and situations, and to lift from the roles of others any effective lines that could not be added to those of the star. The new titles for old plays are instructive: *Twelfth Night*, *Cymbeline*, and *The Winter's Tale* became *Viola*, *Imogen*, and *Hermione*. An actress in *Viola* was accustomed to playing both Viola and Sebastian. Possart turned *The Merchant of Venice* into a revenge play for Shylock. Actors regularly played both Karl and Franz Moor in Schiller's *Die Räuber*, and one actor, Wilhelm Kunst, is reported to have arranged a version of *Hamlet* in which he played both Claudius and the prince. The entire field of classical drama became fair game: lines, speeches, and even whole scenes were transferred from one play to another. The German actor habitually ignored Lessing's dictum that "it is easier to wrest the club from Hercules than to remove one verse from Shakespeare."[24]

The comic stars, for their part, increasingly fell into an especially offensive practice. It was not new; Shakespeare himself had advised the clowns not to speak more than was set down for them. They added jokes to the plays: local witticisms, often crude and frequently obscene. These were never rehearsed. The comic merely said, "Put a red cross at that place and tonight I'll make a joke." No one, not the director, not the rest of the cast, probably not even the actor himself, knew what would be added to the performance. Over the years, Gustav Freytag's *Die Journalisten* had accumulated a number of silly and tasteless jokes with which the comics thought to enliven their acting. At a performance of his play at the court theater in Wiesbaden, Freytag turned angrily to the actor Friedrich Haase and asked, "Who did you say wrote this play?" It was only because of Freytag's strong objections that his play was restored to its original form, for the directors had neither the discipline nor the courage to override the demands of the stars.[25] Intendants used the stars to entice the alienated public back into the theater, and their success was such that people no longer came to see a play; they came to admire a virtuoso in however indifferent a production.

The guest appearance, the logical extension of the star system, proved still more detrimental to the well-being of the theater. There were, to be sure, some genuinely gifted artists from Berlin or Vienna—or even from Paris or London—who visited theaters and played from their repertoire, names like Emil Devrient, Josef Lewinsky, Sarah Bernhardt, and Jenny Lind. In 1857 the American Negro tragedian Ira Aldridge toured Germany, and in 1859 Samuel Phelps brought a company from England. But there were also many actors of the second rank, who having made a name for themselves in one role, traveled from stage to stage in it for the rest of their careers. It was said of the actor Pander, who went from theater to theater playing the foot doctor, Hirsch, in *Heines junge Leiden*, that he was a virtuoso in that part, unbearable in all others. The most famous of all these wandering stars—in the 1880's he "traveled" across the United States from New York to San Francisco—was Friedrich Haase, who played many classical parts, but whose name is always remembered in connection with the hero Thorane in Karl Gutzkow's *Der Königsleutnant*.

These visiting stars brought glamor and excitement for a few evenings, but benefited only themselves. When they left, the resident company was impoverished artistically and financially. The already poor repertoire was destroyed when the actors had to learn the star's version of the proposed play and hold several rehearsals without him. On the day of the performance, the much-traveled star arrived, attended a rehearsal, then took the stage, threw cues to the local actors, and expected them to do as well in their roles as he did in a part he had played a hundred times. The actors saw the usually indifferent public wildly applauding the guest, throwing wreaths and bouquets. Next day they could read in the newspaper an account of the contrast between the brilliance of the guest and their own ineptitude and insensibility. Yet the mania grew, to the point where many theaters almost lived on the appearance of guest stars.[26]

The star lived on the favor of the masses; it was he who got the applause, not only at the end of the scene, but during it. He had to receive wreaths, poems, and bouquets on the open stage lest it be said that he had only been able to earn a *succès d'estime.*[27] This search for public adulation eventually led to a shameful corruption of both the stars and the newspapers.

During the classical and romantic periods only the purely literary weekly and monthly journals carried theatrical reviews and essays on dramatic works. Even then many editors and essayists used their positions to praise or criticize, mention or ignore, theatrical events, by way of bringing writers and players to heel. Adolf Bäuerle, editor of the Vienna *Theaterzeitung*, and his spiteful companion, Moritz Saphir, terrified a generation of artists. As theater activity increased and most of the critics went over from the literary periodicals to the daily newspapers, their influence began to color all theatrical and literary endeavors. "Under a thousand masks, extortion sought to make directors, dramatists, and actors, first submissive, then beholden to the critics."[28]

The stars fawned on the journalists and obliged them with free tickets and invitations. Some critics were for sale, but they demanded tribute. The "visit to the editor" became obligatory. As soon as a guest star arrived in a city, he had to make a personal visit to the local drama critic to pay his respects. No actor, however celebrated, dared flout this custom.* Indeed, some critics were not satisfied merely to write approvingly or disapprovingly about an actor, but felt it was their duty to arrange claques to approve or disapprove entire performances.

Add to all this a censor to whom all plays to be given on the public

---

* Even when this practice was at its height, some editors disapproved of it. It was not uncommon to see the advertisement in the theater section of the newspaper: VISITS TO THEATRICAL CRITICS NOT ALLOWED. Max Kurnik placed a visiting card on his office door: OFFICE HOURS: 2-3 AFTERNOONS. Then he made sure not to be there at that time. Later the Union of Theater Workers freed their members from this subservient duty, but they were never able to force all newspapers to remove the requirement. We know it was still in force in Berlin in 1874 because Ludwig Barnay had to make such a visit when he appeared with the Meiningen company.

stage had to be submitted, and who on moral or political grounds demanded small and large changes or refused permission to stage any drama. Words did not escape his watchful eye, nor did whole plays. Until the middle of the century, *Egmont*, *Wilhelm Tell*, and *King John* were forbidden in Berlin because of their political tendencies. Other plays were banned because of their "immoral" language or social attitudes. *A Doll's House* was not presented until the ending was changed to permit a reconciliation between husband and wife. *Ghosts* was banned entirely until the end of the century. Countless other examples could be given.

Contemporary literary and theatrical theorists viewed the decay in the theater with deep misgiving, some, even, without hope. Most of them agreed with the critic Julius Steiner that by 1849 the great time of the court theater was over,[29] but a backward look reveals that at the very time these despairing words were written, there were emerging in Germany forces strong enough to revitalize the drama and re-animate the theater. From its infancy the German theater regarded itself as a means of education and as a touchstone of the deepest desires and hopes of the nation. After 1850, this mission was vital. The theater became the substitute for those hopes that had been growing in the middle class since 1797, and that had been shattered by the Revolution of 1848. If the burghers could not achieve the political emancipation they hoped for, they could at least shape the theater into a social institution. In the central squares of large cities, citizens raised municipal theaters that rivaled in beauty and magnificence the finest of the old court theaters.

As the newspaper *Grenzeboten* noted, on the occasion of the dedication of the Stadttheater in Leipzig in 1868: "The German theater has achieved increasing importance for the education of the nation. In all outstanding cities, our stages are a regular pleasure, their productions work an immeasurable effect on the thought and sensitivity of the people." Forced into this role, the theater, "as the conscience of the nation, the integration-point of middle-class desires and hopes, the seat of self-identity of middle-class society, has become the subject of general interest."[30] The audience that filled the theater was largely uneducated, the repertoire trivial, and the art of the actor debased, but there was a growing awareness of the powerful part the theater could play in the life of the nation. There were already men active in the field whose efforts were decisive in the reforms Georg of Meiningen would carry out. Seven men in particular directly or indirectly influenced his work: Ludwig Tieck, Heinrich Laube, Franz Dingelstedt, Eduard Devrient, and Richard Wagner in Germany; and Samuel Phelps and Charles Kean in England.

Ludwig Tieck, poet, playwright, and translator, came to Berlin in 1841 at the invitation of the king of Prussia and there turned to directing at the Königliches Schauspielhaus under the intendant Theodore Küstner, himself a reformer. Tieck's first effort in Berlin, Racine's *Athalie*, given in antique dress, was unsuccessful, but the following year he presented *Antigone*, set to Mendelssohn's music, to great acclaim. He followed this with performances of *Oedipus at Colonos*, *Medea*, and *Hippolytus*. These were well received, but it was readily seen that they could secure no permanent place in the repertoire. Tieck consequently turned to the dramas of Shakespeare, many of which he had translated and adapted in a masterly way. Before he retired from the theater in 1847 at the age of seventy-four, he had brought seventeen of Shakespeare's dramas to the stage. Unfortunately, only one of them had any lasting success, the comedy *A Midsummer Night's Dream*, which he set on his idea of the Shakespearean stage. Earlier, with the aid of an architect, he had reconstructed a stage from the plans of an Elizabethan theater, The Fortune, but complicated it with so many stairs and levels that it lost much of the value he had hoped for.[31]

Karl Lebrecht Immermann, who hoped the theater he operated in Düsseldorf from 1832 to 1837 might serve as a model for a national theater, was another early reformer bent on developing the powers of the actor, enriching the repertoire, elevating the theatrical arts, and, by those reforms, educating the public. The dramas of Shakespeare, Schiller, Calderón, and Kleist were among the classics he presented. He introduced the plays of the Austrians Johann Nestroy and Ferdinand Raimund, presented middle-class pieces of stark reality by Friedrich Ludwig Schröder, August Kotzebue, and August Wilhelm Iffland, and produced many experimental plays by Tieck, Christian Dietrich Grabbe, and Byron. Careful rehearsals, the use of original texts, and the introduction of a stage architecturally designed to bring actors and audience closer together were all part of his method.

If Immermann had had more time, received more help, and had more money, perhaps he would have been Germany's first modern director, but theatrical conditions in Düsseldorf and the fanaticism of the man himself—he refused to compromise any detail of his "beautiful theater"—brought about the collapse of the entire enterprise. At the time he said, "Who knows when the spirit of this undertaking may fall and where it may rise again in a new guise?" It appeared twenty years later in Vienna with the appointment of Heinrich Laube as the stage director of the Habsburg court theater, the Burgtheater.[32]

Laube, born in Breslau in 1806, came to the Burgtheater by way of a long road from his father's stonemasonry shop. He had been by turns a theology student, a member of the Junges Deutschland movement (which got him jailed for his political opinions in 1835), a political writer, a magazine editor, a theater critic, a dramatist, and a stage manager. At the Burgtheater, like Tieck before him, he eventually turned to Shakespeare, whose plays he had met as a twenty-three-year-old in the Hamlet of Wilhelm Kunst and the Shylock of Karl Seydelmann.[33]

The times were ready for him. When he took over as director at the Burgtheater on July 26, 1851, it had been nearly fifty years since the middle class had last installed one of their own on the stage of a great theatrical institution. He found the intendant, the Polish Count Lanchoronsky, in full artistic power. The stiff-necked Laube set himself against the over-organized intendant, and for the next seventeen years he battled to maintain strict discipline, create an effective ensemble, and reduce the power of the stars. "The principal duty of a stage director," he said, "is to recognize the pulse of real life. That serves the drama and it serves the actor."[34] Later he asked himself, "What is the essential of a theater director? My wife said, 'Industry, attention, skill.' But I said, 'Creation is essential. Patience and industry belong to it, but only as an aid. Only when theater direction can create will it be respected. For creation I need actors and I need plays.'"[35] Patience, luck, and a great deal of money built a company of the greatest German-speaking actors of the time. Laube's shrewdness and devotion to the best in literature shaped the repertoire.

His style was all simplicity, based entirely on the development of speech, drill, untiring polishing, cultivation through inner and outer discipline, and a strong sense of duty.[36] There was, says Friedrich Rosenthal, much of the Prussian schoolmaster in him, and one of the marks of his management of the Burgtheater was the synthesis of the charm and warmth of southern Germany with the strength of duty and puritanism of the north. This puritanism showed in the severity of his stage pictures. "Laube," said the playwright and critic Paul Lindau, "was all ear and no eye."[37] Laube followed the basic principles set forth in Goethe's words:

I did not look to magnificent scenery, and a brilliant wardrobe, but I looked to good pieces. From tragedy to farce every species was welcome; but a piece was obliged to have something in it to find favor. It was necessary that it should be great and clever, cheerful and graceful, and at all events, healthy and containing some pith. All that was morbid, weak, lachrymose, and sentimental, as well as all that was frightful, horrible, and offensive to decorum, was utterly excluded; I should have feared, by such expedients, to spoil both actors and audience.[38]

Laube himself applied the words "wallpaper direction" to the work of directors like Franz Dingelstedt and Georg of Meiningen. In turn "horse stalls" was the name given to the plain settings he put on the stage. He defended himself with these words:

Décor has worked its way up to become the essential element of dramatic production. The words of the poet become lost in the distractions offered the eye. I have always preferred to spend money for good actors instead of beautiful settings. Scenic luxury and wallpaper direction lead to a dissipation of the attention that the public should devote to the poetry; they lead to a decline of the drama. . . . I don't deny that I really may have sinned in the point of settings during my direction. *King Phillip* [probably Schiller's *Don Carlos*] had really threadbare rooms; I was probably duty-bound to provide better carpets and furniture. But in those days the public was entirely *á la* Goethe; it was satisfied with dusky Spanish furniture. It was more important to hear Schiller's words.[39]

If Laube left to later directors the task of outfitting the stage, that does not detract from what he did accomplish. He united in one person the stage director and the dramaturge; he unified the word and the action to achieve a complete production. He brought to the task, as did Goethe and Immermann, interest, love, and artistic sensibility; but he also brought knowledge and experience, sharp and understanding observation and criticism of theatrical activity. He had a practical view of the necessity and possibility of stage reform in the German theater, and he proceeded positively, but prudently, in his reform efforts.[40]

What made Laube the prototype of the modern director was his system—his manner of work, above all his activity on the set. He selected and produced all his plays himself. His repertoire proved the truth of his famous statement that anyone living in Vienna for a few years could see everything current and precious that the German stage possessed. *Julius Caesar, Henry IV, Coriolanus, The Comedy of Errors, Richard III, Much Ado About Nothing, Twelfth Night, Cymbeline, Antony and Cleopatra, A Midsummer Night's Dream, Macbeth,* and *Richard II* took the stage next to the works of Schiller, Kleist, and the young authors Otto Ludwig, Gustav Freytag, and Karl Gutzkow. The Vienna public showed great interest in social plays, and Laube found in them fruitful soil for intensive ensemble work. Every production, whether a French comedy of manners or a classic, received the same careful attention.

Laube cast everything himself without any consideration of Fach. His independent nature caused him to engage personnel only as "actors." He selected performers on the basis of talent and personality, and it could happen that he entrusted a serious role to a comic or a humorous role to a serious actor. He liked to experiment with his actors, and enjoyed surprising success in unconventional casting. He began every production with a reading rehearsal attended by the entire cast, the prompters, the stage directors, even the orchestra conductor if there was music in the piece. He often read one of the roles himself, for he had a remarkable reading talent. "He can bring tears or laughter," said one critic. "To hear Laube read is a real artistic treat."[41] After the first rehearsal, which he called the "placement rehearsal," he began drilling the actors with only one goal in mind: to bring out the motivation and complexities of the plot by means of the spoken word. Everything was subordinated to clarity and comprehension. He built the ensemble carefully, but used it only to give force and variety to the speech. The ensemble as part of the stage picture held no interest for him; that became the primary concern of his successor at the Burgtheater, Franz Dingelstedt.

Dingelstedt not only continued Laube's work, but added color, music, and romantic passion; his became the first German theater of the painter and costumer. Like Laube, Dingelstedt came to the theater via a long and troubled road. The son of a Hessian prison official, he was at first a schoolteacher, but was dismissed after the publication of a book of poetry. Years of political danger and troubles resulting from his satirical writings, and years of journalistic wandering followed, before he took a position at the court theater in Stuttgart as librarian and reader to the duke of Württemburg. When he was appointed dramaturge at the Königliches-Theater in Munich, the middle-class again saw one of their own in a decisive position.

In Munich, Dingelstedt began the work that was to make him famous. He became "perhaps the only German theater man known to the world and of whom the world—with bated breath—spoke."[42] Lacking Laube's energy and puritanical sense of duty, Dingelstedt never pursued his predecessor's method of drill or paid the same attention to fine detail and to the development of the actor. For him the outer was always preferable to the inner, but he continued Laube's basic principle of developing an ensemble as opposed to promoting the individual actor.[43] He was a master at creating "atmosphere," though that was not his main aim. Sensitive to the lyrical and musical elements of the drama, he worked to illuminate the decorative in the drama as well as in the setting.

For the first German Industrial Fair, in Munich in 1854, Dingelstedt organized a combined guest appearance of many of the great stars of the German stage and coined a new word for his presentation, *Gesamtgastspiel*. Set on his "model stage," the ensemble of stars was to play according to the Dingelstedt art principle, but he was not able to weld a variety of styles into one whole. The stars were too accustomed to playing the virtuoso to submit themselves to group acting. The venture was a critical success, however; both the foreign and the German press were enthusiastic. The greatest works of the German drama were played to sold-out houses until a cholera epidemic brought an end to the Industrial Fair, and with it, to the *Gesamtgastspiel*.[44]

In 1857 Dingelstedt became director of the court theater in Weimar, and in his ten years there he restored the sorry little stage—once Germany's theatrical pride—to a place next to the court opera with its brilliant conductors, Franz Liszt and Richard Wagner. For Schiller's centenary in 1859, he produced the entire Wallenstein trilogy, something not seen in its entirety for decades. Later, Friedrich Hebbel's full *Nibelungen* was given in the presence of the author.

In this same period, Dingelstedt was building the work with which his name is coupled, the presentation of the Shakespeare Histories, from *Richard II* to *Richard III*, in commemoration of the third centenary of Shakespeare's birth. The original eight five-act dramas, connected by both plot and poetry, had never appeared in full on the modern stage, even in England. Now Dingelstedt dared to propose to give all the plays in sequence when the centenary began on April 23, 1864.

This ambitious program aroused great interest throughout Germany. The accomplishment of the ensemble, and the extravagant scenery and costumes, received the highest praise. The critic Adolph Starr thought that as a director, Dingelstedt was "doubtless the best of his kind in Germany," but he disliked the "capricious adaptation." Dingelstedt had used the translation of Wilhelm August Schlegel, but announced that although he would treat the text "piously," he would treat it "freely." This he did, causing the critic Michael Georg Conrad to complain: "It is not enough for him to omit, shorten, and rearrange whole scenes. . . . He discovers new motives . . . adds whole scenes, all with the aim of heightening stage effect."[45] Georg of Meiningen, who over the years had seen much of Dingelstedt's work in Weimar, said only of the cycle, which he saw in its entirety, that it was "interesting."

Eleven years later, Dingelstedt repeated the cycle in Vienna. This marked the beginning of years devoted to the work of Shakespeare, with productions of *The Tempest*, *Antony and Cleopatra*, *Macbeth*, and *The Winter's Tale*. Throughout the remainder of his career, Dingelstedt preferred to direct Shakespeare's dramas, but they were always shortened, cut, rearranged—often, as in the case of *The Winter's Tale*, almost mangled. Set to music by Friedrich von Flotow, as was *A Midsummer Night's Dream*, it became little more than a beautiful operetta with a corps de ballet.

The work of both Laube and Dingelstedt became famous throughout the German-speaking world. Laube wrote volumes, setting forth his aims. Editors, stars, and directors were invited to watch him work, to sit with him at his *Regietisch* (director's table) and observe his methods. Laube-trained actors appeared on every stage in Germany, and on many in France and England. Laube had all the disdain of a middle-class man who had struggled along a hard road to success, for the seemingly easily achieved accomplishments of a ruling prince. He never passed up the opportunity to express that disdain; yet Georg of Meiningen admired Laube as a man and imitated his methods as a director in nearly every detail. He saw countless Laube productions and followed the director to the Vienna Stadttheater when Laube was forced out of the Burgtheater.

Georg knew Dingelstedt's work also, possibly as early as 1854, the year of the Munich Industrial Fair, but certainly by 1857. For one thing, Dingelstedt was a master publicist, who made use of any means available to widen his reputation. But in any case, Georg learned of Dingelstedt's methods from Baron Carl von Stein, the first intendant with whom he worked on the Meiningen stage.

Few Germans, even in theatrical circles, knew that contemporary with Laube and Dingelstedt, in the small provincial city of Karlsruhe, the Residence (or capital city) of the grand duke of Baden, Eduard Devrient was effecting important reforms. If any German theater reformer deserves that often-bestowed title, "a Meininger before the Meininger," that person is Eduard Devrient, a member of a large German theatrical family that included the two celebrated virtuosos, Emil and Ludwig. In 1852 Eduard, who had been a director in Dresden and Leipzig, chose to move to the Baden capital, lying far out of the way of cultural and artistic traffic; it was only there, he said, that he could find a patron willing to give him the freedom to run a theater on his own terms. In 1857, five years after he had taken up his reform efforts, he wrote: "If Karlsruhe lies remote and offers slender means and a public unprepared for, even inimical to, my purposes, surmounting these obstacles is part of my task. And if I succeed, then this will furnish even more proof that a worthwhile theater based on an ideal is possible even under the most unfavorable circumstances."[46]

Laube believed that a large, critical, cosmopolitan audience was necessary for the proper development of a worthwhile theater; otherwise, he wrote, the director pleases himself while, over his shoulder, the actors try to please the audience. In his view, the absence of comparative standards must inevitably result in too much or too little. But Devrient proved this notion wrong. It was Laube, in Vienna, who was forced by the demands of the box office to allow many trivial pieces to be played, whereas in little, provincial Karlsruhe, Devrient molded an audience made up almost entirely of a court accustomed to viewing the theater as a mere pastime. Perhaps because Devrient was of the theater, he did not try to re-form The Theater. He knew that first he must reform the audience. "Although the theater director is not a preacher," he wrote, "in many ways they are alike: they must see to it that the public learns what it should, not what it wants to."[47]

Devrient began his reforms by systematically building a constantly growing fund of well-produced plays, which by periodic revivals could provide a continuing program. He gave his most conscientious care to the works of Shakespeare, twenty of whose plays he staged, nearly all in new revisions, based as much as possible on the original text and discarding the free and capricious revisions then in common use. He showed an equally skillful hand in his treatment of the German classics. He returned Schiller's *Die Räuber* to its original form, rescued Kleist's *Käthchen von Heilbronn* from its "improvements," and restored Immermann's *Andreas Hofer*, long lost to the German stage. He chose freely from foreign litera-ture: Molière, Calderón, and Sophocles. He made room for the popular and prolific German writers Roderich Benedix and Charlotte Birch-Pfeiffer, but only because he felt that their plays offered the actors a vari-ety of demanding and instructive tasks. His standard was excellence, not repute: Gustav Freytag, Otto Devrient, and Albert Lindner all had De-vrient to thank for introducing their works.[48]

Devrient was a master of actors. He possessed the most important tal-ent for a director: the ability to make himself understood. He had been an actor himself, and he knew that he could get the most out of his com-pany by personal instruction and fastidious rehearsal. Devrient found little talent when he came to Karlsruhe, but he soon attracted actors who were eager to receive the kind of training he could give. In return they had to submit to Devrient's ruthless discipline, which meant above all sub-scribing to the view that everything must give way to the good of the theater.[49]

The first thing an actor had to learn on Devrient's stage was that he was not there to grandstand. His task was to interpret the dramatist's in-tention. He had no right to any special roles; categories did not exist on the Karlsruhe stage. How painful all this was to the virtuoso is shown by Haase's rather sour account of a guest appearance there: "At the first re-hearsal I began to portray the picture of my dreams. From the director: 'Herr Haase, I must ask please—a little less realism.' I continued; then, 'Herr Haase, please omit the colorful shadings. You don't want to look like a virtuoso.' Everything had to be ensemble, ensemble! All else was realism, colorful shading, or virtuosity!"[50]

Devrient's settings were simple. Like Laube, he feared that elaborate scenery would eclipse the poetry, but his stage pictures were never so bare as those at the Burgtheater. He was willing to accept certain innovations. For example, after 1865 he adopted the scene curtain, which Laube insisted impeded the flow of the action, something that Georg of Meiningen was to use consistently. As the critic Eugen Kilian noted in 1913, this was not the only way in which Devrient's reforms anticipated those of Georg. "In more than one point," he wrote, "can Devrient be considered a direct forerunner of the Meininger: in the reestablishment of good and accurate classical texts in place of the prevalent slovenliness, in the careful composition of the ensemble, in the struggle against role monopoly, in the principle that actors have to accept subordinate roles in the interest of the whole production, and in many artistic innovations that today are in general use on all stages."[51]

Devrient's penchant for "atmosphere" and his strong sense of artistic unity go back to Richard Wagner, with whom he had worked in Dresden in 1842. Both Devrient and Wagner wrote extensively on reform programs for the German theater, but Devrient wished to work with existing materials, whereas Wagner dreamed of a whole new art form, "a unified work of art," which, under the direction of one man, would call into its service the arts of the architect, the sculptor, the painter, the dancer, the musician, and the poet. Such music drama, said Wagner, would be played in a national theater, which would become a place of pilgrimage for the German nation. Although Georg of Meiningen recognized the grand scope of the composer's plan, he did not agree with it in all details.*

Much of the realism and historical accuracy in the Meininger staging can be traced to the work of Charles Kean, who in his turn worked out of a long tradition in the English theater.[52] More famous, and certainly more flamboyant, than his fellow countryman Samuel Phelps, Kean set out, in the 1850's, to present seventeen Shakespearean dramas at the

---

* Georg knew Wagner over many years, first through Franz Liszt and Hans von Bülow, and later through his wife Ellen Franz, a girlhood friend of Cosima Wagner's. In her diary entry for Nov. 16, 1875, Cosima wrote of a meeting with Georg and his wife in Vienna. Richard, she said, found the duke "completely typical of the old House of Wettin, something firm, reserved, powerful about the features, which one could easily trace back to Widikind." Later that year, Wagner borrowed the Meiningen orchestra to supplement his own musicians for the opening of the Festspielhaus in Bayreuth. Although Georg was not in total agreement, he let Wagner have the orchestra and bought the members new instruments. Georg attended the opening in 1876 and dined at the Wagners', where he heard, as Cosima noted, "Saint-Saëns play the piano." (Cosima Wagner, *Diaries*, tr. Geoffrey Skelton, 2 vols., New York, 1976-77.) By this date, however, Georg's own reforms were well in motion. Rather than say that Georg was greatly influenced by Wagner, it is more nearly correct to say that they were both working under the same artistic influences, which directed the genius of Wagner in a unique way.

Princess Theatre in productions of great "historical truth." With each theater program he provided material explaining the cultural and historical background of the drama and its setting, naming the researchers whom he had engaged to compile the material and giving biographies of designers and scenic artists. His stage was loaded with an excess of ethnographic and archaeological detail.*

With processions and parades Kean crowded the stage in opera-like magnificence. His coronation procession in *Henry VIII* consisted of more than one hundred accurately costumed people moving past a "changing" panorama of London from Westminster Palace to the Church of the Grey Friars in Greenwich; the banquet scene at York Palace and the great courtroom scene were pictures of blinding splendor; and between Acts IV and V of *Henry V* he inserted an interlude in which the King crossed London Bridge in a glittering procession before a moving panorama. For such scenes, Kean devoted great care to the ensemble; to make the scenes living and realistic, he divided his crowds into small groups, each with its own leader, to be individually drilled in the smallest detail. Unfortunately, he did not devote the same careful attention to the accuracy of Shakespeare's texts. Too often the ensemble was used not to illuminate the poet's words, but to set the star: Charles Kean, who with his wife, Ellen Tree, was always the center of attention.[53]

The impression Kean made on German visitors varied. When Josef Lewinsky, a great tragedian of the Burgtheater and faithful adherent of the Laube school, was shown sketches of a planned Shakespearean production with 500 actors and a proposed expenditure of £50,000, he shook his head. "The accessories must inevitably stifle the essentials," he wrote on June 24, 1862. But he found the experience worthwhile for all that. "Thinking about this expenditure has been instructive to me in both positive and negative ways," he said, "and has given me some suggestions about improving the externals on our German stages."[54]

The actor Friedrich Haase was delighted by the color and pomp of Kean's *The Merchant of Venice*, which he saw in London in 1867, and seized the opportunity to borrow from it when he took over the direction of the court theater of Saxe-Coburg:

---

*The first act of *The Winter's Tale*, for example, featured a complete replica of the Acropolis. Kean restored the bear scene, and the critic Dutton Cook recalled that the bear "figured conspicuously, chasing the Antigonus of the time with special zest." Kean himself gravely noted that "the presence of bears in the East is exemplified in the Second Chapter of the Second Book of Kings." *Punch*, which liked to poke fun at Kean's excesses, claimed to have it on the actor's own authority that his bear was "an archaeological copy of the original bear in Noah's ark." (Arthur Colby Sprague, *Shakespeare and the Actors: The Stage Business in His Plays*, Cambridge, Mass., 1944, p. 68.)

I saw *The Merchant of Venice*—the magnificent outfitting, the fresh business of the stage, and the changing pictures—all this awakened my curiosity and held me in breathless suspense. I asked the duke of Saxe-Coburg to give me a large sum of money to present a miniature of this production, a watercolor reproduction of the original oil painting, and after I had given him a long lecture on the subject, he agreed. The house was sold out days ahead. [Among the guests were Friedrich von Bodenstedt and Georg of Meiningen.] The duke of Meiningen was in a rosy conversational mood, and on that evening—so it seemed to me—the resolve formed in this so artistically gifted gentleman to give to the classical drama the cultural decoration that a few years later was to gain the Meiningen court theater a world reputation.[55]

We can easily dismiss as self-serving Haase's suggestion that his production was the genesis of the Meiningen reform, for fully twenty-three years earlier Georg had bought costume plates, and more than twenty years earlier he had sought out "historically accurate" armor, weapons, and other stage decoration. Indeed, in December 1867, the year in which Haase first saw *The Merchant of Venice*, Georg had presented Shakespeare's *Romeo and Juliet*, *Macbeth*, and *King John* in productions that had been enthusiastically praised in the *Shakespeare Jahrbuch*, so he was not likely to have been impressed by Haase's "watercolor." Even more important, nine years earlier, the duke had seen the work of Samuel Phelps in Berlin.

A disciple of Charles Macready, the English tragedian who declared that his life as an actor had been devoted to giving "a clearer and deeper insight into the poet's meaning," Phelps did not have anything like Kean's financial resources. Perhaps this was fortunate. His productions were never so elaborate. His reforms as they touch on the work of the Meininger are four: education of the public, absolute reverence for the work of the poet, creation of a carefully rehearsed ensemble, and the use of what Phelps called "atmosphere" direction.

Like most reformers in the theater, Phelps had much of the schoolmaster in him. In 1843 he chose to establish his theater at Sadler's Wells, in a London suburb where he could expect to attract only an unruly, even rowdy audience, accustomed to and preferring the lightest form of entertainment. Like Devrient in Karlsruhe, he gave people, not what they wanted, but what he thought they should have: Shakespeare. He required absolute decorum in his audience, and within a year he had developed a model gallery, keenly interested in the works of the great poet, and had also attracted to the outlying theater the literary and social elite of London.

In England, as well as in Germany, many of Shakespeare's plays had been rewritten to suit the stars: soliloquies, dialogue, and characters had been moved from one work to another. Lines had been changed, scenes added or dropped, plays shortened. In the years when Drury Lane and Covent Garden had had the exclusive right to mount serious dramas and tragedies, other theaters had been limited to presenting comedies and musical plays. To give the classics under these conditions, many theaters had added music and called them musicals. For example, *Macbeth* had featured singing witches since the seventeenth century. Tragedies and comedies alike were brutally cut to make room for a farce or ballet to follow. All this Phelps discarded.[56] On his stage the audience heard Shakespeare as near to the original as Phelps could make it. Over the years, he made more than one hundred restorations in the texts.

Careful rehearsals at Sadler's Wells produced a living ensemble. Phelps was not himself a great actor, but he was conscientious, thorough, and capable. He knew how to instruct other actors. More than that, he was original and independent in his direction. His staging of the banquet scene in *Macbeth* broke with the traditional setting that the actress Fanny Kemble found so tedious:

From time immemorial the banquet scene . . . has been arranged after one invariable fashion: the royal dais and throne with the steps leading up to it hold the middle of the stage, sufficiently far back to allow two tables at which the guests are seated on each side, in front of it, leaving them ample room for Macbeth's scene with Banquo and Lady Macbeth's repeated descent from the dais and return to it, in her vehement expostulations with him, and her courteous invitation to the occupants of both tables "to feed and regard him not."[57]

Phelps moved Macbeth's throne to stage right and Banquo's chair to the downstage side of the table, flouting the tradition of always positioning a king and queen in no matter what drama at the center of the stage. Phelps's change allowed the crowd to enter into the action, since they were no longer looking upstage.

It was in *A Midsummer Night's Dream*, produced in 1851, that Phelps displayed most effectively his ability to create atmosphere through the use of gauze, light, and darkness. Playing the fairy scenes behind pale green scrim, he achieved an ethereal quality that lent enchantment to the poetry. He also used gauze to good effect for the witches' scene in *Macbeth*, which he produced as Shakespeare wrote it, rejecting the alterations that had been on the English stage since the Restoration. It had been customary, as Fanny Kemble noted, "to make low comedians act the witches and to dress them like old fishwomen . . . with as due a proportion of petticoats as any old women, let alone witches, might desire."[58] Phelps's witches, without the "jocose red faces and broomsticks" Fanny Kemble deplored, were discovered behind gauze, the thickening folds of which produced the effect of the sisters' vanishing when the time came for that. The weird sisters seemed to grow out of the supernaturally induced mist and merge once more into it.[59] In 1852, Kean copied the gauze and the mist.

Georg saw several of Phelps's productions in Berlin in 1859, including *Othello*, *King Lear*, *Hamlet*, *The Merchant of Venice*, *The Merry Wives of Windsor*, and *Henry IV*. They were played in the Friedrich-Wilhelmstädtisches Theater, which was equipped only for drawing-room pieces, farces, and comedies. The English actor brought no scenery and played in shabby wings, so that the productions were far less effective than they might have been, but the critics praised the skillful employment of the crowds. No one commented on the fidelity to the text; but Georg, who had been studying the plays in both English and German for more than twenty years, learned a lesson from Phelps. No director has ever improved on Shakespeare by altering the texts.

As compelling an influence on Georg of Meiningen as any of these men was the social and artistic spirit of the time. The nineteenth century, with its many powerful impulses for change, was dominated by romanticism, which manifested itself, above all, in a search for what the German historian Leopold von Ranke called a "reconstruction of events and institutions of the past as they actually were." By the time Georg began his education, the period was already deeply immersed in history, and no German family with any pretensions to learning was without Karl von Rotteck's massive six-volume history, *Allgemeine Weltgeschichte*, or Friedrich von Raumer's equally massive study of the Hohenstaufen dynasty, *Geschichte der Hohenstaufen*. As early as the 1830's and 1840's, Immermann's *Alexis*, Christian Dietrich Grabbe's *Hannibal*, and Karl Gutzkow's *King Saul*, among other plays, marked a widening interest in moving away from Greek and Roman themes. A rising German nationalism and the desire of the middle class to validate its place in society awakened a yearning for the "simplicity and nobility" of the virtuous "Old German" past; and audiences began to see Turks and other "heathens" regularly fall before the Christian German banners.

Artists, too, turned to the historical. Eugène Delacroix set the tone of the painting of the time. He was convinced that color was more important than draftsmanship, and imagination more powerful than knowledge.[60] Exhibitions of historical paintings toured Europe and influenced people even in their own homes. History was popularized in dioramas and panoramas for which the public developed a veritable passion. The same period saw a great popularity of festival parades in historical costume; and the mania for costume balls reached a new height.

From the middle of the century, the theater—especially in the form of the opera house—replaced the museum as the pantheon of the arts. "The focal point of the new tendency rested on the ideal of the unified-work-of-art, which the Romantics had yearned for, and on the theater as a consecrated place."[61] Bayreuth became the visible symbol of this theater-as-temple ideal. Here was to be realized a democratic festival for the German nation. In the field of theater architecture, the pioneer of the new era was Gottfried Semper, who from the first attempted to rescue all the arts from the individual isolation into which the eighteenth century had brought them. His first famous building, the Opera House in Dresden (1838), was a trend-setter—not in its outer form especially, but rather in its appearance of a unified conception and synthesis of the elements of splendid decoration, feeling, and color. Between 1840 and 1890 most of the great opera houses of the Western world were built, many of them displaying a magnificence that formerly belonged to the royal palace.[62]

Very little of all this artistic ferment reached the theater of the spoken word, but every element for its revitalization was there. The time was right, the theaters built, the audience waiting. If there was little contemporary drama being written, there was a great storehouse of classics, and young actors were ready for a call to excellence. What was needed was a single, sharp-sighted man to reach back to Laube and Devrient and unify their principles. The man who answered that need was Georg II of Meiningen, who built all his reforms on continuing tradition. "The duke of Meiningen gave to that time neither the method of historical truth nor that of the picturesque. He did not discover the historical costume, the scene curtain, the stage floor broken up and framed by a realistic landscape. That all lay ready for him, but at the same time it lay ready for every other director."[63] It is precisely because Georg—a true child of his time—was able to assimilate these theatrical traditions into his own experience, and used them skillfully and imaginatively on his stage to touch the deepest aspirations and values of his audience, that he is honored as the first modern director in the theater.

PART ONE

The Meiningen Triumvirate

ONE

GEORG OF MEININGEN

Seventeen years of touring through-
out Europe by the court theater of the Duchy of Saxe-Meiningen earned
for the ruler of that little land the title The Theater Duke, but during the
time he devoted to the theater, Georg never forgot that his first duty belonged to the people of Meiningen.[1] In September 1891, when he celebrated the silver anniversary of his accession, Georg could look back with
pride on the way the duchy had prospered during his reign. The bitter
struggle over public lands, which had plagued his father for decades, had
long been settled. Industry had been encouraged, and the tax and credit
system reorganized. Education for both boys and girls was required, and
the church's hold on education had been lessened. Every citizen, in many
cases women as well as men, had a vote in the general elections. New
regulations in church and synod had been instituted, and absolute religious tolerance demanded. There was a flourishing cultural life.

Georg inherited his intense love of and devotion to Meiningen and its
people from ancestors going back to the seventeenth century, when the
duchy was carved out of Gotha and established as a separate entity. In
many ways Georg's own reign repeated politically and artistically that of
his grandfather Georg I. Although Georg I's reign coincided with the
French Revolutionary years, which left many ducal houses reactionary or
even oppressive, he was distinguished by his liberal and progressive ideas.
The little country enjoyed a free press, and under ducal auspices liberal-
minded scholars and thinkers found refuge there. Goethe, Jean Paul
Richter, and Schiller were among those received at court. The duke had
firmly believed in education for both sexes and expanded educational opportunities to include all classes. His liberal ideas extended even to the

burial of his mother, whom he laid in the public cemetery instead of the ducal vault because "she was worthy to lie among her subjects."[2]

Georg I disappointed his subjects in only one way; he had no son. Salic law denied the rule to one of his daughters, and the people of Meiningen did not wish to pass to a collateral line. So it was with extraordinary joy that they greeted the birth of an heir in 1800, just three years before the duke's death. Georg named his son Bernhard Erich Freund, the last as a sign that he would always be a friend to his people. Contrary to custom, he did not invite a neighboring nobleman to be godfather to his son; instead, he asked the citizens of Meiningen to stand for the little prince.[3]

Georg's young widow, Louisa Eleanora, born princess of Hohenlohe-Langenburg, ruled as regent with energy, courage, and good sense during the Napoleonic Wars, which for the next decade ravaged the Saxon states. As an ally of Napoleon I, King Friedrich Augustus I of Saxony conscripted Meiningen citizens to fight in Russia and Italy; and first the French, then the Russian armies marched back and forth across the country. Other rulers submitted or fled their principalities, but Louisa Eleanora with her infant son and her two little daughters never left the castle. She used every stratagem to preserve the autonomy of her regency; and when she joined the Allies in 1813, she had saved the duchy for her son, who became the ruling duke of Meiningen eight years later.

In 1826 two important events took place in Meiningen. Because Duke Friedrich IV of Saxe-Gotha-Altenburg had died without an heir the year before, his duchy was now divided among collateral claimants, and Meiningen was enlarged by grants of land, including Hildburghausen and Saalfeld. Even more satisfying to the people was the birth on April 2 of a son to Duke Bernhard and his wife of a year, Princess Marie, daughter of the Elector of Hessen-Cassel. The little prince, named Georg for his grandfather, remained an only child until he was seventeen years old, when his sister, Auguste, was born. Georg spent his first years under the earnest supervision of his parents and grandmother, the redoubtable Louisa Eleanora, who considered it their first duty to instill in the child the patriotic virtues of his heritage and the sense of duty that he needed to rule even a tiny duchy.

Besides a Swiss nursemaid, Rose Reuille, who cared for the child from 1829 to 1835, the family employed a governess about whom nothing is known except that her methods were severely criticized by a court official named Rossman. In a letter to Duke Bernhard, he complained: "Any governess who inflames the fanciful powers of the child too early, who crams him with nonsense and overexcites his imagination will be dismissed. In an artificially darkened room, thrilling tales are recounted. . . . His whole

Fig. 1. Georg II, duke of Saxe-Meiningen (1826-1914), at the age of 72

being is stuffed with fantasies. . . . Piety, respect, and regard for duty are taking second place."[4] Georg was already evincing the attraction for the strange and marvelous that was to characterize his whole life.[5]

When Georg was eight years old, his Aunt Adelaide, the queen of England, joined the family in Bad Liebenstein, where the duke, his wife, and the prince spent their summers. Forty-three years later, when the actor Josef Kainz walked into Bad Liebenstein for his tryout with the Meiningen court theater, he would call it the most charming place he had ever seen, "lying in a laughing meadow and closed in by wooded hills and mountains,"[6] but the English visitors found the frugal and simple life of the religious little court "empty and boring." Lady Brownlow, the queen's lady-in-waiting, was given the queen's girlhood bedroom, which she described as a "bare and comfortless-looking room at which any English maid would turn up her nose." The visitors found the castle in Meiningen "dreary" and thought Castle Altenstein "unpleasant."[7]

The young prince did not view his life as either boring or empty: plain living in Meiningen went hand in hand with high thinking. As soon as he left the nursery, Georg was instructed by a university student, Johannes Michel Klug, who, on long walks through the Thuringian forests, taught him of the beauties of nature and man's place in it. Klug took him to the Tyrolean Alps, whose mighty snowclad peaks seized the child's imagination in an extraordinary way.

In 1835 Moritz Seebeck became Georg's second teacher and one of the most powerful influences in his life. Duke Bernhard had called Seebeck to Meiningen to reorganize the education system and enlarge the secondary schools, but he saw in the earnest, middle-class, thirty-one-year-old Prussian the ideal tutor for his son. Seebeck, quoting Goethe's words, "A prince should not be reared alone, for alone he cannot learn to govern himself, let alone others," accepted the post on the condition that the boy become part of the Seebeck family, which made its home in apartments on the first floor of the castle, and be taught in the company of other boys. In a letter to Duke Bernhard on June 20, 1835, Seebeck laid out the principles he intended to follow:

All excessive indulgence and every sort of coddling that detract from the cultivation of high-mindedness and the growth of character shall be avoided, and concern for physical well-being shall end when it begins to operate negatively against the intellectual and spiritual development of the child. A prince who is to be educated not merely for the drawing room, but for the career of a ruler, must develop a serious and worthy view of life and be given the correct ideas of the great duties of mankind; he must learn to be religious-minded without turning into a zealot, and to be decisive without becoming overbearing, thereby growing up as a noble and lofty man.[8]

For the following nine years Seebeck devoted himself to the prince's education, stressing lessons in German, religion, and history. Georg also studied Greek and Latin, learned to read, write, and speak French and English, and followed a strong course in mathematics, geography, and science. Seebeck's method of teaching by example, "never to reprimand [*schelten*], never to find fault [*tadeln*], never to admonish [*warnen*]," was ideal for the gifted, sensitive prince.[9]

In this loving but disciplined atmosphere, Georg grew up a happy child. He taught Gustel (August) Seebeck, the small son of the family, to play his silver mouth organ, to learn his letters, and to name the animals. He and his piano teacher Reichel joined the family in the evenings to read the works of Goethe and Schiller with assigned parts. As other children were born to the Seebecks, Georg accepted them as siblings. He spent birthday and Christmas celebrations with them, decorated their festive tables, and led them in play. He entertained them with his toy theater so successfully that when Bernhard, Seebeck's second son, was taken to the theater in Berlin, he declared that he did not care to go again, but would rather see Georg act for him in his little theater. Seebeck was gratified to watch the prince play with the children with "naturalness and a complete absence of affectation." He noted that Georg always "knows how to arrange something and is as understanding as he is happy."[10] The close, affectionate home that Moritz and Ida Seebeck made for their four children and for him too became for Georg the measure of a successful family life.

Summers, Seebeck accompanied Georg to the mountains. Here they climbed and walked; Seebeck studied nature with the prince and taught him to know the creatures and the peoples of his native Thuringian forest. Yearly, they visited Altenstein, where great herds of horses ran free, and Georg watched the foaling. By the time he was fifteen, he was a fine enough horseman to set his pony Tamar in a three-way race with his Aunt Ida, the grand duchess of Saxe-Weimar, who rode sidesaddle on a horse "as big as an elephant," and with Seebeck on Duke Bernhard II's Calliope, "each horse straining to be first."[11]

His parents' austere views on child-rearing prevented Georg from attending the theater often. We know little about the plays he saw, only that as a child he was entranced by the theater.[12] He was almost certainly not allowed to see any of the shabby troupes that came and went during the first winters after the opening of the Meiningen city theater in 1831, but he did see the productions of Count Karl Friedrich von Hahn-Neuhaus—whom old theater historians always introduce as "the legendary"—who became its manager in 1836. In his productions, known less for quality than for spectacular costumes and startling effects, Georg would at least have seen that the theater could hold marvels. Three years later he saw Pixérécourt's *Le Chien de Montargis ou le Forêt de Bondy*, the same melodrama that had outraged Goethe's classical taste with its real dog, thrilling events, and exotic scenes. That year he also saw at least one performance of the flamboyant Wilhelm von Kunst, "an original genius," who gave seven performances in Meiningen, including three from his classical repertoire. Besides Lear, Tell, and Wallenstein, he played the leading roles in Karl Gutzkow's *Zopf und Schwert* and August Wilhelm Iffland's *Die Jäger*. The simple honesty and love of home in the last named must have impressed the prince; he produced it off and on all his life.

When he was eleven, the prince stood with Seebeck and a crowd of excited citizens at Bad Ischl to watch an Imperial Entry as dazzling as any procession he would ever put on the stage. Riding in an ornate golden carriage drawn by six magnificent white horses, Emperor Ferdinand I of Austria, with a colorfully garbed mounted escort, passed slowly through the streets of the little mountain resort. Cannons boomed, church bells rang, and military bands broke into music. The noise was deafening, the people wild with joy. Nightfall brought an equally dazzling display, with thousands of candles burning throughout the village, and the mountains aflame with bonfires. Boats large and small, aglow with lights, floated past the emperor's house on the Inn River, and the people on board danced, laughed, and shot off guns, all the while shouting "Long live the Emperor!" A sudden downpour dampened the celebration, but not Georg's enthusiasm for the pomp and ceremony he had witnessed.[13] Much of the glitter of the day would show up on his stage years later.

Georg early showed a considerable talent for drawing, leading the deeply religious Seebeck to believe that God had given the child extraordinary gifts, which should be cultivated carefully even though they seemed to have nothing to do with his future life as a ruler. Friedrich Paul Schellborn, in Meiningen to paint decorations for the theater, was Georg's first instructor. Although not a great artist, he encouraged the child and taught him the rules of proportion and figure drawing.[14] A more important influence was Wilhelm Lindenschmitt the Elder, who came to Meiningen to paint the murals in the newly completed Castle Landsberg, high overlooking the town. Lindenschmitt (or sometimes Lindenschmit) was known above all for his historically correct murals in Castle Hohenschwangau in Bavaria and for his monumental painting of the battle of the Sendlinger peasants in the Sendlinger Stadtkirche. Deeply immersed at the time in medieval history, Georg studied Lindenschmitt's subject matter and methods carefully. The artist recognized the fifteen-year-old's talent and urged him to continue sketching seriously. He corrected the prince's work and professed himself greatly impressed by his efforts, one of which Georg sent to his mother. "Your depiction of *manœuvres* greatly pleased me," she wrote in 1841.[15] Under Lindenschmitt's instruction, Georg began a large historical painting that was to occupy him for years, *Die Dithmarschensschlacht* (The Battle of the Dithmarschens).[16] The sketches for this work as well as the completed painting now hang in the Meiningen Museum and demonstrate how skillful the prince already was in composing groups and showing men and horses in action.

At about this same time Georg tried his hand at theatrics by translating and adapting Shakespeare's *Macbeth* for his class. We know that he cast himself in the leading role and Seebeck in the role of Duncan, but whether the play was actually presented or merely read is uncertain.[17] At any rate, Seebeck wrote that Georg had accomplished so much in German that he no longer needed correction "and writes a very pretty style."[18]

On February 19, 1842, the proud Seebeck wrote to his own mother:

In fourteen days, my prince will be sixteen years old. What a great difference between this day and the first on which I came to him! Then he was a sensitive boy, gifted and lovable, but little developed. Now he is a few fingers taller than I, so robust and hearty that in wrestling it is only with the greatest effort that I am able to pin him. His temperament has acquired ardor and mettle, his judgment clarity, his heart warmth. When I observe what sort of spirit animates him, which interests occupy him, what kind of thoughts he has, then I realize with joy how much, how very much he has advanced to his goal since that long-bygone day.[19]

At that time Georg presented Seebeck with a manuscript of a long, comprehensive tale of an imaginary battle during medieval times at the newly built Castle Landsberg. Seebeck read the successful invention and presentation with pleasure. The characters were well drawn and each was allowed to speak in his own voice. The liveliness of the tale aroused the reader's interest, the "plot was well thickened" and carefully resolved. The story was at the same time complicated and simple. Its basic theme, which was clearly developed, treated the triumph of custom and law over the raw power of the mailed fist. It presented that thesis effectively because it was without premeditated design. It spoke simply and plainly, said the tutor, of a noble frame of mind. Certainly, it contained youthful mistakes in form and content, but it was never exaggerated or effusive. The motivation and complication of the individual incidents were more successfully brought to a balanced unity than most young men could achieve. "I must recognize," wrote Seebeck to his mother, "that he knows how to absorb skillfully what he learns and to mold it so that it becomes his own unique property. The imaginative productivity of his spirit is gratifying."[20]

On May 1, 1842, the sixteen-year-old Georg was confirmed in the Lutheran Confession in the Meiningen Stadtkirche, a rite of passage marked in a public ceremony to which the people of the land were bidden. A ninety-year-old member of the Bach family, who had played for Georg I, was at the organ.[21] Earlier that spring the duke had taken his family to England on one of the many extended visits they made after Adelaide became queen. Georg delighted in these visits. There is no record of his being taken to the theater on these occasions, but his aunt often took him to the circus, for which he developed a lifelong passion.* Georg's absences had long been a source of conflict between the duke and Seebeck, who now refused to have the prince's studies interrupted again. Finally, it was agreed that the tutor would accompany the family, and the prince, in addition to his regular work, would make a detailed study of English life and institutions.

Seebeck made even the journey an education. The party moved through Germany and the Lowlands to take a ship large enough to transport their four carriages. Only Georg, his mother, and Seebeck were not seasick, and the tutor pointed out the different kinds of ships they passed, including one magnificent vessel with thirty sails billowing in the wind, which Georg rapidly sketched. As they approached Dover, a great crowd was gathered on the shore. There was a cannonade from the fortress, high on the rocks. Soldiers in formation made no little noise with their drums, pipes, and trumpets. As an officer in a red uniform came forward to greet the duke, the soldiers presented arms, looking "wonderful in their uniforms of red and white." They were so elegant that to the visitors from the frugal little German duchy, each looked like an officer. Of course, the officers were even finer since they were as bedecked with gold as a Prussian general. From Dover the visitors drove by coach to London behind such horses as were unknown in Meiningen.[22]

The duke and duchess resided in Marlborough House with Adelaide, who was now the dowager queen, but the prince with his tutor carried on his studies in the king of Hanover's residence in St. James's Palace. Georg had a full schedule. Besides continuing his work in French, English, and the classics, he toured the Bank of England, the Royal Mint, the East India House, and other public buildings and art galleries. He went with his deeply religious and benevolent Aunt Adelaide to meetings of the Charity Schools of St. Paul's and the Singing Classes in Exeter Hall.

---

* In 1887 he went to London for Queen Victoria's golden jubilee, which featured, among other entertainments, Buffalo Bill and his Wild West Show. Georg, then more than sixty years old, rode through Regent Street, Hyde Park, and the City on top of the Deadwood Coach, pursued by Indians and protected by Buffalo Bill's men riding shotgun. His wife said the ride was worth the whole trip to England. (Helene, Freifrau von Heldburg, *Fünfzig Jahre Glück und Leid*, Leipzig, 1926, p. 53.)

All this he was storing up and would use in his theater: the pomp of the "family" dinners with Queen Victoria and his cousin, Prince Albert; the splendor of the levees and protocol observed on formal occasions; hunts with his cousins Princes George and Edward of Saxe-Weimar; the bows and the curtseys. He never forgot that living faces lined the road as he was driven in a royal carriage with Prince Albert—right behind that of the queen with his parents—in procession to Ascot. Nor did he forget the sea of waving handkerchiefs underneath the Royal Box at Her Majesty's Theatre. His artist's eye recorded all the detail of a splendid journey around the Isle of Wight in the company of the dowager queen on the steamship *Volcano*, and of the horror that accompanied an accident in which a sailor's arm was torn away from his body as his gun exploded in the volley of a salute. Thus at sixteen, Georg was building up impressions that would prove invaluable to the development of his theatrical imagination; but he was also instilled with notions of the prerogatives of princes that would serve him ill six years later when he was caught up in the Revolution of 1848.

Georg went twice to the zoo, where both he and Seebeck rode on an elephant and were astonished to see animals roaming as freely as the horses in Altenstein. And twice Georg was in the royal party attending the Italian opera, once to hear *Lucia di Lammermoor*, and once *Lucrezia Borgia*. We have no record of his impressions, but he must have found the operas pleasing, because he was to hear both many times in years to come. We also do not know whether he attended the theater. In view of Queen Victoria's great admiration for the actress Rachel Felix,[23] who gave six performances in London during the time the family was there, it might be supposed that she would recommend their seeing the international star, but there is no account of such a theater visit. It is more provocative, but no less speculative, to suppose that Georg saw William Charles Macready in *Macbeth* in Drury Lane. Given Georg's near obsession with the works of Shakespeare * and his close adherence throughout his theater activity to Macready's principles, it is tempting to think that he must have seen the celebrated tragedian.[24] After all, he had only recently translated the tragedy and taken the role of Macbeth; Seebeck, always alert to opportunities to expand his charge's education, would have found the production eminently suitable. The queen had recently seen Macready play the tragedy, but whether or not she advised her young visitor to see it is not known.

* The only reason Georg ever gave for undertaking his theater reforms is his statement, "I was annoyed that Shakespeare was so badly played on the German stage." (Cited in Max Grube, *The Story of the Meininger*, tr. Ann Marie Koller, Coral Gables, Fla., 1965, p. 21.)

Georg was often in the company of his cousin on his mother's side, Prince George of Cambridge, who, seven years older than Georg, had long been visiting all kinds of London amusements and moved at all levels in theatrical circles. By this time the young prince had taken up with the actress Louisa Fairbrother, whom he was to marry several years later. Since she had been acting and dancing for some time in a number of theaters, including Drury Lane, the Lyceum, and Covent Garden, Prince George may well have introduced his young cousin to entertainment other than the circus or the opera. If he did, it was not anything that Georg would care to discuss with his anxiously restrictive parents or the high-minded Seebeck.

Two weeks after the party returned from England, another son was born to the Seebecks. They named him after Georg "as a loving reminder of the time in which we lived with our prince so closely and cordially," and asked him to be the child's godfather. This marked the beginning of a full and exciting year for Georg. In December 1842 he received the uniform of the Saxe-Meiningen Defense Battalion; Capt. Eduard von Reitzenstein became his military governor and shared his education with Seebeck. The following February he attended his first masked ball, for which he planned elaborate costumes for himself and his four cousins, the countesses of Castell. More important, in April, on his seventeenth birthday, he was formally presented to the people of Meiningen. The theater was brilliantly lighted and all present were in glittering attire. Even small Gustel was present with his parents to shout "Vivat!" "Hoch!," but when the ducal family entered the loge, there arose such a storm of applause that the child could not speak; and when the prince, in his open, modest manner, came to the railing of the loge to bow his thanks, Gustel could only weep.[25]

At the beginning of the summer semester in 1844, both Seebeck and von Reitzenstein accompanied the prince to the University at Bonn, where he remained five semesters studying law, history, archaeology, church history, and church architecture. Seebeck still exercised loving but strict control, choosing the prince's instructors, few of whom met his high Prussian standards and several of whom disturbed his middle-class thinking with their radical opinions; he took care to remain close to Georg, even sharing his quarters, a large, well-furnished single room. Georg had been sent to the university for serious study.

Two professors, Friedrich Christoph Dahlmann and Ernst Moritz Arndt, both ardent patriots and fervent supporters of the aspirations for unity then stirring the German states, particularly impressed Georg.[26] Two others, Franz G. Welcher and Gottfried Kinckel, influenced his ideas on art.[27] The prince, already conditioned by the ideas of Seebeck, absorbed their profound reverence for German antiquity and their idealistic hopes for the unity of the nation. Long discussions on German music, architecture, and painting helped him sort out his ideas of aesthetics and questions of art. In Bonn, Georg was introduced to the art of Dürer and others of the northern Renaissance; he made visits to Munich, where he studied the strong lines of the *Nibelungen* murals of Julius Schnorr von Karolsfeld in the castles of King Ludwig I of Bavaria. The composition and movement without vivid colors proved a model to him, and his studies in church history provided him with a subject that he attempted in imitation of von Karolsfeld. He wrote to his mother for details, asking "whether Zwingli wore a suit of armor in the battle of Kappel [1531] or not, or whether the Züricher [Zwingli] carried a flag or not, for I wish to depict him in this battle."[28] Earlier he had sketched on the margin of a letter to his mother a figure of a Bonn lancer in which the details of material and color were distinctly designated.[29]

Georg threw himself enthusiastically into the study of Shakespeare. He and "the Holsteiners" (possibly Prince Friedrich of Schleswig-Holstein and his brother Prince Christian) asked Professor Johann Wilhelm Loebell, with whom they were studying medieval history, to conduct a series of Monday evening lectures. "The first will be an excursion through the works of Shakespeare," he told his mother.[30] Next Loebell took up the individual plays, first *King John*, then the old *John I* and *Richard II*.[31] Professor Dahlmann presented the first two acts of *Romeo and Juliet*, probably at the end of 1844.[32] Georg also reported to his mother that "perhaps *Caesar* by Shakespeare will be read with assigned roles."[33] Whether it was read and whether he received a role he never said.

During the winter Georg visited Cologne, where he heard Mozart's *Don Giovanni* and saw Daniel François Auber's romantic opera *La Muette de Portici* (which impressed him enough to send him back to see it twice more in the next twelve months).[34] He also called on "the aged Schlegel," but said little about their meeting.* If Georg sought to engage Schlegel on the subject of his own studies, the eminent Shakespeare scholar may well have repeated his famous advice: "Let no man lay hand on Shakespeare's works to change anything essential in them; he will be sure to punish himself."[35] Whether or not Georg heard these words at this time, they embody a principle he would abide by in all his future theatrical activity.

With the approach of Georg's nineteenth birthday in April 1845,

---

* August Wilhelm Schlegel (1767–1845), scholar, translator, and friend of Schiller, produced translations of Shakespeare of extraordinary literary quality during the years 1797–1810. Later completed by Ludwig Tieck, his daughter Dorothea, and her husband Graf von Baudissin, these translations established Shakespeare in Germany.

Seebeck suggested to Duke Bernhard that the prince might thereafter dispense with a tutor, such was his progress and demeanor at the university. The duke did not respond immediately, but then in February, several months ahead of schedule, abruptly ordered Seebeck home. Georg had no notion that a separation from his tutor was imminent; Seebeck was closer to him than his own father. On the morning of Seebeck's departure, the prince sat with him for a long while, breaking their mutual silence·only to say, "There is no one to whom I owe more than you." He begged Seebeck not to leave the duchy, but to make his home in Meiningen. He spoke with so much heartfelt friendliness, and was so calm, natural, and straightforward, that Seebeck thanked God for the opportunity he had had in forming the prince's character. That night he wrote his wife: "May God guard him in the future and allow him to fulfill all the wonderful hopes to which he is entitled." [36]

At the end of the semester, Georg began an extended journey through the Netherlands, Belgium, and France, accompanied by Count von Reitzenstein. For the first time, he was not under the supervision of his parents or Seebeck, but his letters to his parents indicate that he was conscious of the trust they had placed in him. He conscientiously visited educational and historical sites, though in Brussels he did find time to go back again to the romantic and melodramatic *La Muette de Portici*. In Belgium he saw the historical paintings of Louis Gallait and the romantic works of Baron Gustav Wappers, but he found little to praise in the excessive sentimentality of those popular and influential painters.[37] His eye had been trained in Bonn to appreciate the old German art, especially that of Dürer and his contemporaries. But in Paris the next month he saw for the first time a number of paintings of the Italian High and Late Renaissance, a period style that was to influence him all his life. The previous year he had visited Düsseldorf, "the Painters' City," where the academic art had put him off, but the richness of the Italian work, the balance and harmony of the composition, and the modeling of figures kindled in him new ambitions. "I like to compose with figures," he later wrote, an inclination his theater sketches bear out.[38]

Georg was to visit Paris many times during his life, but never again would the city appear so fresh and inviting as it did to the handsome young prince in the spring of 1845. He was nineteen and in the artistic and intellectual center of the world. With money in his pocket and his head filled with newly acquired notions of literature and music, he had what seemed to him endless—and better still, totally free—time. He spent his days in art institutions and his evenings in the theater. Thanks to the letters of introduction he brought with him, he became acquainted with artists, actors, and opera singers.

The prince came to Paris with the intention of making a thorough and scholarly study of the Comédie Française, but he found the venerable institution at a low ebb. The aristocratic and educated classes, wearied of the stagnation of that stage, had followed the general public to the secondary and boulevard theaters, and to the Cirque Olympique. Georg did the same. He attended only two performances at the Comédie Française and commented on one: he found Molière's *George Dandin* "excellent." [39] He was not pleased with the free translations of Schiller's *Wallensteins Lager* and *Wallensteins Tod* he saw at the Odéon Théâtre; "*Wallensteins Lager* was given only as a farce," he complained. [40] He was also bothered by the lack of unity in *Maria Stuart* at the opera, which was "arranged completely differently from [Schiller's] tragedy." The costumes were magnificent, but the piece was "very tiresome . . . without coherence and therefore without interest." [41]

What was certainly of interest to him was *La Muette de Portici*, which he saw for the third time that year. Nowhere in Paris could Georg experience a purer expression of the opulence and glitter of the romantic opera of the day. "Hot enough to scorch, gripping enough to enthrall," said Wagner of this extravaganza, which became something of a phenomenon as it swept through Europe after its première in 1828. [42] Georg saw it in Paris as brilliantly staged by Pierre-Luc-Charles Ciceri, who had visited first Naples, to absorb the flavor of that city, and then Milan, to study the stage machinery used at La Scala to produce the erupting volcano. The opera reached a high degree of pseudo-realism: "Vesuvius, revolution, dancing, love, the marketplace, festivals, prayers, all combined—an orgy for the musicians." [43] The effect was increased by "the important part played by the chorus, who took on the appearance of real people whose lives were being changed by the stirring events taking place around them." [44]

Georg was dazzled, but he retained enough critical judgment to write his mother a close analysis of the production, in which he noted especially the integration of spectacle, drama, and music. The composition in particular caught his eye. "In the first act," he wrote, "the richness of the scene unfolded to a far greater degree than in Brussels. Before the wedding there came a crowd of soldiers and peasants who arranged themselves about the stage." [45]

He was no less dazzled by a production of Giacomo Meyerbeer's *Robert le Diable*. Usually considered the first of a new genre—the Grand Opera—this extraordinarily influential piece, with its grandiloquent text by Augustin Eugène Scribe, fairly breathed, as Heine said, "diabolical carnal desire and love." [46] The craze for the strange and the supernatural, which had reached its height in literature and art in the form of the "gothick" in the 1820's and 1830's and then had largely dissipated, was given new impetus in the theater with the improvements in stage machinery, scene painting, and lighting. Doomed heroes still wandered through decayed abbeys and along desolate shores, and the ghosts of betrayed maidens seeking faithless lovers still haunted lonely graveyards; but now they moved in recognizable landscapes, and their bruised hearts and tragic struggles were sympathetically mirrored by nature. Eerie moonlight, crashing thunder, flashing lightning, beating rain, and lowering skies attended the action on stage and seized the audience's emotions directly. Seas boiled, ships rocked and sank, graves opened and spirits walked. And the appropriately passionate music and a corps of brilliant dancers supported the actions of the tormented souls on stage.[47] Georg succumbed to the power of the music, the staging, and the allure of the unholy theme. Thirty years later, echoes of *Robert le Diable* could be discerned in his staging of Franz Grillparzer's *Die Ahnfrau*.

If *Robert le Diable* thrilled the prince, the ballet *Giselle ou les Wilis* charmed him. In his most detailed letter to his mother, he described the picturesque village on the Rhine and the appearance and grouping of the hunters; but what he noticed most was the atmosphere of the graveyard scene:

The decoration was wonderful, disclosing a wood in every detail lying in the night light. In the foreground were clumps of reeds and undergrowth and also flowers. On the left, only the grave of Giselle, indicated solely by a cross. Hills extended on both sides. On the left, in the background, a mysterious lake, lighted by the moon! On the right, a deep forest from which the hunters came. The audience first sees them gradually coming forward from far back in the woods. They pause in order to take refreshment and, at that very moment, the clock strikes twelve. Terror seizes them as they recognize the forbidden place, and they flee. At that the queen of the Wilis rises from the ground and an unearthly light spreads through the forest. Then she touches . . . a branch of the reed, which breaks apart and from all sides the Wilis rise from the earth and fill the stage, the whole company arrayed with butterfly wings. Then the queen moves to Giselle's grave, and immediately the girl rises from it and is received into the company of the Wilis.[48]

Georg commented on the visual beauty of Carlotta Grisi's dancing and pantomime and on the masterly employment of the ensemble. Later, as a director, he made use of what he had learned from the effective interplay of the corps de ballet and the prima ballerina, especially in the ways the ensemble complemented and supported the principal dancers.[49]

In September 1845, as Georg was on his way to Dresden to sketch its baroque and rococo architecture, he made a stop-off in Weimar specifically to see *The Taming of the Shrew*. In Dresden he went twice to the new opera house designed by Gottfried Semper, where he heard Donizetti's *Lucrezia Borgia* and von Flotow's *Stradella*. He also saw and was "greatly impressed" by a performance of Goethe's *Torquato Tasso*.[50]

On his return to Bonn, Georg asked his professors to resume the Monday evening lectures with readings from Shakespeare. It is easy to imagine that he now read the English masterpieces in the light of the exciting staging he had recently seen in Paris. In November he was assigned a role in a reading of *Coriolanus*. "At my request," he wrote his mother, "I have luckily been given a very short role, that of Titus Lartius, who hardly opens his trap."[51] Georg was a good choice for the valiant Roman, who vows "to lean upon one crutch and fight with the other" rather than shrink from battle. More than six feet tall, strong, erect, and athletic, with a massive head and piercing eyes, the prince was already showing the bearing that caused Richard Wagner in later years to refer to him repeatedly as the perfect representation of the "ancient [Germanic] tribe of Wettin," and Paul Lindau to say that whenever Georg entered a room he seemed to have just divested himself of his medieval armor.

Georg's two years in Bonn were happy ones for him, but the political climate there was causing his father increasing concern—from his point of view, with some justice. Georg's close friendship with the crown prince of Baden, a dangerously radical duchy in Bernhard's eye, was symptomatic of what he saw as a perilous atmosphere in Bonn, lying close to the repeated upheavals in France. German universities had long been placed under strict control, especially after the disclosure of a plot in 1833 to seize the seat of the German Confederation; but it was evident that despite official scrutiny many students and some faculty members still preached reform or even revolution.[52] Prompted by his wife and her father, the Elector of Hessen-Cassel, one of the most reactionary princes in Germany, the duke made plans to remove Georg to a politically safer atmosphere: during the Easter break the Prince was to visit his aunt in England, and after returning to Bonn to finish the semester, he would transfer to the University of Leipzig, safe within the boundaries of Saxony.

On this break in London in March 1846, Georg enjoyed none of the freedom of the previous year in Paris. Now as visiting nobility, nephew of the dowager queen and cousin of the prince consort, he was expected to perform duties attendant on that position. He rode out in a coach-and-four to view the Royal Dockyards at Woolwich; he inspected the Royal Horse Artillery as it went through its paces for him. He interrupted his stay with his aunt at Marlborough House and Bushy Park to spend Easter week with Queen Victoria and her family at Windsor. In letters to his mother he reported his rides in the pony cart, his outings with the royal infants, and his visits to the duchess of Kent at Frogmore in such a noncommittal way that it is difficult to know what he thought of the splendor of the English court as contrasted to the simplicity of Meiningen. But there is no lack of enthusiasm in his account of his ride to Slough on the train (more than a decade would go by before his duchy would have its own little railway) for a hunt with his cousins. The color, the movement, the formalities of custom and deportment, were all brought to life in the sketches that adorn his letters. He rode out often with the prince consort, who had known him from infancy as a relative and close neighbor. Georg had much in common with his Coburg cousin. They had both been educated at the University of Bonn, and they had enjoyed a similar education in art and music.

During the month Georg was in England, he was often in the theater, always arriving on time and never leaving until the performance was over. This was something so unusual among aristocratic box-holders as to be noted by the London *Times*, which reported on April 15, 1846, that "His Serene Highness, the Hereditary Prince of Saxe-Meiningen, remained until the end of the performance." The variety of offerings on the program encouraged theater-goers to stop in for that portion they wished to see; many entered and left at will. Even the queen was guilty of coming late and leaving early, often disrupting the action on stage—once during the dagger scene in *Macbeth*—while the royal party settled itself or prepared to leave. Seebeck's uncompromising training would not permit the prince to act discourteously to anyone, even public entertainers.

Georg found that to attend the London theater in 1846 usually meant to go to the opera. As in Paris, the educated and aristocratic classes, led by the court, had largely deserted the native playhouse for the Italian opera at Her Majesty's Theatre and for the "French plays" at the St. James Theatre. Unfortunately for us, the opera never seemed to elicit from Georg the thoughtful letters other forms of art did. He liked the opera and admired many composers and singers; but although he attended performances all his life, he never had much to say about them. He heard Bellini's *I Puritani* at Her Majesty's Theatre and found Giulia Grisi "exquisite." In the same opera "[Luigi] Lablache was powerful . . . and [Giuseppe] Mario's voice was rich."[53] Such generalities as "excellent" and "fine" are enough for the other Italian operas; he gives no details about the setting or music. Of the French plays, he notes only the titles, but a visit to the circus and two ballets stirred his interest.

It was pure delight at Astley's Amphitheatre, where the stars were two amazingly talented pachyderms, and their vehicle *The Rajah of Nagpore or The Sacred Elephants of the Pagoda*. Set in the oriental splendor of India in 1740, this production (as rewritten in 1845) copied an extravaganza presented fifteen years earlier at the Cirque Olympique in Paris by a master of pantomime and circus pieces, Adolphe Franconi.[54] Spectacle, not historical truth, governed a production in which the prime minister of India was named Missouri and one of the elephants answered to Kelly. By the time Georg saw the play, it was famous throughout Europe for the Act II luncheon scene, in which the two elephants, enveloped in elephantine napkins, sit at a table, ring for service, snatch their master's plate and cup, eat and drink. The English version reproduced the spectacular elements of the French original and ended with a magnificent procession of animals and actors, all accoutered *à la* Orient. Georg was as entranced as he had been as a child.

In no city in Europe in the 1840's was the ballet more cherished than it was in London. There Georg saw Marie Taglioni, considered the greatest dancer of her age, but it was the celebrated Lucile Grahn, in her performances of *Éoline ou la dryade* and *Catarina, the Bandit's Daughter*, who put her mark on his imagination.[55] The young Danish ballerina was one of the four "incomparables" who in the previous year had turned their performance of the *pas de quatre* before Queen Victoria into a historic event.[56] She was at the height of her powers as a dancer and mime. Grahn had trained at the Copenhagen Ballet, whose director, August Bournonville, had long been flirting with realism by incorporating elements of national dances into his productions and staging them in historically accurate and colorful sets and costumes. Further, the company had abandoned the custom, almost universal in other companies, of subordinating everything—ensemble, sets, and especially the male dancers—to the ballerina. Grahn was a brilliant soloist, but she could work with strong male dancers and an ensemble. In her Georg saw a great star who kept her place in a unified work of art.

The theme of the half-mortal, half-supernatural being torn between the desire of a human lover and the jealousy of a malevolent spirit reaches back to the ballets of Louis XIV; but *Éoline* as Georg saw it in 1846 retained few of its classical trappings. Grahn's *Éoline* was danced and mimed in the preternatural atmosphere so prized by the Romantics. The extravagant display of violent passions culminated in a wild *mazurka d'extase*, but in Georg's eyes even Grahn's masterly dancing did not surpass the effect of her forceful miming. The silent acting with which the despairing Éoline accepted death, tied to a burning tree by the vindictive king of the gnomes, proved more powerful than words.

In the second ballet, *Catarina, the Bandit's Daughter*, Grahn impressed the prince not by the artistry of her mimicry, but by her vigorous mobility. At the climax of the ballet, the choreographer broke with the usual movement of the corps de ballet directly across the stage or diagonally toward one corner. Catarina drilled her brigands in a series of military exercises; then they abruptly turned and ran upstage, where they scaled a rock formation—the lookout. Poised thus a moment, they reversed themselves and stormed furiously toward the audience. Georg learned a vivid lesson on the use of movement on stage: how anonymous and powerless the brigands looked as they scrambled away from the viewers, how strong and threatening as they rushed toward the footlights.*

Georg makes no mention in his letters of seeing any of Shakespeare's plays.[57] During his stay Macready appeared at the Princess Theatre in *Macbeth*, *Othello*, *Lear*, and *Hamlet*. It is hard to believe that someone who would make a stopover in Weimar just to see *The Taming of the Shrew* would fail to see England's greatest tragedian, but there is no evidence that he did. Further, Georg makes no reference to seeing Madame Vestris, that important innovator, although the actress was a great favorite of Queen Victoria's.[58]

As planned, Georg returned to Bonn to finish the semester, and sometime in those months "bought a collection of Swiss costume plates for twenty Franken."[59] By October 1846 he was at the University of Leipzig, where he studied law and national economy. He found the old city, with its many bookstores, publishing houses, and strong musical history, pleasing. He lived in the household of Felix Mendelssohn and felt that life there, with its simple Biedermeier comfort and hominess, suited him. The deep affection between Mendelssohn and his wife, Cecile, and the composer's close family ties with his sisters touched the prince. He was attracted to the circle of happily married men around the musician—he himself was destined to become a family man, never so happy as when surrounded by children and grandchildren.

Georg had not given up the serious study of the piano. Through years of searching application to the study of Beethoven's works, he evolved certain principles that guided his reception and evaluation of art throughout his life. These he had set forth in a letter to his mother while he was still in Bonn:

This Ninth Symphony is probably the most exalted and most incredible of all Beethoven's symphonies. Certainly, such a work, . . . like a deep imprint, does not permit itself to be understood without effort and the expenditure of labor. We must study it thoroughly just as we study a difficult book; we must listen to the symphony many times with concentration in order to fathom the depth of its meaning. Unless we do that, we cannot find it beautiful, for how can we find anything at all beautiful if we don't understand and comprehend it? You will say, music should not be difficult! But why should music see the light of day simply as a superficial creation? Should poetry then do the same? Certainly not! Now why

---

* Even 30 years after Georg saw Catarina, audiences were still astonished at the Meininger's "innovative" use of this movement, which critics contrasted to the usual crowds "goose-stepping" across the stage, parallel to the footlights.

then should the art of poetry have as its warrant the right to elevate itself so much higher than music? Just as Goethe or Schiller could scarcely have created light, shallow, superficial things, but instead through their spirit raised such stuff to higher spheres, so Beethoven's spirit could hardly find a place in the province of the insipid elements lying at hand; instead art must aspire to what is higher and more impressive than the ordinary.[60]

In this youthfully spirited, even vehement defense of the "higher spheres" of art, it is not hard to discern the fervor that Georg would later bring to his work in the theater.

Although Georg's favorite composers were then, as always, Bach and Beethoven, he listened with great interest to Mendelssohn's opinions of the "new" music. Three years earlier in Berlin he had seen a production of *Antigone* with Mendelssohn's then starkly modern music, and now he learned of the doubts the composer experienced while composing it. He also heard of the difficulties of presenting a drama under the direction of several strong-minded men, as Mendelssohn described the battles that raged among Ludwig Tieck, the historian August Böckh, and Eduard Devrient during rehearsals. If the accounts of the near-violence that accompanied the production did not teach the prince that a single, resolute hand was necessary to stage a classical drama, then the report of the intransigent and irresponsible conduct of King Friedrich Wilhelm IV of Prussia, who had commissioned the work, must have done so.[61] Mendelssohn found in the prince a gifted amateur pianist, and Georg attended weekly concerts at the Gewandhaus. There he was surprised to hear Mendelssohn play from memory a piano arrangement of Beethoven's *Ninth Symphony*, in which he found such profound meaning, but of which Mendelssohn said, "It gives me no pleasure."[62]

Georg went often to the theater. He wrote his mother a thoughtful letter after seeing the disturbing new drama *Uriel Acosta* by Karl Gutzkow, that controversial champion of religious and intellectual freedom. Georg's conservative rearing and deeply held religious views gave him cause to question the theme of the drama, but his critical honesty forced him to concede its artistic worth. The piece, he said, was very interesting and absorbing, "even if the current of thought is not to be praised. The piece relates to religious conditions of the present time and defends radicalism. On the whole, however, it is an important drama and has beautiful places and fine language."[63]

Georg's twenty-first birthday on April 2, 1847, marked the end of his university studies and the beginning of what he thought was to be his life's work in the military. He made a study tour to Italy during the summer and in December took up his duties as a first lieutenant in the Guards Regiment at the court of Friedrich Wilhelm IV in Berlin. Here he had time to continue his art education. When he began a new painting, *Die Schlacht am Lechfelde gegen die Hunnen* (The Battle at Lechfeld Against the Huns), he was fortunate in having the advice of the painters Peter von Cornelius and Wilhelm von Kaulbach, whom he had known at Bonn.

Georg followed his usual pattern of frequent theater-going. Shakespeare's *A Midsummer Night's Dream* "pleased him especially," and *Antigone* "worked a monstrous effect" on him, moving him to tears. The opera *Wilhelm Tell*, which impressed him as "very true," was distinguished by its "magnificently" painted decorations. He found the characters in *Othello* well delineated and the scenery exciting. "In the final scene," he reported, "there comes a bombardment of Cyprus by the Venetian fleet, something very well staged. The ships, which the audience sees in the distance, rock to and fro on the waves and shoot accurately from the harbor toward the city lying on the distant, romantic shore." The ballet *Esmeralda* also made an impression. It was based on Victor Hugo's *Notre Dame de Paris*; the action was set in a square before a realistically painted façade of Notre Dame Cathedral and presented a magnificent picture of fifteenth-century Paris. The color, the shifting masses of gypsies, vagabonds, soldiers, market people, and students, remained in Georg's memory and appeared on his stage years later.[64]

At the beginning of 1848 there appeared on the political scene events more disturbing than anything Georg could see on the stage. For some time Duke Bernhard II had found Georg's friendship with the princes of Oldenburg and Coburg unsettling; both houses were closely allied with Prussian politics, which Bernhard neither trusted nor admired. Equally worrisome to him was his son's continued friendship with the crown prince of Baden. But the February Revolution of 1848 in Paris drove these worries from his mind and turned it to the dangers in which the ruling princes of Europe found themselves. In March he wrote Georg a letter in which he set out what he saw as the only two courses the rulers might take with their dissatisfied subjects: conciliation or force. On March 10 Georg replied in a letter to his mother:

What Papa expressed in his letter as a fear that in a few weeks it might be too late to make common [that is, unified action by all the rulers] or suitable concessions, I am afraid that now in the course of a few days, his prophecy will come true. Events push in, and every hour brings news. Thrones are rocking too much, and it is hard to know whether concessions should be made or not. If concessions are not made, it could cost the monarchy; but if some concessions are made, the people will want more, and the mob will want to go far beyond the will of the people.

Everything in Georg's conservative training and background forced him to take a stand against violent revolution. He ended his letter: "From my point of view, if someone had bombarded Paris and changed half of that city into a heap of ashes, it would have been better than the probability that the whole world will break into revolution." [65]

His father ordered him home. Filled with all the outrage of an imaginative twenty-two-year-old prepared for righteous combat, Georg answered angrily: "If the German princes are to be pushed from their thrones—something that does not seem unlikely to me—and we all fall, it would be shameful for me if, in Germany's greatest need, I sat at home like a milksop [*milchpuppe*]. . . . No one would thank me, but rather I would be despised every day of my life, and I would curse myself. *This is to me a holy combat!* . . . If the people of Meiningen want me to pull out with our battalion, tell them that with a great army I can accomplish more important things." [66]

Duke Bernhard was not impressed by his son's heroics and again ordered him home. A few days later Georg took part in subduing an uprising, which resulted in sixteen revolutionaries dead, and thirty mortally wounded. The bloody episode appalled him and destroyed forever the notions of glory in warfare. On April 3 he wrote his mother: "A town militia in Meiningen! How much has changed in a few days!" But now he was glad to go home. The March Revolution made a profound impression on Georg; and when he returned to Meiningen a second lesson was brought home to him. The fires that had raged through Western Europe had touched the duchy very little. The citizens had even put aside an old controversy over public lands in order to support the ducal house; repeated efforts by radical groups to incite rebellion had pushed the middle class over to the side of the aristocracy. But Georg realized that the power of the old feudal system was dead, and that the thrones of Europe now rested not on the ancient idea of divine right, but on the support of the people.

In the following year, during Prussia's conflict with Denmark over Schleswig-Holstein, Georg, with the rank of major, led eight hundred Meiningen troops under the command of Duke Ernst II of Saxe-Coburg north, but saw no action. In May and June they guarded the coast as reserves. Georg walked over the countryside, sketching landscapes and studying the architecture. The flat land, so unlike the rolling hills of Thuringia, and the seascapes provided a variety of unfamiliar views for sketching. Released from military duty, Georg spent September in Norway, traveling from Christiania along the Oslofjord to Drammen, where he produced a number of paintings. He came back with a deep interest in the northern lands. [67] It was an interest he did not lose: sixteen years later, at his instigation, the Bibliographisches Institut in Hildburghausen published the first collection of Björnstjerne Björnson's works; and Georg was one of the first directors to present the plays of the Scandinavian writers.[68]

The following years were important ones for the prince. He resumed his military career in Berlin and there became engaged to the niece of the king of Prussia, Princess Charlotte, eldest daughter of Prince Albrecht of Prussia and his wife, Marianne, born princess of the Netherlands. It was a love match between the twenty-four-year-old prince and his nineteen-year-old fiancée, and their engagement was a short one. They were married on May 18, 1850. Among the wedding gifts was a splendid old villa and showplace on Lake Como from the mother of the bride, renamed in Charlotte's honor the Villa Carlotta. The couple spent the next five years in Berlin and in Potsdam (where they made their home in the Marmor Palais), though they returned to Meiningen for the birth of each of their three children.

Charlotte was as ardent a theater-goer as Georg and had acted with him in amateur court theatricals during their engagement.[69] But whether they regularly went to plays in these years Georg's letters do not say. He indicates no more than that on January 16, 1853, he saw the first of four performances of the American Negro tragedian Ira Aldridge, who appeared at the royal command of King Friedrich Wilhelm IV. Playing in English while others in the cast spoke their native tongue, Aldridge was phenomenally successful, especially as Othello and Macbeth. His acting and miming, the natural tone of his voice, and the nervous play of his hands deserved the highest recognition, said the reviewer in the *Preussische Zeitung*. "What abandonment, passion, beauty, greatness, and sense!," he wrote. Billed as the African Roscius, Aldridge proved himself as capable in comedy as in tragedy. His Mungo Park in Isaac Bickerstaffe's one-act blackface farce, *The Padlock*, made "the old chandeliers shake with laughter, and the gas flames shake with laughter."[70] Georg was impressed enough to invite the actor to appear in Meiningen, which he did five years later.*

---

* In January 1858 Aldridge appeared on the Meiningen stage as Shylock, Macbeth, and Mungo Park. Georg was so impressed with these performances that he induced his father to honor the actor, who received the Saxon Order with the medal in gold. As the *London Illustrated News* of July 3, 1858, reported: "What enhances this great distinction is that Mr. Aldridge is the only artist, native or foreign, so decorated." (Herbert Marshall and Mildred Stock, *Ira Aldridge, the Negro Tragedian*, London, 1958, pp. 181-83.) Georg's appreciation of Aldridge is emphasized here because Marshall and Stock make a good case for Aldridge's having materially influenced the European theater through his influence on Georg. "In 1878 [sic] the Meiningen Company, which had already become famous, came to London and earned great acclaim, then to Moscow, where it influenced the young Stanislavski, and so the ripples of reform spread—the initiation of some of which may be attributed to the Chevalier Ira Aldridge, Knight of Saxony, as he ever afterwards called himself" (p. 211).

Political affairs continued to absorb Georg as conditions between Prussia and Austria destabilized. His parents, always distrustful of Prussia, were resolutely pro-Austrian, but by this time Georg was familiar enough with Prussian politics to regard their attitude as impractical. He feared that in an open conflict between Prussia and Austria small states like Meiningen would suffer most. In 1854 he voiced his concern to his mother in a long letter ending with these words: "Don't be angry, but it seems clear to me that you are almost one-sided and not entirely correct in your judgment of present political affairs. To be sure, it is very desirable for Austria and Prussia to follow the same politics—yet I do not think one can call it treason if Prussia follows a direction vetoed by Austria. . . . Since both states are Great Powers, one can certainly expect that both cannot go on together without there being treachery by someone on one side." [71]

In 1855 personal tragedy drove all political problems from Georg's mind. On January 27, his second son, Georg, nearly three years old and a special favorite of his father, died. Three months later, Charlotte died in childbirth, her infant dying with her. Georg was inconsolable; for the next two years he moved restlessly about. He did not return to Meiningen, but spent long periods at the Villa Carlotta. From April 1855 to January 1857 he wandered through France and Italy. He was in Paris in September 1855, but says nothing about the theater. Later that year he visited theaters in Nice and Marseilles, and then spent time sketching in Spain and Algiers. Back in Italy in December, he saw *Don Pasquale* in Florence. From January to July 1856 he painted seriously at the Villa Carlotta under the direction of Andreas Müller, who had been recommended to him by von Kaulbach. Georg returned to Meiningen early in 1857 to attend a gala performance of *A Midsummer Night's Dream* for his thirty-first birthday.

Georg knew that he must marry to provide a mother for his two small children, Prince Bernhard and Princess Marie. Accompanied by Baron Rochus von Liliencron, a member of his father's staff, he began a three-month journey to Paris and London on what Liliencron called a "bride search." [72] Georg wrote few letters from Paris, and almost nothing about the theater. Liliencron himself saw some farces, conversation pieces, and ballets, but it is not known whether or not the prince accompanied him. Georg did remark on *Psyche*, a classical piece at the Opéra Comique, which was already old-fashioned when August von Kotzebue complained about it more than fifty years earlier. [73] Adelaide Ristori's powerful performance in Ernest Legouvé's *Medea* proved a revelation of realistic acting. At the Théâtre Lyrique he enjoyed von Weber's *Obéron*, written in 1826 and a favorite of the prince since his university days. An example of the early Romantic opera, *Obéron* was filled with oriental splendor and ended with a *danse turque* in full costume.*

He wrote his mother that he had found a factory, Granget et Cie, "which perhaps is the only one in Europe where armor is fabricated. I stayed there for a long time and looked over everything carefully. Every sort of armor is there reproduced and certainly in the correct strength and quality." This factory, he reported, provided "all the great theaters of the world with armor, coats-of-mail, and ornaments, also weapons." Georg later ordered much of the Meininger's armor from Granget. Also in Paris he found a shop where the silver-glittered stockinet used to give the appearance of chain mail could be bought.[74]

The prince and Liliencron proceeded to London for the baptism of Queen Victoria's last child, Beatrice. Again the prince wrote almost nothing, and we must rely on Liliencron's rather rapturous descriptions of his proximity to royalty, both the English and the large expatriate colony of the deposed French. Georg visited the newly completed National Portrait Gallery and the Victoria and Albert Museum, then known as the Museum of Ornamental Art. He liked the movement in Charles Kean's production of *Richard II*, he said in a letter to his mother, and also the attempts at reality and historical accuracy, but he found the decorations excessive, the text mangled to enhance the star, and Mrs. Kean's crinolines under her fourteenth-century costumes ridiculous.[75] It is interesting to notice that the extravagance Georg accepted at the opera and the ballet without complaint and at the circus with delight, he deplored when it violated what he saw as the soul of a serious drama. He ended his letter by saying "the acting left much to be desired; only Kean, son of the famous Edmund, played Richard very well."

He went off to Astley's with hopes of having some fun, and he was not disappointed. *Richard III* was given as a circus piece with the celebrated horse, White Surrey, playing a major role. Everything that had charmed Georg since childhood was in this production: color, music, excitement, performing horses, even a bit of Shakespeare. The great scenes, says A. H. Saxon in his excellent account of the hippodrama, took place at the battle of Bosworth Field in Act III. "The actors appeared on horse-

---

* Georg was amused at a conversation with his barber on the morning after he heard the opera. "Is it an Italian opera?" he asked the barber. "French, of course, monsieur," the man replied. "Who is the composer?" the prince asked. "I don't know," was the reply, "but it's by a Frenchman and entirely new." The prince later laughed with Liliencron and said, "Of course, if it's new to Paris, then it's new to the world." (Anton Bettelheim, *Leben und Wirken des Freiherrn Rochus von Liliencron*, Berlin, 1917, p. 112.)

back whenever opportunity afforded, and Richard, mounted on White Surrey, triumphed over several valorous opponents before his steed was 'wounded' and died on stage. To the blare of music from the orchestra pit, Richard and Richmond clashed in battle against the background of human and equine bodies, the docility of the stud meanwhile being exhibited in the 'pertinacity with which they retain their semblance of death.'"[76] Even the farce with "dancing girls" that the prince and Liliencron saw later must have seemed pretty tepid after this.

The following year, 1858, while he was on a journey to Italy, Georg met Princess Feodora of Hohenlohe-Langenburg, whose mother, also Princess Feodora, was a half-sister of Queen Victoria's.[77] They became engaged almost at once. But it was not a happy choice for either: Georg had never become reconciled to Charlotte's death; and Feo, as she was called, was not temperamentally suited for the life she was expected to lead. As Georg was quick to discover after their wedding on October 23, 1858, he had married a sweet, nineteen-year-old child. The youngest of four children, petted and spoiled, always called Baby and treated like one, Feo had no intellectual or artistic attainments and no interest in developing any. With his usual energy—probably terrifying to a young woman like Feo—Georg set about educating her. Her mother found it "very sensible of him indeed to arrange for his bride to be much occupied with lessons, to take drawing lessons, and to hear lectures on history,"[78] but it was soon apparent that Feo would never be another clever and witty Charlotte. Three sons were born to them, but only the first two survived. After the death of the third within days of his birth in 1865, Feo stayed away from Meiningen as much as she decently could.[79] But Georg remained fond of her. When she contracted scarlet fever in January 1872, he was genuinely distraught and sent telegrams to her parents twice daily. Feo died on February 10.

During these years, Georg wrote very little about theater-going. In 1859 he saw six performances of Shakespeare's plays in Berlin; but he gave no details other than to note that they were produced by Samuel Phelps. Likewise, Dingelstedt's tercentenary cycle of the Shakespeare Histories, which he saw in Weimar in 1864, elicited the single comment, "interesting." To be sure, there were things to keep him home. For one thing, he continued his military career, becoming a major-general on November 22, 1858, and a lieutenant-general on January 29, 1863. For another, he continued to be preoccupied with politics, and had watched with growing anxiety as his father's hostility toward Prussia became more and more open. Georg's years at the Prussian court had given him an insight into the strategies of that state, and as early as 1854 he had warned his parents of the folly of a land so small as Meiningen challenging Prussia's might. Meiningen, he pointed out in a letter to his mother, lay geographically near Prussia, and prudence dictated that the duchy moderate its hostility toward its neighbor. It would be wise, he thought, for Meiningen to do willingly what it would be forced to do unwillingly.[80]

Soon after Bismarck's appointment as premier in 1862, he made it clear that he intended to push Austria out of the German Confederation—and out of German affairs. By 1866 he was ready to provoke war to do this. Georg did not indulge in any of the rhetoric that had marked his conduct in 1848; now his only concern was for the future of Meiningen. He was convinced that the duchy could not defend itself militarily; Austria lay far away, and his little country was in danger of being swallowed up by Prussia. Such a fate did in fact overtake his grandfather's land, Hessen-Cassel. Bernhard did not agree; and when war was declared in June, he was one of the fourteen princes in the German Confederation who stood against Prussia.

Events moved quickly. Bernhard's father-in-law was arrested, and Bernhard, with most of his officials, fled to Bamberg in Bavaria. On July 19 Georg wrote to his father, begging permission to enter the Prussian army in order *"to save for our house what can be saved."*[81] His father refused to allow it. The Prussian army rolled over Germany and defeated Austria in seven weeks; for the time being, Bismarck had reached his goals. The king of Prussia wrote Bernhard a friendly letter beginning, "My dear Cousin Bernhard," and signing himself, "Your Cousin Wilhelm," but making it clear that Bernhard was no longer the ruling duke of Meiningen. On September 20, 1866, Bernhard abdicated in favor of his son, and on September 21, the crown prince became Georg II, duke of Saxe-Meiningen, Hildburghausen, and Saalfeld.

The abdication announcement Bernhard sent to the people of Meiningen concealed a profound bitterness. He had never known any life other than that of a ruling prince. Not yet three years old at the time of his father's death, he had grown up watching his mother bend every effort to secure the throne for him. By 1866 he had ruled for more than forty years; and although he pointed out to the people of Meiningen that new times required new ideas, and asked them to accept his son with love and trust, much of his anger and bitterness was directed toward Georg. Georg's message was a model of love and conciliation:[82]

To my beloved people of Meiningen!

Deeply affected that the pitiless events of this year have moved my greatly beloved father to lay down the duties with which he has been blessed for almost fifty years, I enter my high office. I beseech God to strengthen and enlighten me, to give me vigor to administer that office with the same exceptional loyalty and devotion that made my beloved father a shining example to princes. I come to you with love and trust. Support me in my arduous calling with your trust.

Meiningen,   Georg.
September 21, 1866.

Problems arose almost at once. Bernhard may have laid down his office, but he had no intention of laying down the power that went with it. He was confident that only he knew what was best for Meiningen, and he fully expected to rule through his son. For two reasons Georg would have no part of such an arrangement. He knew Prussia would never allow Bernhard any position, no matter how unofficial; but more important, he intended to be a duke in his own way. In reply to his father's warning that as an inexperienced ruler, he would be at the mercy of flatterers and self-seekers, Georg wrote: "Unpalatable truth is generally not imparted to princes, [but] I can only repeat to you that I wish to have only those people near me who will sincerely speak the truth. Those who gratuitously push themselves forward and offer commonplace advice while they ignore concrete questions—such persons I have always appropriately rejected and I shall always appropriately reject—even if the person be a wife or clergyman." [83]

This letter laid down the principles that guided Georg throughout his life. He was never satisfied with half-measures or with anything indecisive. He listened to opposing opinions, but as we can see from his letters, no one ever made a final decision for him on policy. He pursued a lifelong study of national and international politics, and sought always to do what seemed to him to be to Meiningen's advantage. Bernhard never accepted his son's position, and they remained estranged for many years after Georg's accession. [84] Not until 1879, when Georg's life was despaired of during a siege of pneumonia, was there any lessening of Bernhard's hostility.

After Prussia's victory, Georg set about strengthening Meiningen as a defeated duchy living by Berlin's sufferance. In the 1840's he had belonged to an organization of ducal sons whose aim was the unification of the German states under the king of Prussia; then their plan came to nothing. Now in a letter to his cousin Ernst of Coburg-Gotha, he set out his reasons for renewing the proposal. "Southern Germany would be bound to a German emperor," he wrote Ernst on December 21, 1866, "and we would cease to face Prussia as, one might say, the conquered, for an emperor of Germany is quite different from a king of Prussia." The next day, in a letter to the same effect to another cousin, Karl Alexander, grand duke of Weimar-Eisenach, he added: "With an emperor we would win back the South Germans and bring them nearer to us . . . especially in Bavaria, where the aversion to Prussianism is great. An emperor would also have an interest in all those who lived in his empire, not just those living in his hereditary states, whereas the king of Prussia cannot possibly have this interest. Therefore, the idea must suggest itself to him and his government to loot our conquered lands for the profit of Prussia."[85] The proposal came to nothing; Bismarck was not yet ready to unify the German lands. Georg II had to wait five years and fight in still another war before he stood in the Hall of Mirrors in Versailles to see Germany become a unified nation.

In the meantime, he set about strengthening Meiningen from within, an endeavor that remained his primary purpose and to which he devoted his greatest energies for the next forty-seven years. He never allowed artistic pursuits to absorb any of the attention or the means that properly belonged to the Duchy of Saxe-Meiningen and its citizens. His reign was marked by simplicity and frugality. Its just and liberal quality is demonstrated by the fact that in nearly half a century of government, he had only five state ministers, and each of these was appointed only on the retirement of his predecessor.

At the same time he turned his attention to the duchy's cultural life, already richly diverse. Princes of the Wettin dynasty in Thuringia had fostered theatrical activity since at least the end of the sixteenth century. At that time, critics were already listing among the sins of the nobility extravagant buildings for "play-giving and dancing," and complaining that many nobles had "their own drummers, lute players or zither strummers, bagpipers, or fools, whom they dressed in green, red, gray, or blue and outfitted them in new hats." Even the ravages of the Thirty Years War did not prohibit them from "erecting for pleasure: riding schools, indoor tennis courts, libraries, and music rooms."[86]

Amateur court theatricals received new impetus in Meiningen in 1776, when the ruling duke Karl Augustus built a stage in the ballroom on the third floor of the castle. He and his younger brother, later Georg I, not only took part in the court productions, but had printed a special edition of the works performed. When Georg II's grandfather became the ruling duke in 1782, he assumed direction of the plays. Descriptions of the careful use of decoration and costume by Duke Georg I, who was said to "talk theater" constantly,[87] give credence to Max Grube's assertion that his grandson's theatrical interests were "truly atavistic." In 1785 Johann Friedrich Schönemann brought the first professional company to Meiningen; others followed.[88] The theater gradually drew more support from

Fig. 2. The old Meiningen court theater, which opened in 1831 and was destroyed in a fire in 1908. Georg made plans to rebuild the theater two days after the fire; it saw its first production in 1909.

the middle-classes than from the court, but the duke never lost interest in the productions. When Hildburghausen and Saalfeld were annexed to Meiningen, they brought theatrical traditions as ancient as those of Meiningen. But there was little activity in the years following Georg I's death in 1800; his widow, Louisa Eleanora, was too much occupied during the Napoleonic wars to concern herself greatly with the theater.

As a ruling duke, Bernhard II supported the theater, although he had neither his father's nor his son's love for it. He preferred the opera, but comedies and dramas interested him if they were well done. He did not care for tragedy unless some virtuoso appeared as guest. Finding regular performances in the castle becoming increasingly inconvenient for those living there, he determined that the town should have a theater of its own. A sale of stock in the undertaking was successful, and the theater opened on the duke's birthday, December 17, 1831, with a gala performance of Auber's opera *Fra Diavolo*. The first paid public performance took place three days later; the vehicle was *Hans Sachs* by the Austrian playwright Johann Ludwig Deinhardstein. One month later, Pius Alexander Wolff's *Preciosa*, a gypsy drama based on Cervantes' *La Gitanilla* and set to music by Karl von Weber, was given on the Meiningen stage as a benefit for Therese von Weber, identified in the papers as "probably a relative of the composer."[89] This was destined to become one of Georg's

57

favorite plays, but whether the five-and-a-half-year-old prince saw it at this time is not known. On February 8, 1832, four weeks before Goethe's death, a performance of *Faust* marked the end of the Meiningen public theater's first season.

Troupes came and went during the following years, and only one director remained for a second season. A few productions were good, but most were so bad that in 1860 Duke Bernhard restored the court theater and appointed his aide-de-camp, Baron Carl von Stein, intendant. Von Stein did not want to accept the post, saying he knew nothing of theater management; indeed, as he later said, he had never been inside even one of the best German theaters.[90] But Bernhard insisted, and von Stein went to study with two of the ablest instructors in Germany: Franz Dingelstedt, then general intendant of the Weimar court theater, and Eduard Devrient, director of the court theater in Karlsruhe. The unknowledgeable von Stein wisely engaged a stage director, Dr. Karl Locher, about whom nothing is known except that he fostered some sort of ensemble playing, could take leading roles, and on stage led a group in crowd scenes. Although von Stein did not have the luxury of a permanent company because the theater played only during the winter season, he succeeded in adding a fair number of plays to the repertoire, including several classical pieces.[91] Some of the performances were good, many excellent. The opera was the weakest part of the court theater because of its scanty means, but von Stein depended on the excellent reputation of his conductor, John Joseph Bott, to attract enough strong artists to produce grand opera successfully.[92]

This was the situation in the Meiningen court theater when Bernhard abdicated in September 1866. How was it, asks von Stein, that within seven years he (von Stein) had been able to transform a faltering venture into a vigorous, artistic achievement? Because, he answers, ignoring his own considerable contributions, "already the crown prince was the *spiritus rector* of the new enterprise and was breathing his inspiration into it. Without daring to step in openly, the crown prince found in the intendant a thankful and teachable instrument (*Werkzeug*) to carry out—as far as the means and circumstances would permit—his ideas."[93] During this time the Meiningen court theater took a respected place among German theaters, so that when Georg became duke and could support the theater more generously, there was no great or sudden change.

Four years earlier, in 1862, the prince had formulated his artistic principles in a letter to von Stein:

Artists are nothing; only art has worth. This means that only the artist who uses art for the benefit of humanity deserves support. That other kind of artist, however, who approaches art carefully and uses it to delude mankind—he should be fought and rendered harmless. My anger is now—and always will be as long as I live—directed against everything frivolous in art. He to whom God has given a talent should not bury it. I too shall use that little ability in art that I possess in the service of the highest. If I look on art as higher than many others do, that should not be charged against me less than against those others who do not regard art as holy.

These words are identical in spirit to those the nineteen-year-old Georg had written to his mother from Bonn when, from his study of Beethoven's *Ninth Symphony,* he had worked through to the truth that "art must aspire to what is higher and more impressive than the ordinary." Now, twenty years later, in this letter to von Stein, he had accepted for himself the obligation this truth imposes. It remained for him only to apply this principle to the theater to develop what the literary historian Robert F. Arnold calls "one of the two most important [theatrical] phenomena of the century."[94]

The exact division of duties between von Stein and the prince was never made clear by either, but a letter Georg wrote to the intendant in January 1864 seems to indicate that the prince had been turning his attention to the Meiningen stage for some time and had, in fact, been taking a hand in directing it. He says he has added to the meagerly outfitted property room and is now ready to supplement the scanty store of weapons with pieces from his own collection. He begins the letter with the authority of someone already in charge: "Concerning the opera *Margarete* [*Faust*], allow me to make some observations that I would like you to refer to the stage manager." Then he attacks point by point the weaknesses of the performance and offers suggestions on how best to make the staging clarify the substance of the work. The war scene with its goose-stepping troops is "a horror," he concludes.[95]

Georg's revitalization of the cultural life in Meiningen effected changes in three spheres: he created epoch-making reforms in the theater; he gave a strong impetus to Germany's musical life; and he worked for the benefit of all the other arts, including even the industrial arts. For nearly fifty years he devoted himself primarily to the first. He dropped the court opera to devote all his modest means to the spoken drama. He did this, not because he did not like music; the history of the Meiningen court orchestra, called by Wagner "the best in Europe," and the Salzunger Choir, characterized by Liszt as "remarkable," disprove that.[96] Besides Liszt and Wagner, the composer Brahms was closely connected with Meiningen; Hans von Bülow was long conductor there, and under his baton the Meiningen court orchestra became as celebrated throughout Europe as the theater company. Richard Strauss began his career in Meiningen, and the duke himself was a fine pianist. Paul Lindau said, "How he could listen!" But he was resolved to support the theater from his private means, never allowing it to become a burden on the people. He intended too to keep the price of admission low enough for all the citizens of the duchy to attend performances. Above all, he recognized that a small theater could not spiritually support opera and operetta as well as drama.

The duke began his work in the theater, not because he wanted to reform it, but because he loved it. His training in painting and music, as well as more than thirty years of theater-going, shaped his views. He knew definitely what he wanted to see on his stage. Everything must be part of a unified work of art. The decorations must never be too magnificent, but must be correctly suited to the drama; the content of the piece must not be superficial, but beautiful; the speech and playing of the actors must not be pathetic or empty, but true to life and authentic. He set out detailed analyses of pieces that interested him in these considerations and mentioned their positive aspects.[97] He saw Shakespeare's dramas above all others as a profound reservoir to be plumbed by study and illuminated on stage for the education and pleasure of the public.

On November 4, 1866, the duke opened his first season with *Hamlet*, hardly a new piece on the German stage, but as von Stein says, new in the sense that "a new spirit hovered over it."[98] The engagement of several superior actors permitted the introduction of a number of classical works, most of which were well done.[99] The Oedipus trilogy and *Julius Caesar* were theatrical events. Georg never lost his interest in *Macbeth*, which he had translated and adapted before he was sixteen years old, but at this time he began work on *Julius Caesar*, the play most closely associated with his name and with which he worked all his life.*

In February 1867 he sent a letter to von Stein, asking him to write a newspaper article describing each piece of scenery and its significance, for "the public must be prepared for the performance of *Caesar*." He followed with a detailed discussion of the three sets. *Julius Caesar* had never been given in Germany as it was on March 10, 1867. The first view of the stage set the audience in ancient Rome and established the mood for the evening. The scenes in Brutus's garden, the murder of Caesar before the Forum, the speeches of Brutus and Mark Antony, and the battle of Philippi may later have been improved on, but they never made a greater impression. The powerful plot, historically true settings, and vigorous crowd action held the audience's closest attention.

Yet the Oedipus trilogy in the antique form without scenery, pauses, or

---

* Just two years before his death, the eighty-six-year-old duke returned to the protagonist of his first great success when he directed his final play, Shaw's *Caesar and Cleopatra*.

scene changes was just as effective. As he had with *Caesar*, the duke himself conducted the rehearsals after he had worked through every phase of
the drama until it stood as a complete entity in his mind. He concentrated
entirely on the poetry; the staging was simple to the point of sparseness.
The three tragedies, *Oedipus Rex*, *Oedipus at Colonus*, and *Antigone*,
were given on successive evenings, which closed the season.

At the end of the season von Stein, who had never felt comfortable in
the theater, took up duties as the duke's chamberlain, and he remained
his confidant and friend. Georg found a new intendant in the person of
Friedrich Bodenstedt, whose reputation as a poet and Shakespearean
scholar convinced the duke that he would add prestige to the Meiningen
stage.[100] At the same time, Karl Grabowsky, who had come to Meiningen
as an actor and stage director in 1863, became stage manager and art
director.[101]

Bodenstedt arrived in April 1867, engaged new personnel during the
summer, and opened his first season on October 20 with *Romeo and
Juliet*. There were nine works by Shakespeare in the 1867-68 season, together with four German classics and one Greek tragedy.[102] They were
not so beautifully mounted as they were to be in later years, but the principle of harmony between the meaning of the work and the staging—
between what was heard and what was seen—was carefully followed.
Perhaps, says von Stein, it was left to the actor to use his talent and inspiration, but nothing was left to chance. From the first reading rehearsal
to the performance everything was devoted to a common goal.[103]

Wilhelm Oechelhäuser, Shakespearean scholar and for many years
president of the Shakespeare Society in Germany, saw three of the English masterpieces and praised them highly, especially *King John*, which
he saw on December 17. Since Bodenstedt believed that every word written by Shakespeare must be spoken, he restored many scenes never before
played in Germany. Oechelhäuser cited not only the sensitivity to beauty
in the productions, but the historical accuracy; and he pointed to Weimar, Karlsruhe, and Meiningen as models for Berlin, Vienna, and Dresden—theaters producing Shakespeare in the traditional manner. "What
good are masterly individual performances," he asked, "when the text,
staging, outfitting, costuming, and casting of secondary roles, ensembles,
and crowds are usually deplorable, and at best mediocre?"[104]

By the third season, Georg had enough confidence in his productions
to invite two important men to see the performances: Professor Hermann
Köchly of Heidelberg, Germany's leading authority on the time of Julius
Caesar, and Karl Frenzel, one of the most influential drama critics in the
German-speaking countries. Many years later, Frenzel wrote of how
greatly impressed he had been:

I saw at that time the comedy *The Taming of the Shrew* and the tragedy *Julius Caesar*. These productions delighted me. I had seen nothing similar in Berlin or Dresden, nor in Munich or Vienna. . . . The Italian comedy was thoroughly charming and colorfully picturesque, the Roman tragedy overpowering. It is difficult to give the present-day public any idea of the Meiningen magic. For everything that delighted me—the truth, the movement and the force of the folk scenes, the swelling tide of the revolution, the magnificence of the processions, the historical truth of the costumes and setting—has now become general on every middling stage; no one can think of a theater production in any other frame. . . .

The first performances that I saw won me to the new methods. In no way was it the glittering exterior, the historical appearance, that impressed me; it was the spirit of the poetry that rose out of the picture on the stage. Here really unrolled on "those boards that mean the world" a piece of the history of a bygone day, although, of course, in condensed form. The finely felt, judiciously shaded ensemble, which permitted no individual to monopolize the stage, expressed the unity of the drama far more effectively than the distracting and mechanical playing of subordinates grouped around a virtuoso without taking any part because they know all the attention rests on the star and they will not share in the applause. Here, as far as it was humanly possible to do so, the poet spoke in his own words; all his intentions and allusions were embodied.[105]

By the time the highly successful 1869-70 season ended in April, the duke was already making plans for improvements; but owing to the Franco-Prussian War, he was not to see any performances on his stage for some months.* It had become clear to him well before this, however, that Bodenstedt's appointment had been a mistake. He had done some good things, such as expanding the classical repertoire and introducing a number of new dramatists to the Meiningen stage; but as an internationally acclaimed poet and a friend of the king of Bavaria, he was not prepared to defer to the demands of a mere duke. More important, there was no theater blood in his veins. He did not know how to deal with actors; he rarely learned their names, and he was so unprepared for rehearsals that they often deteriorated into embarrassing confusion.

The duke treated Bodenstedt correctly, but Georg was not a patient man, especially when he knew he could do something better. The two had been at odds at least since December 1868, when the duke had suggested that the intendant be more practical in his approach to the theater

---

* Georg fought in the field as a general, accepted the capitulation of the mayor of Chartres, and was present in the Hall of Mirrors when the king of Prussia was named emperor of the German Empire. But even in battle his mind was not far from Meiningen, to the point where Bismarck felt obliged to remind him that "the use of the field telegraph to send messages anent the concerns of the state theater cannot be permitted," adding that he seemed to have nothing better to wire about than "forest nurseries, chorus girls, and horse dealing." (Emil Ludwig, *Bismarck, the Story of a Fighter*, tr. Eden and Cedar Paul, Boston, 1929, p. 331.)

and demanded that Bodenstedt lay before him a proposed program every two weeks. Bodenstedt made the mistake of blaming his employer for his difficulties. On December 2 he wrote a sharply worded letter to the duke, replying that the fault lay, not in his work, but in his equivocal position. He ended by saying: "If I had the power of an intendant as well as the title, the theater would have a different character. Everything would be operated according to fixed principles and not be ruled by changing influences. The theater, the box office, and the public would be the winners. Then I'd show whether or not I'm practical."[106]

The duke fired back a letter the same day, which left no doubt who was going to be master on his stage:

Your clarification concerning your practicality has—I use the word in its Gothic sense—amused me. Concerning the matter of the leadership of my stage, you complain that you do not have a free hand. Don't you think that you possess enough latitude for your activities? You can prepare the plays to be given according to your judgment. You can instruct the actor individually—have him read, recite, and act for you. You can arrange everything at rehearsals as you wish, direct the speech, the gestures, the movement, and the grouping of the performers, create in the staging such new things with the materials at hand as you please. You stand at the peak of the managerial organization and have the unrestricted right of fining [the actors] up to 5 fl. [gulden]. . . . Had you as a practical man informed yourself of the extent of the authority given an intendant here before you accepted the post, you would have known before accepting that never during my lifetime would you acquire that most important right: the establishment of the repertoire and the engagement of personnel. Since the repertoire is established so far in advance, it cannot be a substantial hindrance for you that I reserve the right to approve the plays. Since it is I who provide the 25,500 fl. in the budget for theater purposes, is it not only fair that no plays that displease me shall be given and no persons whose acting offends me shall play before me?[107]

Things did not improve, and on December 31, 1868, the duke wrote: "Because of the unnecessary screaming, the actors have become completely confused doing something that can be done calmly and quickly if the *Regisseur* [Grabowsky?] makes a plan in advance and writes down those things that are necessary, as, for example, the names of the actors in the order they are to seat themselves at the table, etc., instead of following the inspiration of the moment."[108] At this point, the duke may well have turned to the actor Ludwig Chronegk to assume many administrative duties. Bodenstedt did not retire formally until 1873, but by late 1869 he was no longer an important member of the theater administration.* The duke effectively took on much of the intendant's work; and

---

* On Nov. 17, 1869, Bodenstedt had the following announcement placed in the *Berliner Fremden- und Anzeigeblatt*: "As the *Regierungsblatt* announces, Herr von Bodenstedt

even in France during 1870 and part of 1871, he managed the theater through Chronegk. On his return, he appointed Chronegk stage manager and began to devote even more time himself to the Meiningen theater. He had now decided to send his company out for a series of appearances in Berlin.

For this he had three reasons. He wanted the nation to learn from the reforms he had effected on his own stage; he wanted his actors to compare their efforts with those of the actors in the capital and thereby develop their art; and he hoped that a successful engagement would provide funds for further reforms on the Meiningen stage. But he waited a few more years before he felt satisfied that his company was ready for Berlin. Only after Karl Frenzel returned to Meiningen in September 1872 to see *Macbeth*, *The Merchant of Venice*, and *Twelfth Night*, and pronounced the troupe ready to present to the world, did the duke begin to firm up his plans.[109] He was certain that established theaters would not welcome his revolutionary changes, but he was confident that he had charted the right course for the German theater to follow. In this belief he was supported by two colleagues—his third wife, the former actress Ellen Franz, and his new stage manager, Ludwig Chronegk.

---

has at his own request been removed as intendant of the ducal court theater and choir and has been placed on call. The reason for the change on our stage is not to be sought in any disagreement, as Herr von Bodenstedt, at the request of His Highness, the duke, will continue to use his influence on the stage, just as he will continue to enjoy his full salary. It may be assumed, rather, that the intendant believed that he did not find that freedom of movement in his administration that he finds necessary." (Friedrich von Bodenstedt, *Ein Dichterleben in seinen Briefen, 1850-1892*, Berlin, 1893, p. 166n.)

TWO

ELLEN FRANZ AND LUDWIG CHRONEGK

𝕴f Ellen Franz, the duke's third wife, had set out to educate herself for the role she was to play in the work of the Meininger, she could hardly have devised a better program than the one she followed. Born on May 5, 1839, in Naumburg an der Saale, she was the first child and only daughter of Hermann and Sarah Franz. Her father, a highly educated member of an old and distinguished Thuringian family, had been a tutor in an English nobleman's family. There he married Sarah Grant, already recognized as a poet,[1] and brought her back to Naumburg. Both their children were born in that city, but when Ellen was eight years old, the family moved to Berlin, where they became part of a circle of artists and musicians.

From her earliest childhood Ellen received the most careful education, especially in music and the German and English classics.* Her first wish was to become a concert pianist. She entered the Berliner Konservatorium, where her teacher, Ernst Kullak, recognized her unusual gifts and recommended that she apply to Hans von Bülow for lessons.[2] "Trembling and shaking," she later wrote, "I played something for the master. When he wished to hear something of Bach and I told him that Kullak thought I should try Bach a little later, Bülow spoke these beautiful words: 'Bach is our daily bread.' What I managed to cook up for him must not have seemed too tasteless, for he took me as a pupil."[3]

Through von Bülow, Ellen became acquainted with Franz Liszt, who called her Little Albion, and she formed a lasting friendship with von

---

* Ellen Franz formed an attachment for all things English, especially the drama and poetry. Her letters are full of descriptions of visits to England, as well as quotations from and references to English literature. In them we see her real anguish during the First World War.

Bülow's wife, Cosima, Liszt's natural daughter and later Richard Wagner's wife. In the next years, as her knowledge and love of music grew, she developed a keen critical judgment. Von Bülow's teaching was rooted in the work of the German masters, but in the struggle over the new composers, he championed Liszt, Wagner, and later, to a far greater extent, Brahms. Ellen was fervently caught up in the battles to establish the validity of these artists. She was present at the scandalous concert in which a Liszt symphony was hissed, and von Bülow called from the podium, "The hissers are asked to leave the hall." Only the forceful personality of the conductor restrained the audience from the violence that had broken out on similar occasions. "How I admired him," she later said. "How I feared for him." [4]

Ellen matured in a close, loving family, a serious young woman immersed in music and in the talk of art, literature, and politics that went on in her father's house. An ardent patriot like her father, she supported his aims as a co-founder of the Nationalliberale Partei and remained a loyal member of the party for forty years. Otherwise, she lived the life of any well-bred, middle-class girl of her time. She was an enthusiastic walker and nature lover, she went to parties and social gatherings, and she passionately loved to dance. After nearly fifty years she remembered her literature class:

In my time we went to school much longer than now, at least in Prussia, and I went almost to the end of my seventeenth year. We had an extraordinary teacher for literature, to whom I am much indebted. He loved the poets himself with his whole soul and knew how to awaken that love in us. I still remember how we looked forward to him from class to class and were often in suspense over what he would give us each time. I can feel even now my glowing cheeks as he had us read *Maria Stuart*, and I read with him the great scene in which the queens quarrel after Maria has knelt at Elizabeth's feet—the whole class was fire and flame. [5]

Ellen did not attend the theater until she was sixteen years old, and then all thoughts of becoming a concert pianist disappeared. She was seized with an ardent desire to become an actress. It was her good fortune that Frau Minona Frieb-Blumauer, a leading actress at the Königliches Schauspielhaus in Berlin, took her as a pupil. "Die Frieb," trained at Karl Immermann's experimental theater in Düsseldorf, was a resolute opponent of the star system, and though not a true ensemble player, she was at her best when playing with strong actors. To see her balance her artistry against such a talent as Theodor Döring was said to be "a treat." Frau Frieb-Blumauer was a real original, and Ellen absorbed much of her natural manner and the humor of her native Swabia. Under the older actress's tutelage, she learned the great roles of the German stage and showed so much promise that Heinrich Marr was persuaded to undertake her further instruction.

Marr had a long and distinguished career as an actor, but he is best remembered as a director and an educator of actors. Like all his students, Ellen learned on stage. The reading rehearsal was the foundation of his work. He demanded pure articulation and a scrupulous regard for every nuance of dialogue. From the first, he insisted that everything immaterial be cleared away, and at every rehearsal he forced the actors to the core of the drama. Accustomed to say that a good director must have schoolmaster's blood in him—and a little of the drill sergeant's too—Marr conducted rehearsals in a strong, dictatorial way. He was all over the set, directing now with stentorian voice, now with pantomime, growling, "Here!" "There!" "More spirit!" Crossness, searing malice, biting wit, were the elements of every tense rehearsal. Standing in front of the prompter's box, chewing on a nail, he kept his pale blue stare on the scene, and his cold, inexorable "Once more!" drove the performers until they were exhausted. He was willing to work a scene endlessly if it did not go.[6]

Marr had an uncanny ability to recognize talent, and he knew how to develop it.[7] After watching him work with actors, an admiring Friedrich Hebbel felt that Marr had the truly remarkable ability of breathing his own creative spirit into others in whom it was missing. Marr resisted every form of the Weimar declamatory style of acting and lived every role through with the actor. His strength and earnestness called forth an esprit de corps that forged a tight and effective ensemble. "Each actor," he said, "is a stone in a great edifice. Each must adapt himself to the whole." In order to ensure the success of the ensemble, Marr did not disdain to become an extra himself.[8] His disciplined view of the art of the theater and the demands that he made on the company made him feared by young and old, yet every actor who worked with him recognized his efforts with deepest gratitude. He was the idol of every aspiring beginner.

Marr had no eye for scene decoration or appropriate costume; he probably did not even notice the deficiency of historical exactitude. It was this disregard for the picture in favor of meticulous enunciation and painstaking attention to dialogue that made him the forerunner of Heinrich Laube, a greater director. In fact, one historian suggests that Laube, who was theater critic for the *Leipziger Tageblatt* in 1844-48, came to what he called his "careful, energetic manner of direction" from observing Marr, then the director of the Leipzig Stadttheater.[9] If this is true, then Marr's work influenced the theater reforms of the duke of Meiningen through Laube as well as through Ellen Franz.

Blessed with a supple, expressive voice, Ellen proved an apt pupil in a system that stressed enunciation and purity of tone. She was already knowledgeable in French, English, and German literature and language; Marr extended her knowledge and deepened her view of the art of acting. She learned to observe herself and others on stage, and accepted Marr's philosophy of theater. If she did not come to regard the stage as an altar and the actors as priests in a ritual, as Marr did, she at least developed a deep respect for the art of the actor. She accepted Marr's belief that the theater was rooted in the soul of the people and represented much that was beautiful in their lives. Especially, she came to see that the spirit and personality of the director formed the company and ensured the success of its undertakings. How well she learned these lessons and how well they remained with her we can see on the stage of the Meiningen court theater fifteen years after she left her teacher.

During her years with Marr, Ellen made only one solo appearance. At a concert conducted by Franz Liszt, she recited Heinrich Heine's poems "Schön' Hedwig" and "Heidenknaben" to the music of Robert Schumann. When she was twenty-one years old, Marr pronounced her ready to try her first role; but it took both Liszt and his daughter to convince the reluctant parents to allow their daughter to accept a part in Coburg-Gotha. On September 10, 1860, Ellen made her debut, playing Jane Eyre in Charlotte Birch-Pfeiffer's *Die Waise von Lowood* on the stage of Germany's oldest court theater.[10] The celebrated virtuoso Emil Devrient was Rochester. The beginner was successful enough to earn six friedrichsdor and a contract for three years. But disappointed by the roles she was given, she did not stay out her contract. After a short time in Stettin, she found a congenial engagement at the artistic court theater at Oldenburg. Here there still remained some of the glory from the time when a faithful follower of Immermann's methods had served as intendant.

October 1862 found Ellen rehearsing twice a day "a very fine role" in Hebbel's folk drama *Die Dithmarschen*, homesick and maintaining herself modestly on a beginner's salary. "I can send you only a ducat," she wrote her brother, Reinhold, on his twenty-second birthday. "Your first birthday away from home! Terrible isn't it?" To the court and public she was something of a mystery: an actress so reserved and quiet, living, it seemed, only for her work in the theater. Nightly, she accepted the flowers and bouquets sent to her, but she made no inquiries about the senders. Still, she was popular with the public. At one benefit she received 143 bouquets and 43 laurel wreaths on the open stage. Despite her retiring life and her devotion to her work, two suitors were not discouraged.

That winter Ellen's mother wrote her brother that "Ellen has had three proposals, but she refused them all. . . . One is named Stockhausen, a conductor and, so it seems, a famous singer." Julius Stockhausen, later founder of the music academy in Frankfurt am Main, came to Oldenburg for one concert, but did not go away again. Instead he wooed Ellen with his beautiful voice, and evenings she heard Schubert's serenades under her window. The court was certain that there would be an engagement, and the grand duchess was so pleased that she sent Ellen a long chain of coral studded with pearls. Ellen hesitated. What passed between them at last is not known, but Stockhausen left Oldenburg. Count von Wedel, the grand duke's adjutant, then began a passionate pursuit of Ellen.

The next year was a demanding one for Ellen, and she was happy to escape in June with her parents. In a letter showing weariness and indecision, she wrote to a friend in Oldenburg: "Do not think, dear friend, that I don't want to return to Oldenburg. Oh, no! I know what joys and pleasures await me there. . . . And I love my work above all other things. I have the most serious and best intentions to work with new courage and cheerful spirits." She returned in September to begin rehearsals on Laube's *Graf Essex*, and a month later she wrote the same friend: "I have an important message, which may change everything. . . . This evening I must make a decision." The following morning she announced to her friend that she was engaged to be married to Count von Wedel, though "for the moment" they must keep their plans a secret. Almost at once it became evident that "the moment" would stretch into years. They could not afford to marry, and the count was jealous of Ellen's work. She saw her art shattered on years of indecision and her hopes indefinitely suspended. Resolving to leave at the end of the season, she accepted an engagement in Mannheim, but she was not to act there for some time to come.

In October 1863, while she was playing the queen in Schiller's *Don Carlos* as a guest in Frankfurt an der Oder, she made a sweeping final gesture and prepared to leave the stage. The rush of air from the rapidly falling curtain caused the gas light to flame up and catch her wide sleeve. She was enveloped in flames and burned so badly that her arm was kept bandaged for nearly two years. During this time she learned how much she was loved in Oldenburg, as a letter from her mother to Reinhold shows: "During Ellen's illness, the grand duchess has inquired about her every day. On the order of the grand duke, the ducal gardener has been told to send her asparagus daily. The best people send her ices, flowers, and all sorts of delicacies. As soon as the public heard that she was improving and would act again, it was agreed among them that they would greet her with flowers and call out, 'Stay with us.'"

In his chronicle of the years 1862-63, the Oldenburg intendant, von

Dalvigk, wrote: "During her two years here, Fräulein Franz has through her many-sided talents almost dominated the stage. The list of principal roles she played in that time indicates her extraordinary range."[11] Her success in such diverse roles as Gretchen in *Faust*, Imogen in *Cymbeline*, and Elizabeth in *Don Carlos* confirms his judgment.

It was not until two years later that she was sufficiently recovered to step on stage again. On September 20, 1865, she wrote her brother from Mannheim that she was busy in her new engagement. "Last Thursday I played again in [Paul Heyse's] *Hans Lange*, last Monday in [William Jordan's] *Durchs Ohr*, and on Friday we'll have *Romeo and Juliet*. Next week, I'll have a difficult, but very wonderful role, Lucretia, in a new piece, [Albert Lindner's] *Brutus und Collatinus*, the best modern piece I can remember reading." During the next two years she did little but work. She widened her repertoire and developed a witty comic style, but the events in Oldenburg and her long convalescence had left emotional scars. In March 1867, she wrote her brother, addressing him with the nickname she had used from childhood:

Don't think, dear Lynn, that I live a full life of pleasure and happiness. It is instead a life of fulfilling my duty. I am twenty-eight years old, not young for an unmarried woman, and I shall be poor as long as our parents live, something I hope God will grant for many years. For I shall never, never take anything from their hard-earned capital. I have made myself a pledge to be independent. I have been twice bitterly disappointed in love, and I think I can say with certainty: I can look forward to no real happiness.

Three months later, Friedrich von Bodenstedt was announced to her one morning. When she sent out regrets that she could not receive him— her hair was up in curl papers—he sent back word that he was in Mannheim only a short time and wished to speak to her about her performance as the princess in Goethe's *Torquato Tasso*, which he had seen the previous evening. When she received him, he made her an offer for the Meiningen court theater. She later described the meeting to Max Grube: "He knew how to speak so well about the artistic life and activity there, about the duke's intellect and artistic knowledge, that he rendered me, so to speak, numb. I signed an agreement that did not guarantee me a substantially higher income. On the whole I had no reason for leaving Mannheim. I pleased the public there, and for that reason it pleased me."[12]

The duke was not pleased when he saw a photograph of the new artist, who had none of the conventional beauty then generally admired. The rigid pose demanded by the photography of 1867 reveals a somewhat forbidding young woman, plainly dressed in a wide white crinoline with only a locket on a black ribbon as an ornament. A generous mouth and a small up-turned nose are there, but the photograph does not reproduce the feature most remarked on by everyone describing her: in Max Grube's words, "those great, wonderful dark brown eyes from which wit and spirit flashed, in which roguishness and loving-kindness sparkled." [13]

The Mannheim *Stadt und Land* for July 5, 1867, described Ellen's farewell appearance as a festive occasion. The crowded house, which saw her departure with deep regret, poured out its affection and almost buried her in bouquets as she stepped on stage. After her performance, she sang a song, accompanying herself on the piano; the playwright of her final role spoke a farewell and in the name of the city begged her to return. Thereupon the crowd echoed his words by throwing wreaths and bouquets to the stage.

Two months later, Ellen Franz descended from the tiny train, passed Goethe Park, moved up the Bernhardstrasse, and shooing the geese from the courtyard, entered the stage door of the Meiningen court theater for the first time. On October 20, 1867, she played her first role, Juliet. The great success she enjoyed that evening remained with her during the next six years. Her charming appearance, her great talent, her untiring industry, her unusual education and training, and her enthusiasm for everything connected with theater set her apart from her colleagues. She was a great tragic actress, but she was also excellent in conversation plays and comedies, and so a variety of roles fell to her. Roles that demanded warmth, kindliness, and wit were especially suited to her talents. Her Beatrice in *Much Ado About Nothing* was said to be brilliant. Max Grube, who began his career as an eighteen-year-old in Meiningen, remembered her in one role in particular:

The first piece I saw was *Tartuffe*. Besides [Joseph] Weilenbeck only the actress playing Elmire pleased me—but she exceedingly so. I have never again, not even in the Théâtre Française, seen such a perfect Elmire. She appeared so spirited; yet one felt a real undertone of loving-kindness. And still one more thing she possessed, a charming magic in her voice and an art of speaking the like of which I had heard only in Pauline Ulrich—which allowed the words to slide from her lips like a string of pearls. Ellen Franz was not beautiful, but in addition to a slender, attractive figure, she had a pair of wonderful brown eyes. [14]

Ellen spent her first years in Meiningen in rooms in the Henneberger House on the Georgstrasse. Thanks to her mother, who came to live with her to free her from all duties except those in the theater, she was able to devote herself to the work she saw growing on the Meiningen stage. When, in 1870, the critic Karl Frenzel came to see the productions, he found Ellen Franz the only person in the company besides the actor Ludwig Chronegk who could appreciate the duke's ambitions and support his aspirations. Her years with Marr had trained her to understand what Georg wanted to do, and her experience on stage complemented his intuitive but untested endeavors. Her wide knowledge of German and foreign dramatic literature, a dedication to the idea of acting under a strong, even dictatorial director, a devotion to ensemble playing and to a pure and natural manner of speaking, provided a practical basis on which Georg built.

Ellen Franz was thoroughly a person of the theater and numbered her closest friends among her colleagues, but her family background and education enabled her to move in official and professional circles where actors were rarely welcome. She brought a letter of introduction from Mannheim to the privy councillor, and through his family she met Cäcile Sebaldt, wife of the duke's counsel general, with whom she formed a life-long friendship. It was at a festive evening at the home of Friedrich von Bodenstedt that she first met the duke outside the theater. He appeared unexpectedly at a party given on the twentieth birthday of von Boden-stedt's son, who at the time was entertaining a boyish enthusiasm for the actress and had asked as a birthday gift to be allowed to take her in to dinner. When the duke offered his arm to Ellen, the young man had to defer to age and rank. A strong friendship based on common interests grew up between the duke and the actress.

After the death of his wife Feo in February 1872, Georg spent all the time not required by his official duties in the theater. He directed all stage rehearsals himself and worked with the actors on the interpretation of their roles at the reading rehearsals. Later that year, Karl Frenzel returned to persuade the duke that the company was approaching the point where a Berlin appearance should be considered. All efforts were doubled. When Ellen was not on stage, she sat in the auditorium near the duke, advising, suggesting, prompting, as he directed. By the end of the year his appreciation and respect had grown into a love strong enough to over-come any qualms he had about the difference in their stations. He pro-posed that they be married in England the following summer.

When Bernhard had learned of his son's attachment to an actress, the bitterness he had nurtured since his forced abdication had increased. Now he saw a way to strike back at Georg, and what better way than through Ellen? His campaign of innuendo soon turned into vicious lies. He was supported by Bodenstedt, still smarting from the loss of his posi-tion as intendant,[15] and by Rochus von Liliencron, who had served the old duke in a number of offices and who had accompanied Georg to France and England in 1857.* The tiny capital was treated to watching the sorry conflict between father and son: the father determined that

* With one exception, Georg never forgave those who attacked Ellen at this time. When the post of curator at the University of Jena fell open in 1877, the state minister of Weimar nominated Liliencron for the position. The dukes of Saxe-Weimar, Saxe-Coburg-

Ellen Franz be driven from Meiningen, the son equally determined that she remain as his wife.

The rumors about Ellen, her family, and her relations with the duke reached scandalous proportions; she decided to relieve him of her part in his painful conflict with his father. Unknown to him, she signed a contract with the Stadttheater in Hamburg. Unknown to her, he made preparations for a marriage to take place at once. On March 17, 1873, Marie Berg appeared on the Meiningen stage as a guest in one of Ellen's best roles, the lead in *Maria Stuart*. The house was packed with Ellen's opponents—friends of Bernhard and members of the court who did not wish to see an actress installed as *Landesmutter*—and with the merely curious. The old duke bowed from the ducal loge, and the guest was greeted with shouts of approval and nearly smothered with flowers, which Bernhard had brought in two wagons. As the audience left the theater, they found scrawled on the walls and houses: "A new star appeared tonight far better than the 'former' Ellen Franz," and "A new star has been engaged to take the place of the 'fired' Ellen Franz." [16]

Bernhard's efforts had just the opposite effect from the one he desired. Late that same evening, Georg went to the Henneberger House and then left at once for Bad Liebenstein; Chronegk went to the little village of Schweina. Ellen and her mother experienced a terrible night; stones were hurled against their windows, and they could hear the ruffians hired by the old duke's partisans shouting for them to leave town. Very early the next morning, Ellen drove her mother to Eisenach to put her on the train for Marburg, where Reinhold was to meet her. Ellen went to the jewelers' to pick up the rings Georg had ordered, then drove alone for three hours in an open carriage through one of the worst snowstorms on record to meet the duke in Liebenstein. Chronegk arrived from Schweina with Pastor Karl Wolff, who had earlier promised Georg to perform the marriage ceremony. The duke himself had prepared an altar and before this, dressed in a black velvet costume from *Emilia Galotti*—she had not had time to obtain a wedding dress—Ellen and the duke repeated their wedding vows. For the text Pastor Wolff chose the lines from the Book of Ruth, "Whither thou goest, I shall go . . ." That evening they wrote letters to Georg's parents and his daughter, and to the state ministers.

Gotha, and Saxe-Altenburg agreed, but Georg as fourth co-regent of the university refused to approve the nomination, so the post went to another. The one exception was Moritz Seebeck, who greeted Georg's marriage with bitterness and anger, convinced that his *Zögling* had made a serious mistake in marrying an actress. But when he came to know Ellen and realized that the marriage was successful and happy, he bent every effort to bring about a reconciliation between son and parents. (Baroness von Heldburg to Sophie Seebeck, Dec. 19, 1919, in Helene, Freifrau von Heldburg, *Fünfzig Jahre Glück und Leid*, Leipzig, 1926, p. 222.)

Fig. 3. Helene, baroness von Heldburg (1839-1923), née Ellen Franz, in 1873, the year of her marriage to Georg

When night had fallen, they heard singing beneath their window. Two actresses, the only friends to whom Ellen had entrusted her secret, stood in the snow serenading them with Ferdinand Gumbert's old *Wanderlied*, "When thou hast a true heart found." The duke opened the window to beckon them in, but they disappeared into the darkness.[17] By the time the news of their marriage was made public, Georg and Ellen were in the Villa Carlotta on Lake Como. When they returned in the fall, they set to work immediately on the repertoire that they would send to Berlin the following May. Their closest associate in the venture was the actor turned stage manager Ludwig Chronegk.

Ludwig Chronegk was "one of the most remarkable phenomena ever to appear in the theater," in the judgment of Ludwig Barnay, who knew the regisseur for more than thirty years and acted under his leadership during the tours of the Meiningen company.[18] When Barnay first knew him in 1860 in Budapest, Chronegk was just a run-of-the-mill comic. Yet by careful work, untiring effort, and an unswerving loyalty to the goals of the duke of Meiningen, he was able in just a few years to become not only the stage manager of a model company, but the leader of the difficult tours that were to earn him the respect of the Western theatrical world.

Born in Brandenburg an der Havel, on November 1, 1837, Chronegk moved as a child to Berlin, where he attended the Dorotheenstädtische Stadtschule and was a classmate of Paul Lindau. The critic later remembered that as boys of nine they fought in the street and were called "hooligans" by the celebrated singer Henriette Sontag.[19] Chronegk received a good education in Berlin and Potsdam, and when he was eighteen, he went to Paris for a year. Unlike the crown prince of Meiningen, who had first visited that city ten years earlier, Chronegk brought no letters of introduction to intellectual and artistic circles. He spent a large part of his time with German student artists, musicians, and writers, who gathered in the cafés to talk and to read German newspapers. He perfected his French and was often in the theater, backstage as well as in the audience; but he began his real theatrical training when he returned to Berlin for an apprenticeship under Karl Görner. He made his debut at Krolls Établissement in 1856.[20] Then, for some ten years, he followed the usual rounds of theaters in Germany, Switzerland, and Hungary with a comic routine.[21] Dressed as a girl, he sang falsetto, danced, threw himself bouquets, and thanked himself with bows and smiles. Max Kurnik saw him in Breslau in 1865, "a little comic who enchanted audiences as the 'false Carlotta Patti,'" but who otherwise did not give any inkling of having "the genius that would bring him to the high company of the best dramaturges of the new times."[22]

In 1866 Chronegk was engaged through an agent by the Meiningen court theater to play humorous character parts, especially in Shakespearean works; he made his first appearance on the Meiningen stage as Guildenstern in *Hamlet*. The first season, he made fifty-three appearances in forty roles, not all comic. Among these were characters created by Schiller, Goethe, Sophocles, and Shakespeare, as well as by Ferdinand Raimund, Ludvig Holberg, Karl Gutzkow, and others long forgotten. His roles were not large; usually he played "an officer," "a messenger," "the third citizen," "a murderer," and the like, though he had a few more demanding roles, including the Fool in *King Lear*.[23] He was not a gifted actor, but he was always good-natured, friendly, and fully prepared when he stepped on stage.*

When Ellen Franz came to Meiningen the following year, she recognized that a highly intelligent man lay behind the façade of the short, fat comic; and they became fast friends. In 1868, when Karl Frenzel came to see the company perform, he immediately appreciated that an intendant like Bodenstedt was a "fifth wheel" in a theater with Meiningen's aspirations. A practical theater man was needed. The next year the duke effectively removed Bodenstedt and assumed the duties of intendant himself. The largely uneducated but experienced Karl Grabowsky, who had been stage manager since 1866, retained that post; and the company was astonished when the duke accepted Ellen Franz's recommendation that Chronegk be appointed regisseur. Only one member of the company, the old and experienced but nearly blind Joseph Weilenbeck, recognized the good sense of the appointment, but even he did not realize that all that was to follow would have been impossible without Chronegk.

By 1873 Chronegk had developed an astonishing appreciation of the duke's ambitions. He was the first to recognize the innovations being made in Meiningen as revolutionary changes that should be shown to the world, and he was ready to accept responsibility for his part in the preparation. The company returned that September from the summer holidays to find a tightly knit administration of the duke, Ellen Franz (now the baroness von Heldburg), and Chronegk deep in plans. That winter the repertoire was primarily classical; rehearsal time was doubled, discipline was strengthened, and magnificent new scenery and costumes were prepared. The duke was present at every rehearsal from the first word to the last, and followed the action on stage with the closest interest and concern. Chronegk never left the stage during the long rehearsals. Each mo-

---

* Still, for all his limitations as an actor, he subsequently became famous in several important roles: Launcelot Gobbo in *The Merchant of Venice*, Sir Andrew Aguecheek in *Twelfth Night*, and Flute in *A Midsummer Night's Dream*.

ment he was aware of every movement and was quick to translate any wish of the duke to the actors. As Karl Grube said, everything *klappt militärisch*.[24]

The baroness had a wide knowledge of literature and training in criticism, which neither the duke nor Chronegk possessed; but Georg knew Greek, German, English, and French dramatic literature well and Shakespeare thoroughly. Chronegk had little knowledge of literature as such and participated in play selection only as far as the practicalities of staging were concerned. The baroness did the necessary literary research, the duke designed the sets and costumes, and Chronegk's work began when the play was in rehearsal. He advised on the workability of the sets and costumes; and if there was a disagreement among the three, or if Chronegk brought a complaint from one of the actors, they tried several suggestions and then used the most effective one.

Chronegk took an active part in casting the plays. There was no such thing as a Fach book, and the duke's casting was intuitive and original; but as a professional actor, Chronegk often objected and frequently overruled the duke. Although the final decisions were Georg's to make, Chronegk was confident that his advice would be taken. He did not hesitate to approach an actor about coming to Meiningen, nor did he hesitate to engage one for at least a tryout. Before the decision to take the company to Berlin was publicly announced, he wrote to Barnay asking him "to join the party" and to play Mark Antony in *Julius Caesar*, Macduff in *Macbeth*, and Henry of Navarre in *Bluthochzeit*, and act "in one other piece." "I have not mentioned my proposal to the duke," he wrote, "since I wanted to have your agreement first. As soon as I receive that, I'm sure I'll have the approval of His Highness."[25]

On stage and in the handling of the cast and crew Chronegk was invaluable. Unlike Bodenstedt, he knew actors. He was a thoroughly professional man and had, in Max Grube's words, "a clear understanding that quickly found the simplest and most natural solution to every question touching setting or acting. He had a gift of explaining to the actor in short, pertinent words—often in drastic ways, but therefore all the more easily understood. He could play out for an actor a scene in the way it should be played."[26] He drilled the crowds, and only after they were well prepared did he turn them over to Grabowsky. He carried on rehearsals once the play was set in broad lines, always led a group, and often played a role.*

---

* Chronegk made six appearances on the tours, appearing for the last time on April 27, 1875, as Trissotin in Molière's *Les Femmes savantes*. He made his last appearance in Meiningen on Jan. 16, 1877, as Sir Andrew Aguecheek in *Twelfth Night*.

Fig. 4. Ludwig Chronegk (1837-91), actor, director, and tour manager, ca. 1880

To Stanislavski, Chronegk's methods of drilling the actors and keeping discipline seemed harsh and often unfair. But Chronegk and his actors understood one another, not least the Meiningen citizens who often played members of the crowds and the "little roles," and were as proud of their theater as he was. He was a humorous, good-hearted, lovable man, full of gentleness and kindness, but he could be hard, unpleasant, and inconsiderate to the extreme when it came to a question of the honor of the theater or the interests of the duke. Still, there are few records of any actor's complaining to the duke about some action of Chronegk's.*

On the tours he was indispensable; without him there would have been no tours. It was unthinkable that a ruling German prince would accompany a band of actors wandering across Europe. In Chronegk the duke found a man who guarded his interests in every detail. Indeed, he was so closely associated with the Meininger that many people believed he was the moving spirit behind the enterprise. Stanislavski fell into this trap when he titled his chapter on the Meininger in *My Life in Art*, "The Genius of Director Kronek."[27] Chronegk tried on every possible occasion to correct the mistake, but the duke never contradicted it.

Every summer Chronegk moved the entire theater—actors and all they needed—on sixteen wagons to Bad Liebenstein, where the company played for the spa guests. Once the company started on tour, he made all the logistical arrangements required for moving eighty to ninety people with a trainload—even a shipload in the case of the London appearance—of sets, costumes, and properties. In each city he drilled the temporary extras, many of whom spoke no German, and few of whom had ever been on a stage. Ludwig Barnay's description of getting *Julius Caesar* on in Drury Lane in 1881 could have been said of any of nearly three thousand other performances: "In London . . . began the same pressure of feverishly busy preparation as with our first Berlin appearance, only now much more noise, because Chronegk did not speak English. Nevertheless, he personally took charge of the foreign-speaking extras. Even now I can see before me that untiring man, standing on a shaky chair, surrounded by his English cohorts, attempting by all sorts of gesticulations to remake the English *Soldaten* into Roman citizens."[28]

Cronegk carried on all correspondence, and on tour reported daily to the duke on the condition of everyone and everything. There were crises: the theater burned in Frankfurt am Main, ruining much of the scenery;

* A notable exception was the actress Therese Grunert, who after being dismissed by Chronegk for insubordination in an argument over a role, took her case to the theater association and was awarded compensation. See *Die Meiningen'sche Theater-Intendanz gegenüber dem deutschen Bühnenverein* (Meiningen, 1879) for an account of the legal process.

the theater in Prague had an odor so repulsive that no amount of disinfectant could dispel it. Members of the troupe became ill; one died. Josef Kainz's father was killed while the company was in Breslau. Olga Lorenz insisted on getting married in St. Petersburg although her contract expressly forbade such a move. She appealed to Chronegk in tears; he appealed to the duke; all ended happily. Hundreds of such letters and telegrams exchanged over the seventeen years of the Meininger's tours attest to the multiplicity of problems Chronegk faced. He had only one standard for solving each of them: what best served the interest of the duke of Meiningen.

In Chronegk the duke had a financial if not an artistic genius. Some have found the regisseur flawed in this respect. Said Karl Grube: "If on the tours, the coarse sometimes overcame the spiritual, lay it to him." [29] The letters streamed back to the duke to report the successes, the curtain calls, the income and the expenses. From London he wrote, "The great honor that the theater has won here in London belongs to Your Highness and to you, dear Frau von Heldburg; in contrast I have brought about only the smallest results, and for that I must thank you; yet over this point we have often argued." But two lines later he voiced his real concern, "that the financial success has not kept up with the artistic has given me many unhappy hours and really angered me." [30] His pious wish, uttered in Cologne in 1877, shows where his heart really lay: "May it rain here on Pentecost; then the theater will be full for *Fiesko*." [31] He accepted every burden of the Meininger as his own.

Not the least of his burdens was the duke himself. Every day Georg dispatched a telegram, often several, full of advice, instructions, changes. "Buy a plush curtain for London. None to be found here," he wired to Chronegk in Bremen on May 5, 1881. Later that day, "Under no circumstances let Nesper play Jaromir [*Die Ahnfrau*] in Bremen tonight [Nesper had a bad throat] and if possible keep him out of *Die Räuber* tomorrow." To Vienna: "Let Fräulein Pauli be accompanied during the rehearsal of her song and longer if she is still worried." To Dresden: "Since the Residence theater is so small, use fewer extras." When Björnson's son fell into financial difficulties and appealed to the duke for an advance on his salary, Georg wired Chronegk: "Out of friendship for Björnson's father, whom we hope to see in Norway next summer, I assent to Björn's request as a gift from me; that is too trifling an amount to call an advance. It seems that he is in deep debt and does not have a kreuzer to his name." [32]

If Chronegk looked on all this as interference, covering details that he could more easily have dealt with on the spot, he never gave any indication of it. Indeed, his most attractive quality was his absolute loyalty. Dingelstedt tried to hire him in 1876, and when he refused, the Burgtheater director wrote to Georg: "The simple loyalty with which the worthy man threw back my attempt put me to shame."[33] The relationship between Georg and Chronegk, a ruling prince and a middle-class theater man, was based on mutual reliance, dependence, and deep admiration. The duke treated Chronegk as a good, trusted friend, but for all the cordiality and frankness, Chronegk never forgot that he was speaking to a duke. In 1899, eight years after Chronegk's death, the baroness wrote to Max Grube: "As for us, the longer we live, the more experience we have, the more we know what we had in him, and the more thankful we are."[34]

All that, however, lay in the future as Chronegk joined the duke and his wife in September 1873 to plan for the first appearance of the Meiningen company in Berlin the following May. That winter he played twenty-one roles in thirty-three appearances. Most were the classical roles: "the third citizen" in *Julius Caesar*, Sir Andrew Aguecheek in *Twelfth Night*, Launcelot Gobbo in *The Merchant of Venice*, and Grumio in *The Taming of the Shrew*, among others. But he also created roles in the works of three new dramatists: Franz von Alençon in *Bluthochzeit* by Albert Lindner; Jacoppo in *Papst Sixtus V* by Julius Minding; Blume and Adalbert in two plays by Adolf von Wilbrandt, *Die Maler* and *Unerreichbar*. He was to perform the Lindner and Minding roles throughout Europe, but the Wilbrandt dramas, though they remained favorites of the duke's, never left Meiningen. Chronegk was still an actor, but the season of 1873-74 saw him assume the most important role of his life, that of manager of the soon-to-be-famous Meininger.

PART TWO

The Meininger at Work

THREE

THE PLAYS AND THEIR SETTINGS

𝔐any theater historians contend that the only reason Georg of Meiningen produced so much Shakespeare and Schiller is that their plays lent themselves to elaborate effects and spectacular scenery. But the duke's own words belie this accusation. In a letter to Paul Lindau, one of his sharpest critics, he said: "This I can assure you: that for me the picturesque or the outfitting is not the important consideration in respect to a poetic work. On the contrary, I am inalterably opposed to any tendency to concentrate on externals."[1]

There is no denying that those plays offering the possibility for beautiful staging appeared most often in the Meiningen theater, but the actor Ludwig Barnay came nearer the truth when he named the duke's "noble goal: to set in its proper place the holy legacy of our literature."[2] Georg knew that if he was to reestablish that "holy legacy," he had to do so within the framework of contemporary taste. If he was to develop in audiences an appreciation of what was valuable in dramatic literature, he must first entice them into the theater, and that would be done on their own terms. Worthwhile dramatic literature would be written only when there was an audience for it.[3] That audience Georg set about creating by presenting excellent productions with all the visual beauty and artistry so prized by the age.

Further, we cannot disregard the enormous success that *Twelfth Night*, *Le Malade imaginaire*, and *Les Femmes savantes*, all presented in the simplest of settings, achieved by the excellence of ensemble playing alone; or the critical acclaim that a *Ghosts* set on a modern stage with neither spectacle nor crowd scenes received even from those who were bitter critics of the Meininger. The number of contemporary writers introduced on the Meiningen stage and made known internationally through the company's tours refutes the charge that Georg was interested only in those classical works that could be splendidly mounted.

Of the forty-one plays taken on the tours, five were given only twice: Edward Moore's folk play *'Tis Nothing*, Paul Heyse's one-act *Frau Lucrezia*, Henrik Ibsen's *Ghosts*, August Iffland's *Die Jäger*, and Otto Ludwig's *Der Erbförster*. Julius Minding's *Papst Sixtus V* was given four times, Richard Voss's *Alexandra* and Arthur Fitger's one-act *Rosen von Tyburn* five times, Gotthold Lessing's *Miss Sara Sampson*, Ibsen's *The Pretenders*, and José Echegaray's *El Gran Galeoto* seven times, and Ludwig Ganghofer's *Der Herrgottschnitzer von Oberammergau* eleven times.

There were various reasons why these plays were not more successful. The folk plays were probably chosen because a large number of actors in the company spoke the Bavarian dialect well; but the plays were not really compatible with the Meininger concept and were not attractive to audiences where the dialect was not easily understood. The one-act plays did not fit in easily, for most Meininger productions did not need a curtain raiser. Several of these were probably chosen because the authors were close friends of the duke and his wife. Max Grube says that where their friends were involved, the ducal couple set aside all critical objectivity.[4] The other one-act plays, Otto Franz Genishchen's *Lydia*, Pius Alexander Wolff's *Preciosa*, and Björnson's *Between the Battles*, were only moderately successful.

Of the remaining plays, nine were by Schiller, *Die Braut von Messina*, *Fiesko*, *Die Jungfrau von Orleans*, *Maria Stuart*, *Die Piccolomini*, *Die Räuber*, *Wallensteins Lager*, *Wallensteins Tod*, and *Wilhelm Tell*, and six by Shakespeare, *Julius Caesar*, *Macbeth*, *The Merchant of Venice*, *The Taming of the Shrew*, *Twelfth Night*, and *The Winter's Tale*. Heinrich von Kleist and Franz Grillparzer, who had almost disappeared from the German stage, were restored, Kleist with *Die Hermannsschlacht*, *Das Käthchen von Heilbronn*, and *Der Prinz von Homburg*, and Grillparzer with *Die Ahnfrau* and the fragment *Esther*. *Bluthochzeit*, by the contemporary German writer Albert Lindner, proved popular, as did Fitger's *Die Hexe*. Of three foreign pieces, Molière's *Le Malade imaginaire* was a great success, but his *Les Femmes savantes*, and Byron's *Marino Faliero* in Fitger's translation and adaptation, were less so. Although plays by Goethe and Lessing appeared every season on the Meiningen stage, only *Iphigenie auf Tauris* and *Miss Sara Sampson* were taken on tour because their other plays, Goethe's *Egmont* and *Götz von Berlichingen* and Lessing's *Minna von Barnhelm* and *Nathan der Weise*, were given every year at the Königliches Schauspielhaus in Berlin and appeared often everywhere else in the German-speaking world. The most serious omission was the work of Friedrich Hebbel; Georg admired his plays and produced them on his own stage, but he never felt that he had the right personnel at any one time to cast them for the tours.[5] The works of Karl Gutzkow, Gustav Freytag, and Ferdinand Raimund appeared regularly in Meiningen but never left it.

Among the modern foreign writers, Ibsen and Björnson made the deepest impression on the duke, whose personal taste foreshadowed much of the coming naturalism. Georg's admiration for the comedies of the eighteenth-century Norwegian-born Danish writer Ludvig Holberg (whose *The Potboiler Politician* provided Chronegk with one of his most effective roles) and his journeys to the Scandinavian countries made him especially receptive to these writers. In 1867 his was the first German production of Björnson's *Between the Battles*, and two years later he gave the first complete showing on any stage of the trilogy *Sigurd the Bastard*. He selected *Between the Battles* for the company's first appearance in Berlin. Two years later, on June 3, 1876, the Meininger introduced Ibsen to Berlin with *The Pretenders*. (The play had been performed once before in Germany, however, by a troupe in Munich on April 10 of that year.)[6]

Prejudice or censorship played virtually no part in the choice of any play. The duke was one of the most liberal of German princes; besides, his curiosity was so intense and his interests so wide-ranging that he wanted to see everything old and new. He did not hesitate to show Lindner's *Bluthochzeit*, with its strong flavor of the current struggle between the Prussian government and Rome (the *Kulturkampf*), or Fitger's *Die Hexe*, with its radical attitude toward established religion. Two of the plays that had limited runs on the tours—*Ghosts*, and *El Gran Galeoto*—were banned by the censors. Karl Gutzkow's plea for freedom of religious and political thought, *Uriel Acosta*, which Georg had first seen as a twenty-year-old university student, played regularly in Meiningen, as did Otto Ludwig's work, with its ethical and philosophical searching, and the ruggedly realistic plays of Ludwig Anzengruber.

Selecting a play was far easier than preparing it for the stage. To allow the public to hear a play as nearly as possible in the poet's own words meant to free it from any "improvements" it had suffered over the years, especially at the hands of the stars. The baroness von Heldburg brought her wide knowledge of German and foreign literature to this task; and Georg called on other experts for help. Karl Werder, a literary historian on the faculty of the University of Berlin, often stayed for long periods at the Castle Elisabethenburg in Meiningen to advise on textual problems; and when necessary the baroness did not hesitate to write one of the contemporary authors to ask about his intent in a certain passage.* Although Georg was not so pedantic as Bodenstedt, who demanded that every word the poet wrote be spoken, his adaptations of the dramas, which later appeared in thirty volumes, demonstrate the greatest respect for the words and intentions of the dramatist.[7]

There is no record of the method used in the collation of versions or any of the basic principles observed in the adaptations of the plays.[8] The plot of the drama seems to have been the deciding factor in scene divisions, as we shall see, for example, in *Julius Caesar* and *Twelfth Night*, where two different methods were used. Dramatic effectiveness dictated some curtailment; lack of censorship and lack of prudery restored many traditional cuts. Some alterations seem merely arbitrary, but where the words of the dramatist could be determined, they were used. When critics or actors pointed out the "improvements" in the text, the duke was accustomed to say, "I'd rather be wrong with the poet than right with the editors." This was evident on stage, as the London *Times* for May 31, 1881, pointed out when remarking that the perfect reverence for Shakespeare's text in *Julius Caesar* might serve as a model for the English theater managers. "The original text was followed, not only in the sequence of scenes, but also in every stage direction. There is no exit, no flourish of trumpets, no acclamation of the people, which is not realized on the stage with more accuracy, no doubt, than Shakespeare himself dreamed of."[9]

Georg used a variety of devices to ensure as much as possible the purity of the text. He weeded out arbitrary changes, cut and rearranged scenes—not always successfully—or employed a unit set, dropped any music and ballet not intrinsic to the drama, and restored scenes cut earlier as being "indelicate" or "crude." In every instance his goal remained the same: to put before the audience the drama as the writer intended it.

But if the words were those of the writer, the picture into which they were set spoke to the spirit of the time. Georg was confident that once he beguiled the public into the theater, the power of the dramatic poetry would hold them there; but the first appearance had to be visual and it

---

* See Helene, Freifrau von Heldburg, *Fünfzig Jahre Glück und Leid* (Leipzig, 1926), pp. 29-71, 170-96, for letters to Paul Heyse, Richard Voss, and Arthur Fitger. In addition, Georg and the baroness carefully read all the reviews of their own productions as well as those of other theaters and made use of the hints therein. According to Max Grube, in their preparation of Kleist's *Die Hermannsschlacht* in 1875, "the princely pair had carefully observed Frenzel's remarks about the Berlin [Königliches Schauspielhaus] production. They read all reviews with the greatest attention." (*The Story of the Meininger*, tr. Ann Marie Koller, Coral Gables, Fla., 1965, p. 72.) The Meininger, said the critic Hans Hopfen, were not afraid to accept good advice "even from their most resolute opponents" (*Streitfragen und Erinnerungen*, Stuttgart, 1876, p. 272.)

had to be current. Truth, internal and external, was the principle on which the Meininger staging rested; the stage pictures were as real as any contemporary painting. Yet it is not enough to say only that the Meininger set designs mirrored contemporary popular historical painting; both the painting and the realistic staging were an expression of the deepest desires of Germany during the second half of the nineteenth century. The middle class had taken over the newly rich economy, but still insecure politically and socially, they longed for an external representation of stability.

The Prussian state, too, sought to validate its legitimacy in the past. Too often, in architecture, in painting, and in the practical arts, magnificence and splendor were substituted for the authentic. In many instances, historical paintings, historical plays, and current political events were hardly to be differentiated—all splendidly "arranged" processions and dramatic happenings out of the "glorious past," each detailed with historical accuracy to give the impression of the genuine.[10] At the same time, the ideal of the unified work of art remained a potent force in the intellectual and artistic spirit of the age. These concepts—the realistic and the material, and the visionary and the romantic—provided the basis of the Meininger staging, something new to the German theater.[11]

For Georg, historical realism in art was best expressed in the strong, clear lines of Peter von Cornelius. In a letter to his mother echoing Cornelius's ideas, he admitted the charm of the popular Karl von Piloty but was put off by the artist's bold color and surface realism. "There is more to art," he wrote, "than the titillation of the senses. It is there to awaken all the noble powers of mankind."[12] From the works of Cornelius, Georg got a schooled eye for composition and line; but he was also inspired by the fluid style of Wilhelm von Kaulbach[13] and the balance and harmony of the Renaissance Italian painters. Indeed, it was his studies in Bonn and especially his meetings there with the Boisserée brothers, whose collection of early northern Renaissance art was to form the basis of the Alte Glyptothek in Munich, that conditioned him to be receptive to the religious and philosophical teachings of the Nazarene art movement, and specifically to the work of Cornelius.*

---

* It is almost impossible to overestimate the influence Cornelius exerted on Georg's view of art in all its forms. An early enthusiast for the northern painting of the Renaissance, Cornelius (1783-1867) was inspired by the drawings of Dürer and others of his time to illustrate German epics in graphic art. He was a member of the order of St. Luke, known also as the Lukasbund or the Nazarenes, a group of German painters who resolved to paint in the old German manner and thus renew the religious basis of German art. They proposed to achieve their aim by observing "the way of fantasy" as represented by Michelangelo, "the way of beauty" as represented by Raphael, and "the way of nature" as represented by

But more than thirty-five years of theater-going had taught Georg that the theater has its own laws, and that he must set about harmonizing artistic principles with the practical demands of the stage and the audience. Fortunately, there remains a record of his methods. Plans for staging were never written out in Meiningen, but the Brückner brothers, Max and Gotthold, who made nearly all of the Meininger scenery, lived in Coburg, and much of their correspondence with the duke and his staff is extant.[14]

Before Georg became active in the Meiningen theater, all the scenery was made either in Meiningen or in Weimar, but he seems to have moved to the Brückners very soon after they opened their atelier in 1865, for we find Intendant von Stein reminding them, in 1866, that "the gracious Lord is a little impatient."[15] The brothers worked with their father earlier for Ernst II, who had provided the means for the younger to make an art study trip; so it is possible that Ernst recommended them to his cousin in Meiningen. Their father, Heinrich Brückner, who had been employed for many years in the court theater in Gotha, had painted the scenery for the Gotha première of *Tannhäuser*.

The older Brückner brother, Max, was only twenty-nine years old when he opened the atelier that was to make the scenery for the Bayreuth Festspielhaus, as well as for nearly all the great theaters in Germany. Precisely what part the younger brother performed in the enterprise is not clear: the duke directed all his orders to Max, although the replies were always signed "G. u. M. Brückner." Chronegk usually addressed both. Since Gotthold was the more masterly landscape painter, we may suppose that he prepared the backdrops. In any case, there were numerous assistants in the atelier, something that did not please the duke, who always strongly requested that Max work on the sets personally. Since the artist usually acceded to the duke's request, it was probably his consistent point of view that gave the Meiningen scenery its unique harmony.[16]

Georg was not an easy employer. Not only did he send back every poorly done piece of scenery; he expected the scene painter to have a high degree of sympathetic understanding for the sentiment of the drama. Max Brückner was constantly and forcefully directed to literature con-

---

Dürer. (Elizabeth Gilmore Holt, *From the Classicists to the Impressionists*, Garden City, N.Y., 1966, pp. 93-101.) In 1860 Georg wrote his mother from Trieste: "I am convinced that Cornelius's name will shine through history with that of Raphael and Michelangelo. I have seen his cartoons in Munich in the Ludwigskirche and the Glyptothek and have not seen their equal during this trip to Italy." (StBBH: K8 M72 B19-20, n.d.) He did not alter that judgment. On Oct. 10, 1937, Prince Ernst, Georg's son and himself a successful artist, wrote to Heinz Isterheil: "My father, even into his old age, considered Cornelius the greatest artist of the last century; indeed, he once said to me that he was the greatest German artist since Dürer." (Isterheil, "Die Bühnendekorationen bei den Meiningern," Ph.D. dissertation, University of Cologne, 1938, p. 41.)

cerning the drama under consideration. Further, Georg demanded the closest attention to his wishes, and he was always in a hurry; but the greatest difficulty for the scenic artist was Georg's way of working. He kept changing and improving the staging, and just as often he changed the scenery. It was not unusual for him to make a radical alteration so close to a performance that it was too late to return the scenery to Coburg; then one of the Brückner assistants was summoned to finish the work in Meiningen.*

The danger of fire was a constant worry for both Georg and the Brückners. Especially on tour, Chronegk feared the destruction of the sets, a catastrophe that did befall the troupe in Frankfurt am Main in 1878.[17] Four years later, Brückner was still struggling with the problem: "The entire question of fireproofing is difficult to solve, and it is not yet satisfactorily worked out."[18] He could not guarantee success if he merely coated the flats. It seemed better to him if he first painted the scenery, then treated it; but that proved ineffective. The duke complained that "the means now being used are useless. In the heat the stuff falls off the canvas and makes the actors even hotter."[19] Still worse, treating the scenery after it had been painted mottled the paint and left streaks. When the borders and backdrops for *The Winter's Tale* arrived in Berlin damaged from fireproofing, Chronegk called for help: "You will have time," he wrote, "and even if you haven't, you must [find some] out of friendship and interest for us."[20]

In every case, Brückner willingly helped out. If he had to refuse a request because he was too busy, the duke accepted another painter—the Viennese decorator Johann Kautsky or Angelo or Simon Quaglio in Munich—but never for an important production. The trust between Max Brückner and Georg was mutual and grew with the years. In 1869 the duke was prepared merely to tell Max formally that he "was satisfied" with his accomplishments, but three short years later he was ready to lavish praise on his set maker, reporting from Bad Liebenstein that "your outstanding decorations have caused a sensation here among the spa guests."[21] In the same letter he alerted Brückner to the possibility of a guest appearance in Berlin, "so that you may paint especially well the works that I shall entrust to you." The salutations of the letters indicate the good footing on which they stood. At first the duke addressed his letters to "Herr Brückner" or "Sir," but it was not long before he was writing "Dear Brückner." By 1875, when the painter wanted to pass on

---

* It was not until he had been directing for some years that Georg realized that the indecision wearied the actors; from then on he tried to make as few changes in large sets as possible.

the work for *Die Hermannsschlacht* to another artist, the duke preferred to postpone the production until Brückner could do the job, "because I have more trust in you than I have in any other painter." In 1885, when he was especially pleased with the sets for *Die Braut von Messina*, prepared for the first Russian tour, Georg wrote: "Wonderful, wonderful, entirely Brücknerish." And as late as 1894, when Georg was planning a model production of *Der Freischütz*, he wrote that the whole thing would fall through if Brückner had no time, "for I know of no other painter who can prepare the necessary decorations so satisfactorily." Many years after the tours had ended, the baroness von Heldburg telegraphed Brückner: "Without you the Meininger could never have conquered."[22]

It was Georg's good fortune to find Max Brückner, whose sympathetic involvement with all aspects of the set design may have put that unique stamp on the Meininger scenery remarked on by all critics, but it was the duke himself who developed a stable scenic principle. He began systematically to divide the stage area as economically as possible. Levels, step units, and platforms broke up the flat surface. Movable scenery in front of a diorama or panorama perspective created natural open landscapes. For the blue borders—he called them "ozone rags"—he substituted tree limbs extending across the stage, or banners, arches, flags, and in the alleys of southern cities, washing hanging on lines. Chairs, tables, and chimneys were now practicable: "Don't paint me any furniture on walls," he told Brückner.[23]

In place of the square, closed room that the German theater had borrowed from the French stage, Georg turned to the English style, making rooms more interesting by using diagonally placed walls, niches, and window nooks. The rooms themselves became better proportioned. "According to old theater practice," he told his painters, "it was usual to make a room larger than usual and houses smaller. That tradition must be completely broken."[24] Interiors should look livable; "corners are always good," he wrote in 1882. No longer did ghostly hands open and close doors; now they were locked with iron keys in real locks. The columns and portals of ancient Greece and Rome were not the familiar hanging pieces of canvas, but were either three-dimensional or heavily stiffened canvas on weighted frames. The beloved "grassy bank" of every German theater, standing sofa-like in every landscape, was replaced by practicable rock pieces, blocks, or stones.

When Georg began planning a set, he had the historical background well in mind. His intent was to set the piece in the period in which the events really took place. If, on one occasion, he acceded to the wishes of the adapter, Arthur Fitger, to allow his version of *Marino Faliero* to play three hundred years later than the doge in that drama lived, Georg at least demanded that the atmosphere of the historical period be retained in the setting.[25] When pictures or maps of the historical scene were available, as for Domrémy, the birthplace of Joan of Arc, or for Castle Fotheringhay, where Mary, Queen of Scots, was imprisoned, Georg prepared a full set of plans and sketches so that the painters might become acquainted with the entire layout of the area even if parts of it were never to appear on the stage. Only in this way, he thought, could they have a "feel" for the whole set.

A letter, often pages long and liberally decorated with sketches, described in detail what he expected. For example, on May 12, 1886, he sent Max Brückner a description of what he wanted for *Bluthochzeit*, along with a sketch of the Louvre at the time of Henry II with many details never to be seen on the stage: the moat, the gallery leading to the Tuilleries, and so on. He then sent Max books and manuscripts so the painters could familiarize themselves with the atmosphere of the time. Georg himself had used the time when he was stationed in Paris at the end of the Franco-Prussian War to study buildings, décor, costumes, furniture, weapons, and armor of the time of Henry II. All this he used in designing *Bluthochzeit*. "I was astonished," Albert Lindner wrote after seeing his play on stage. "I had delivered the 'soul,' but not this 'body.'"[26] No detail was insignificant. Armorial devices were to be painted on Stauffacher's house in *Wilhelm Tell*, but "only those devices of the cantons that belonged to Switzerland in 1300," for the *Book of Peerage* had accorded incorrect devices to the house.[27]

An exchange of letters between the duke and Ibsen in 1886 provides a record of his method. In November the duke informed Ibsen of his plan to present *Ghosts* at Christmas and asked the author if, in view of his own practical theater experience and intimate knowledge of Norway, he wished to make any suggestions on the staging of the drama. A grateful and flattered Ibsen replied:[28]

Most Gracious Duke!
  With great joy I have received the communication from Your Highness concerning the proposed production of my drama *Ghosts*.
  May I be permitted to express to Your Highness and to your wife my deepest thanks for the gracious invitation. I shall certainly not fail to be present at the performance in Meiningen.
  The interior decoration of Norwegian country houses today shows no distinctly pronounced national character. The living rooms of the oldest family houses of this class are usually papered with dark-colored wallpaper. Below this, the walls are finished in *simple*, polished wood. The ceiling as well as the doors and window frames are finished in this manner. The stoves are large, *ponderous,*

and usually *cast iron*. The furnishings are often in the style of the First French Empire, but throughout the colors are darker.

In general, this is the way I have thought of the living room of Mrs. Alving's house. Should the concerned official of the court theater wish additional or different information, I am at his disposal at any time.

> With respectful thanks,
> Henrik Ibsen

On the flyleaf of Ibsen's letter, the duke immediately sketched a set drawing, a floor plan, and a detailed picture of the stove, which he sent to Max Brückner with these instructions:

> For the drama by Ibsen I request, my dear Professor, that, guided by the description in his letter and by the model of my sketch, you prepare a closed room [i.e., a box set]. *Ghosts* will be sent to you by Privy Councillor Chronegk; in it you will see how the room should appear in reference to the doors and window. In the back of the room is to be a window garden, and it is best to have in it real flowers. Through the back window is seen a Norwegian landscape, for which I can use a prospect from *Tell*. The rehearsals for this piece begin December 3.[29]

Unlike *Ghosts*, most pieces played in multiple sets, and shifting became a major problem. Georg made every effort to limit the number of scenes and, therefore, set changes.[30] In his view, and certainly in the mind of the audience, long pauses destroyed the illusion and reduced the effectiveness of the drama. Since he had no revolving stage or heavy hydraulic machinery, he sought to expedite scene changes by uniting the wings and borders into arches—the so-called *Bögen*—and by doing away with the clumsy ceiling in pieces with a number of changes.[31] Over the years, he devised other expedients to cut down the time for shifting.

One common device was to leave parts of one set up while covering them with a quickly erected set for an intervening scene. Such a construction solved the difficulty of keeping up the Bohemian forest set in Schiller's *Die Räuber*, which is punctuated by four short interior scenes. The duke placed shallow rooms with breakaway walls within the already erected exterior. Extending over the whole back wall of Moor's bedroom was a painted Gobelin. A heavy red curtain, half covering the old bed, provided the one lightening color in the gloomy room. The bed and spinet, hidden by rock pieces, remained on stage during the following scene in the Bohemian forest, a March landscape with snow. "A quick change in this endlessly long piece is not to be undervalued," he wrote Brückner.[32]

The second consideration was the construction of the play itself. He kept firmly in mind that the scenery must serve to keep the attention of the audience "always concentrated on the heart of the drama." For that reason he instructed the artists to avoid frescoes as wall decorations in *Die Piccolomini* because they tended "to divert the viewer's attention away from the plot." He also instructed them to keep the balcony on which Wallenstein shows himself to the rebellious troops out of view "so that the action in the room [on stage] will not be disturbed." [33] It was on this principle that the duke broke most sharply with his English predecessor Charles Kean. In Kean's productions the spoken text seemed to Macready "more like a running commentary upon the spectacle exhibited, than the scenic arrangements an illustration of the text." [34] A glance at the list of instructions that the duke gave Paul Lindau, intendant of the Meiningen court theater from 1894 to 1899 (see Appendix B, doc. 5), shows how committed Georg was to removing anything destructive to the illusion of reality or to the intent of the dramatist.

Instructions, sketches, and reading materials were sent to Max Brückner, who prepared further sketches and sometimes a model. These Georg frequently changed, sometimes entirely. He might write out a whole set of new instructions, and as the work progressed there would be a continual exchange of letters, sketches, and models between Meiningen and Coburg. Frequently, as the duke changed his instructions and he himself became more deeply immersed in the staging, the letters arrived in Coburg from almost anyone connected with him: others in the theater, his military aide-de-camp, and even those totally unconnected with court or theater. One such note runs: "Sir: His Highness, the Duke of Saxe-Meiningen, leaves it to you to find the best way. You may make the background next. Respectfully and humbly, Kann, ducal forester." [35]

"Just look how gray and cold everything is; more color is needed in the mise-en-scènes," wrote Arsène Houssaye of the Comédie Française in 1849; and although Georg agreed, he had no intention of enlivening the stage with brilliant color. He did not use a blending of many colors on stage, but selected a ground tone of cassel brown, which with its saturated reddish hue was characteristic of all Meiningen sets. This neutral color was unusual enough for the critics in Brussels to find the decorations dark (*La Nation*, June 4, 1888) and in London to judge "that the color wanted depth" (The *Times*, June 17, 1881). The duke found such criticism complimentary. Against the basic brown he built a composition and created mood by a skillful use of colorful detail. Aloys Prasch relates an incident that occurred in Düsseldorf, "the Painters' City":

When the Meininger appeared in Düsseldorf, the painters were especially interested in the performances and could not see too often the magnificent and splendid pictures that the duke, with his artistic eye, knew how to conjure up. The arrangement of the Bible scene [in *Die Räuber*], long cut on the German stage but now restored, aroused general admiration. The famous painter [Wilhelm] Camphausen, however, moved uneasily in his seat and finally whispered to his neighbor, "I don't know what it is, but some color is missing in this scene to make it complete." In a few minutes he said, "I have it; there should be some white in the picture." At that very moment, the door opened and Hermann entered, dressed from head to foot in a white Croatian cloak.[36]

In the court scene of *The Merchant of Venice* the scarlet of the judges' robes was balanced on the other side of the stage by Gratiano's beret, which lay on the floor throughout the scene. In *Fiesko* Leonore's bright red cap in Act V not only served as a patch of color, but also had the practical purpose of allowing the audience to follow her as she was swirled across the stage in a crowd. Ernst von Possart remembered the duke's calling out to Chronegk on one occasion, "That violet coat the extra behind the third wing is wearing—the little one next to the scarlet senator—it wrecks the whole picture. Away with it."[37]

The painted background, no longer a beautiful but independent picture, now became an integral part of the scenery and supported the action on stage. At the same time the duke did not overlook any chance to present replicas of actual places to a public yearning for the faraway and "real." In 1874 he sent plans for *Fiesko* and a number of photographs to Max Brückner, with this note: "Among the photographs of Genoa is a view of the place where Fiesko landed; this place is very picturesque. We cannot miss an opportunity to present this historically important view to the public. Instead of the southern view of the city, you will wish to choose this view for the backdrop, appearing bright in the sunlight. Look at this picture through a magnifying glass so as to identify the beautiful particulars."[38]

In *The Winter's Tale*, King Leontes looked out through the columned halls of his castle—and the audience with him—at a magnificent view of Taormina stretching over land and sea. In another view, the Sicilian landscape lay in the evening sun; in still another, the audience saw a Sicilian street scene. Other outdoor scenes were as pleasing to the eye. In *Wilhelm Tell*, cutouts in the backdrops allowed storms to gather, a moonlight rainbow to appear, bonfires to blaze, and the sun gradually to rise against the snowy mountain range. The upper Danube in June with vineyards and cornfields lying in the red of the evening sun for *Die Räuber*, the hills in back of the tattered and patched brown and yellow tents in *Wallensteins Lager*, the stony heath for *Macbeth*, the idyllic garden at Belmont for *The Merchant of Venice*—each backdrop was as different as the action that played before it.

Even when Georg had no historical information, he used factual mate-

Fig. 5. Georg's sketch for Shakespeare's *The Winter's Tale*. The written instructions call for a forest of chestnut trees and an expanse of moorland to be painted on one backdrop; and for rose hedges (the bracketed areas) and the tree in the foreground to be set pieces.

rial to support his imagination. In Kleist's *Die Hermannsschlacht* he could do what he wanted, for no one knows exactly how the old Germanic tribes lived. The houses were to wear "the soft color of the Alpine huts that approaches a beautiful black-brown-red" and to have painted thatched roofs.[39] For the last scene, the Teutoburg Forest in shambles, Georg sent Max Brückner a photograph of Meiningen ravaged by fire in 1873, so that he could depict the disaster naturally. The scenes in the Teutoburg Forest achieved a unique quality by the abundant use of artificial reeds and bushes. The duke's conjectural settings seemed so characteristic of the time and place that the critics found them "entirely true."

Georg rarely sketched an empty room or an unoccupied area: Mrs. Alving's living room in Ibsen's *Ghosts*, Marwood's bedroom in Lessing's *Miss Sara Sampson*, Polonius's chamber in *Hamlet*, and the Danube area in Schiller's *Die Räuber* were rare exceptions.[40] For his peopled sets, he provided the actors with places to sit, stand, or crouch.* Fountains, steps, even rooftops, were made strong enough to hold the crowds. He narrowed the set and closed in the acting areas to concentrate the action and to make the crowds thicker.

The Meininger played all interiors in box sets and developed what became known as a "Meininger room," very shallow so that it could be placed inside another, more complicated set, thus simplifying the shifting. Sometimes, as was true of the hall for the banquet scene in *Macbeth*, this was hardly more than a corridor. The same device was used in exteriors. In *Wilhelm Tell* the backdrop was hung far forward so that the complicated fortress of Uri was already set up behind it to allow other scenes to be played between the two prison scenes. But even ingenious measures could not do away with shifting entirely, and the Meininger traveled with their own crew. No one else, says Max Grube, could find their way through so much complicated machinery. A contemporary journalist agreed:

Above all I was astonished at the great number of workers who were busy here, and in spite of the seemingly happy freedom, new palaces and cities were being built in the background of the open stage, and new gardens and forests planted in the side wings; deep in the underground of the traps the machinery was being set up, and high above on the rigging new halls and rooms prepared—everything with admirable industry and skill. And scarcely had the scene curtain fallen than everyone fell to on stage, and as if by ghostly hands the new background on the sides, in the background, from above, was put into place and completed. Everyone, actors and directors as well as crew and extras, lent a hand. Two minutes were enough to root out the wilderness, to raise the mountain, and to erect a prince's shining chamber. A sharp glance of the intendant, a peal of the little bell, the curtain rose, and the tumbling, noisy whirlwind of workers, who a few minutes before had filled the stage, made way for the actors. The important pieces for a play fill the rigging loft and the side stages. The heaviest square piece flutters like a piece of canvas in the air, and the colossal "marble" columns would not stand erect in the breeze of an open door, if they were not anchored with iron weights. Closely observed, the scenery is neither better nor worse designed and made than on any other stage, but the tasteful painting calculated to the exact dimensions and lighted with imagination deceives and charms the eye.[41]

It was not enough for the scenery to provide a place for the actors to move. Georg wanted it to provide an atmosphere as well. In 1872, for his production of Schiller's *Don Carlos*, he knew exactly how the room in

* All scenery was scaled to the stage of the Meiningen court theater, built in 1831, burned in 1908. (See photograph, p. 57.) For the population of the town, about 10,000, it was large: the auditorium held 700; the stage was 18.4 m wide (proscenium opening, 11.20 m) and 12 m deep. There were 6 bridges, and 2 large and 2 small traps. At the end of the 1870's, the duke had the backstage expanded (15.06 m by 7.85 m) with a sixth trap.

Fig. 6. A typical shallow "Meininger room": Georg's sketch for the banquet scene in Shakespeare's *Macbeth*. A trap at stage left permitted the murderers to talk to Macbeth as he leaned over the railing, effectively hiding them from the banqueters.

which Posa is shot should look: the chamber was to be in Spanish gothic, backed by a large practicable iron grill giving a view into the castle courtyard; the walls were to be of blackened stone with roofed niches holding gothic saints. "The room must make an uncanny, gloomy, worn impression," he wrote Brückner. "Create something really striking, reminiscent of the inquisition, of funeral pyres, monks, and ascetics."[42]

The duke liked to say that a set should characterize the people who lived in it, and he was never more successful in showing this than in the three bedrooms he created for Lessing's *Miss Sara Sampson*. In the words of a Berlin critic:

Scarcely another drama points out so convincingly as *Miss Sara Sampson* how significantly the Meininger proceed with the staging and outfitting of their performances, what a meaningful, characteristic atmosphere they spread over every single scene, how everything is present for the plot, and how it carries, raises, and completes the performances of the actors. . . . This room [Mellefont's] is a picture of his situation, disgraced and ruined, just as he is. The gilt wallpaper, cracked and chinked, hangs forlornly from the walls. Sara's room is somewhat better, but it still shows the modest station of the inn she has chosen for her dwelling. It stands in an affecting contrast to Marwood's luxuriously decorated, rococo chamber, a contrast that extends no less to the clothing of the two rivals as well as to their entire surroundings. Not the least is this evident in the contrast of the true Waitwell and the saucy Hannah, who half as procuress, half as perniciously lurking fate, first aids her mistress, then from the threshold of the bedroom watches and follows her every move with a burning look. The last scene plays in Sara's bedroom. She sits and dies in an armchair that stands in front of her fourposter bed, the silent witness of her guilt.[43]

Furniture and properties carried out the same function to simulate history and create appropriate atmosphere. Georg's means were not unlimited, but not only frugality dictated that things be made as simply as possible; time was important and ease of transportation a consideration. Chests, chimneys, and that sort of thing were made from painted canvas and usually consisted of three sides and a top. If such articles had to be strong, then either pieces of wood were added or the whole piece was made by a cabinetmaker, with only those parts seen by the public painted or carved.[44] If neither of these suited, Chronegk called on the duke. "We desperately need two high chests," he once wrote. "The two painted ones just won't work. Couldn't the theater have those two chests that are on the first gallery of the castle? They now have dishes on them, but it seems to me that they are crudely carved and not really valuable."[45] The duke himself gave up what he considered too expensive. For *Julius Caesar* he wished to commission a statue of Pompey, but he abandoned the idea when he learned that it would cost 2,000 marks.

Although the duke was frugal, he never let his careful money management lead to foolishness. When the admiring director of a *Gasfabrik* in Leipzig offered to contribute 5,000 marks for a new lighting installation, asking in return that he be made *Kommerzienrat* (commercial councillor), Chronegk advised the duke "not to allow this man to lay the new main at his own expense—perhaps in future years Mr. X will give himself the pleasure of outfitting the stage at his own expense in return for the title of *Geheimrat* [privy councillor]."[46] Georg did not accept the enticing offer. But he did not hesitate to plunder his own museums and castles. From these came armchairs, chests, carpets, and hangings. With great care he selected other properties: porcelain, caskets, boxes, writing implements, table covers, wall hangings, pillows, screens, ornaments, and books. These details, he believed, served the actor more than the audience, since much of the detail was lost on the viewer. For *Die Räuber* the duke himself made sketches in the Dresden castle for the portraits. For *Maria Stuart*, he had Arthur Fitger paint a Holbein-like portrait of Henry VIII, which looked down on Elizabeth as she sat in the half-darkness to sign the ill-fated queen's death warrant.[47]

Closely connected with the scenery and complementing it were the effects the duke achieved by the use of scrim, lighting, sound, and music. "Who can forget," wrote a contemporary critic, "the realistic crowds, the bier scene with its sad tolling of the bell in *Der Prinz von Homburg*, the storm with its flying clouds in *Tell*, the rain shower in *Das Käthchen von Heilbronn*, the noise in *Wallensteins Lager*, the burning of Paris in *Bluthochzeit*, the uprising of the populace in *Fiesko*?" He went on to praise "the storm in the forest near the smoky charcoal heap from which Count von Strahl frees Kunigunde in *Das Käthchen von Heilbronn*, the moonlight on the Rütli in *Tell*, the burning of the castle." [48] Just as bedazzled was an Austrian critic, who found the transition from midnight to daybreak in the garden scene of *Julius Caesar* "an optical masterpiece." "Never have we seen anything like this in Vienna," he told his readers. [49]

Much of this effect was achieved by lighting, especially of the focused lamp, which was almost unknown in Germany when Georg came to the theater, but which he may have seen in England twenty years earlier.* In 1869 he ordered a "transportable gas flame" that could be connected by a rubber hose to the gas main for lighting. By 1872 he was using an electric focused lamp for the ghost of Hamlet's father, moving a gray figure against a gray background and then picking up the face with a beam of light. Scrim and electric light were used in 1874 for the ghost in *Julius Caesar* and again in 1876 for the ghost in *Macbeth*. In the first, the ghost of Caesar, standing invisible at the back of Brutus's red tent in a red toga of exactly the same color, appeared when a beam of light fell on his face, a specter "that made the public momentarily shudder." [50] In *Macbeth*, Banquo's ghost glided in on a small wheeled cart behind a scrim opening in the wall and appeared when the light struck him. Since the banquet scene was played diagonally upstage, the downstage area was dark enough to make the appearance effective.

Moonshine was produced by an electric light in a glass ball hung above the stage; and if a sharp ray of moonlight was desired, a metal tube directed the beam. A slight mist or fog, used, for example, in the night scenes of *Julius Caesar* or for the smoke of the poisoned candles in *Bluthochzeit*, was produced by drawing a piece of mottled, grayish glass in front of a lamp. Sunrise or sunset could be effected with different colored

---

* This is not the incandescent lamp, which was not commercially produced until 1879. (See Terence Rees, *Theatre Lighting in the Age of Gas*, London, 1978, for a full description of the technical aspects of lighting during the early period of Georg's theatrical activity.) The theater in Meiningen was not fully wired for electricity until it was rebuilt in 1909. Hugo Bähr, "the father of stage lighting in Germany," became known in large part through the Meininger tours, because his work was credited in the programs.

glass. The strange appearances in Act I of *Julius Caesar* and the impressive moving clouds were merely a shadow play of colored glass turning in front of a light and reflected on the backdrop. This extravagantly admired illusion was emphasized by the sound of pouring rain.

In general, the duke used three kinds of lightning effects, each produced in a different way. Nearby lightning, blinding and dazzling, was made by kindling gunpowder behind the first wing. Jagged "chain" lightning, farther away and hanging snakelike in the background, was made by a magic-lantern image projected on the backdrop. Summer "sheet" lightning was merely a rapid play of light behind the wings. *The Winter's Tale* and *Wilhelm Tell* featured spectacular storms with wind, rain, and lightning. In *Wilhelm Tell* the appearance of the signal fires, gradually growing behind the cutouts of the mountain backdrops, seemed like magic to the audience.[51]

For *Twelfth Night*, the duke directed Brückner to make practicable doors and windows. He also wanted the windows to be transparent so the light from the candle could fall into the garden and mix with the moonlight to form a magical night scene. But he overlooked one thing, as the critic Paul Lindau quickly noted when he saw the production in 1874: "The . . . lighting reveals great artistic taste. The contrast between the full moonlight and the lamplight shining through the panes works a beautiful, pictorial effect, but the careful director should remember that the branches of the tree that towers over Olivia's house must be lighted by the moonlight, not the lamplight." [52]

There were other uses for lighting besides creating a beautiful atmosphere. In Act II of *Die Jungfrau von Orleans*, an electric projector was placed behind set pieces to throw the image of the English campfires on the backdrop, which had been painted with a yellow overtone to make the flames more easily visible.[53] A masterly stroke in *Das Käthchen von Heilbronn* was the burning of the castle, with the whole section of the windows and balcony collapsing in flame, an effect achieved by the use of scrim and light. In Act II of *Der Prinz von Homburg*, an entire village burned in the far distance. Buildings had been burning on the stage since the eighteenth century, but Georg's imaginative and skillful use of the new lighting apparatus achieved unheard-of effects.

The novelty of the new methods did not keep the duke from using the very old and often mixing the two. A review from 1886 shows that torches, lamps, and electric lights worked very well together in *The Merchant of Venice*:

The atmosphere of the Rialto was especially effective. It is the evening twilight; night approaches and gradually covers the scene, while the green and red of a few modest signal lanterns are seen in the area. As lanterns hidden behind the wall begin one after the other to light up, an arm of the canal visible in the deep background through an opening in the wall takes on a bright light, which finds its reflection in the transparent green water; this breaks the night's darkness of the foreground, where under the high Rialto Bridge the gondolas quickly pass. The boatmen, standing high up on the bow, work rudder and oar with energetic movements, while the torch in each vessel that shows the helmsman the direction lights the faces red, thereby thickening the surrounding darkness even more.[54]

A brilliant use of torches was also seen in the last act of *Julius Caesar*, where from high on a bridge the conquerors, lighted only by their torches, looked down on the defeated enemy lying in the shadows. All of this was made more effective because Georg darkened his auditorium, a practice not universally followed.

Along with the innovative use of lighting, the Meininger were masters at using sounds of many kinds to heighten the intellectual and emotional tone of the drama. For thunder, wind, and rain, Georg employed methods commonly used on every stage. To simulate thunder, a sound he found difficult to reproduce accurately, he suspended a large drum topped by several billiard balls high above the stage; when the drum was struck, the rolling balls produced a dull sound of thunder, which grew louder as the strokes were stronger. Rain was imitated by rolling dry peas in a sieve.

The conventional means of imitating the crackle of gunfire, by using a wooden roller or by scraping a light board with a nail in it over a barrel organ, did not produce the sharp, irregular rattle of a weapon precisely enough to please the duke. For this, he attached small fireworks to the back of set pieces. The sound of bells or drums was familiar on the Meininger stage. "Especially effective," one critic judged the sounds of the bells on the Alpine cattle. "In such things they are successful in making the sound come from the right side and from the right distance. The effects are so appropriate and inexpensive that no stage director should overlook them. Only everything must be done carefully and handled skillfully; otherwise, it would be better to keep quite away from such attempts and show the public by writing on a piece of canvas what each item should represent."[55]

Quite another mood was produced in the gothic tale, where "no one was spared the terror of the drama *Die Ahnfrau*: the creaking of the weathervane, the howling of the wind, the flickering of the fire, the whining and wailing, the moaning and groaning in innumerable places, the squeaking of the doors at the entrance and exit of the Ahnfrau, and the strange and melancholy sound at her appearance. . . . All this was achieved with so much truth to nature that even a person with very strong nerves had to shudder."[56]

Still another mood was evoked by the wild beating of the angry seas buffeting the little boat in *Wilhelm Tell*. The audience looked toward the Vierwaldstättersee against a realistically painted landscape backdrop.* Originally, the action of the waves was imitated simply by having actors under a large painted canvas move their bodies violently, giving the appearance of thrashing waves. Later a system of profiles of waves was operated, but even with the howling of the wind and rain synchronized with the pitching boat, the duke was not satisfied.[57] On February 2, 1886, he wrote Brückner: "I should like to see at any price the skiff disappearing under the water." Happily for Georg, in that very year the painter Hermann Burghart, who fashioned many of the decorations for the Vienna court opera, devised a satisfactory way to make the seas undulate by using a lighting effect behind a transparent perspective.[58]

Although Georg did away with the orchestra that customarily played between acts, he used music extensively on stage. But again, the music was part of the whole, not simply an ear-pleasing, audience-pleasing technique.† A common practice that was followed in playing Brahms's "Variations on a Theme by Haydn" over and over again in *Die Jungfrau von Orleans* gave the impression that the procession was lasting longer than it really was. Other music—the great choruses in Schiller's *Wallensteins Lager* and *Die Räuber*, the small song in *Twelfth Night*, the simple shepherd's music in *The Winter's Tale*—each added its characteristic tone to each production. *Preciosa* was a musical experiment, a play on the borderline between musical and spoken drama. With the music, as with everything else, the duke was making changes up to the last moment. In 1887, while the company was in Dresden, he wired Chronegk: "I am sending you three tom-toms, which have a wonderfully deep tone, far better than anything we now have."[59]

The scenic designs Georg put on the Meiningen stage were not revolutionary, but they united much of what had been developing during the past century. In an age of reality, an age when pure and applied science

---

* The word realistic must be used relatively when describing Meininger scenery. The paintings represented an actual scene accurately enough, but the landscapes, especially, tended to be romantically beautiful.

† Here, too, the duke was bent on historical accuracy, as is clear from Barnay's account of their disagreement on the fanfares for *Hamlet* (see Appendix B, doc. 2). In the theater program for *Maria Stuart*, the march used when Maria goes to her death is called the "Hexenmarsch" and is said to be the music played while a witch burned. It is further explained that this music had only recently been found in the British Museum. However, in this case the duke (or someone) was badly misled: there is a letter from the British Museum in the Meiningen Landesarchiv describing the piece as an old folk tune, "Joan's Packet," and stating that no music was played at the execution of Mary, Queen of Scots, though some song—perhaps this one—may have been sung by the crowd outside the castle park.

flourished, no symbolic stage forms could be born. If Georg of Meiningen wanted to animate the spirit of the drama in the nation, he could not rely alone on the fire of the poetry or the warmth of the actor; he had to build a bridge to the understanding of the audience on a kind of "reality" they would accept. In order to make his viewers "hearers," as Laube wanted to make them, he had first to make them "see-ers." Even Dingelstedt, who had pioneered the use of spectacle on the German stage, realized that something different was being shown in Meiningen, and wrote to ask "if Your Highness would graciously permit me now and then on your Highness's authority to reproduce some details. The German theater has never possessed such scenic designs as those Your Highness has placed on the stage." [60]

In the Meiningen conception of unified staging, the costumes figured as a necessary complement to the scenery and properties. Authentic and historical costumes were not new in the theater, but Georg's use of them to serve the actor was. The costumes were designed to show the actor the characteristics of the person he was portraying. At the first rehearsal, the actor received a sketch by the duke showing how the garment was to be worn, how any ornaments were to be attached, how the belt was to be fastened.[61] In his memoir, *Die Meininger*, Karl Grube recalls the words of a note he received from the duke along with some sketches showing mustache styles in the Napoleonic era: "In Napoleon's time the *whole* world wore the chin clean-shaven! H. Grube must make himself look older; he now looks too young for a trusted general of N.'s." [62]

In contrast to the practice of letting an actor take anything out of the costume room that he thought appropriate for his role, or more likely, that he thought would look best on him, the Meiningen theater furnished its actors entire costumes, complete down to the smallest detail—including, as Josef Kainz wrote his parents, even the linen (and at a tryout performance at that).[63] On the duke's stage, the actor was allowed to wear only what had been expressly designed for him in one designated role, and he was forbidden to alter it in any way. The tenor style of high heels (the *Stöckelschuhe*) was proscribed, as were the customary thin silk tights. The latter might be worn only with splendid costumes of pomp and then only with undertights, so that even in the sharpest light the skin would not show through. Even though many an actor nursed an injured vanity when he looked "historical" but not very "beautiful," the duke allowed no self-decoration that did not fit the role.

Aloys Prasch remembered the duke's remarks to an actress playing Armgut in a *Tell* rehearsal: "What does this mean? You have a new head scarf on! Take it off! With such a scarf Armgut would have no need to beg

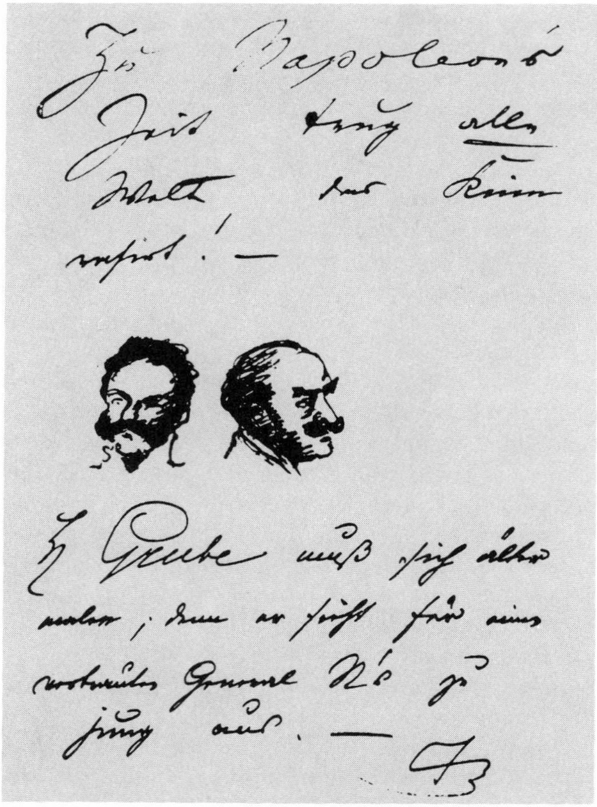

Fig. 7. A note from Georg to the actor Karl Grube asking him to change his makeup: "In Napoleon's time the *whole* world wore the chin clean-shaven! H. Grube must make himself look older; he now looks too young for a trusted general of N's." Every Meiningen actor found such notes and sketches on his dressing table.

bread for her children. She'd need only sell the scarf and then she'd have not only bread, but cheese."[64] But if the roles called for beautiful garments, the stage could present a charming picture. After the Grand Duke Constantine saw the exquisite scenes in *The Winter's Tale,* he wrote Georg from St. Petersburg: "There were the all-too-familiar figures of Giotto, of Masaccio, of Benozzo Gozzoli. . . . Rarely have I left the theater with such a strong impression."[65]

Only the best materials were used for the costumes: "Heavy cloth, real velvet, the heaviest silk, good fur instead of the usual rabbit. Ponderous upholstery materials woven according to old patterns brought into Germany during the Renaissance were scarcely obtainable there until the appearance of the Meininger."[66] The duke ordered the materials from Lyons or Genoa, often having them woven to his instruction. To wear a Meininger costume was in the fullest sense of the word no light task, especially since each was lined with heavy material and sometimes boned for stiffness and a more genuine look.

The costumes were tested in full lighting. The greatest care was taken to ensure the correct fall of the drapery, especially of the toga. The celebrated actor Siegward Friedmann recalled the experience he and the tragedian Ludwig Dessoir had in Meiningen when they played Cassius and Brutus for the duke:

We had naturally—snobs in the provinces—brought our own Königliches Hoftheater costumes and weapons with us. We were informed that the duke, in order not to destroy the harmony of the pictorial effect, preferred that we use his costumes. The prudent Dessoir had his toga brought into the dressing room on the day before the costume rehearsal. What followed showed us how wise his foresight had been.

Our Berlin togas were on the order of a middle-size coffee-table cover. With terror I remember the size of the Meiningen monster. This real toga measured thirty ells, was of heavy woolen material, and weighed—I don't know how much! We had to ask the costumier for a private lecture on how to make such a toga wearable and becoming by gathering and arranging the folds and how to move in it. With my slenderness and twenty-eight years, I soon managed. Indeed I found the unusual constraint that the bulk and weight of the real garment laid on me truly useful. My too lively movements were profitably rendered more difficult and therefore curbed. My Cassius was more commanding, more sedate, more Roman. I believe I never played the role better.

As the monstrous antique garment unrolled threateningly before the astonished eyes of Dessoir, he looked helplessly first at the toga, then at the costumier, then at me, and finally his confused glance moved entirely around the costume room, seeking help like a child. . . . I had to stand as a model and let myself be draped in order to orient him to some extent. . . . At last he seemed to understand how it was to be done. He let himself be wrapped and gathered up; but the results of our combined efforts were lamentable!

With his mighty skull, his broad upper body, and his short legs, he looked in the padding of the Meiningen authenticity like a Roman nutcracker wrapped in swaddling clothes. As he viewed himself in the mirror, he laughed out loud. I burst out in laughter too, and the dresser also. . . . After a long consultation, we cut enough from the togas so that Brutus would not make a comic appearance. He certainly wasn't handsome, but at a performance by Dessoir the public soon forgot all externals and were seized by the power of his acting.[67]

The other actors learned as well, as the London *Times* noted on May 31, 1881: "The manner in which the Roman senators envelop themselves in their togas proves that the actors as well as the designers have studied

Examples of Georg's attention to costuming (all the sketches are his).   Fig. 8 (facing page). The captain in Franz Grillparzer's *Die Ahnfrau*. "Make the cloak in a harmonious color," the duke wrote on the sketch.   Fig. 9 (above left). Roman soldiers in Shakespeare's *Julius Caesar*. Note the duke's details on the armor to specify differences in rank. Fig. 10 (above right). Headdress for Schiller's *Fiesko*.   Fig. 11 (below right). "Cleopatra enthroned." Georg made this sketch for his last production, Shaw's *Caesar and Cleopatra*, when he was 86 years old.

to some purpose." Karl Frenzel remarked that "the public saw nothing of the shabby pieces of cloth that pass everywhere for a toga; nothing of the modern hairdress on the actresses, nothing of the medieval pikes and halberds used to represent weapons of the legions: everything up to the light in Brutus's tent, up to the Medusa head on Caesar's cloak, has an antique character." [68]

The proper shoes and headdresses were sought out with the same care as the weapons and armor. Instead of the "drawing room" shoes worn on all stages even "in the woods," the Meininger introduced heavy footwear for the outdoors, and instead of the customary imitation leather boot tops, high knights' boots of real leather. In the selection of hair styles and head covers, the complexion of the make-up as well as appropriateness was an important consideration. As usual, the duke was changing all this up to the time the actors went on stage. In 1875, just before *The Merchant of Venice* opened in Berlin, he wired Chronegk: "Silver and gold nets for all women, powdered hair strongly forbidden. No flowers or pearls in hair. Pages with wigs . . . only Portia and Nerissa with loose hair." Later the same day a telegram advised Chronegk to add humor to the last act by having Portia and Nerissa enter "wearing large, clumsy shoes." [69]

Pikes, swords, halberds, lances, and spears were all manufactured in Paris according to exact instructions. Armor was no longer knitted "chain-mail," but correct in all details. Any actor who portrayed an armored hero in Meiningen was fully convinced of the authenticity of his heavy coat of mail, with its steel-ringed leg and iron pieces. A letter from the duke to his wardrobe inspector shows that Georg was not so much interested in the costume itself as in the actor's relationship to it:

Please have the raincoat that Hessel wears as ferryman in *Tell* suitably shortened and costume him generally as I have sketched, doing away with the high boots and peaked hat. Cock feathers on the gray cap. Görner, who in the Rütli scene stands right in front with his back to the public, must look properly dressed, . . . a peasant cudgel in his hand or a club with spikes. . . . The arms of the peasants are in general too knightly. Too many carry swords. Flails, cudgels, and the like would be better mixed with swords and axes. If you cannot borrow them from old collections, etc., have them made. . . . On the enclosed drawing you can see how the flail is to be carried. Two with clubs set with iron spikes, two with cudgels, and two with flails will be enough—the wood painted brown to look weathered. The garments of the peasants in *Tell* are generally of a more domestic nature. The actors could lend a hand in dressing themselves.

For Gessler, Rudenz, and the six hunters, one of whom should carry a hooded falcon on his leather-covered hand, I made a sketch for you before you left, and I believe sent it direct. [70]

Fig. 12. In this sketch for Schiller's *Wilhelm Tell*, Georg indicated how he wanted some of Gessler's followers to be dressed, grouped, and moved across stage. Note the detail at left for the hooded falcon to be carried by the third hunter.

Stanislavski was impressed by the way the duke reduced the significance of the king of France in *Die Jungfrau von Orleans* by putting him on a huge throne that dwarfed his person. This technique was also used in *Le Malade imaginaire*, where to point up the absurdity of Dr. Diaforius's pride in his stunted son, the young man sat on a stool so high that, try as he might, he could never quite get his feet to reach the floor. Georg used this device in costumes as well. In Björnson's *Mary Stuart in Scotland*, the costumes of the court fool were padded and exaggerated in all detail. He wrote his costumier that "Herr Ruprecht as the court fool must appear very dwarf-like; therefore, a very large ruff, very large cuffs, very large sword." In Schiller's *Maria Stuart*, the graceful, perfumed, and colorfully garbed French ambassadors contrasted sharply in national spirit as they entered the stiffly magnificent court of Elizabeth. Even persons of the same nationality and station were differentiated, as, for example, were the old and young shepherds in *The Winter's Tale*.

If ragged garments were needed, old things were not used unless they were appropriate; new garments were designed to fit the character and then were torn and dirtied. In *Die Räuber*, Old Man Moor had traditionally been buried in a shapeless shroud, but to the duke it was un-

Fig. 13. Georg used several devices to make an actor appear smaller or more insignificant on stage. In Molière's *Le Malade imaginaire*, he made the doctor's
foolish son look even sillier by perching him on a high stool where he could never
quite get his toes to touch the floor (sketch by C. W. Allers). For Björnson's *Mary
Stuart*, he wanted the court fool to appear dwarf-like: "therefore, very large neck
ruff, very large cuffs, very large sword."

thinkable that a nobleman would be put to rest in such a garment. He
designed an elegant parade coat, had it carefully made of the finest materials, and then had it systematically shredded and dirtied to illustrate the
"frog's life" the old man's son had forced him to live.

The effort the duke put into designing appropriate costumes, like the
effort he put into designing scenery, arranging effective lighting, and de-
vising suitable sound effects, worked toward one goal, that of realizing
the dramatist's intention. Too many people saw only the painted scenery,
splendid furniture, and beautiful costumes, but one Bavarian critic recognized Georg's aims when he wrote of the Meininger:

First to them is always the spirit of the work of art, of the dramatic poetry to be
placed on the stage. With the greatest reverence, with all imaginable conscien-

tiousness, they subordinate everything to the spirit, to the intention of the dramatist. Every expenditure of means has to serve one goal alone: to render the poetic idea most creatively and to embody as truly as possible the dramatic fantasy picture as it hovered before the poet. This fact must be vigorously emphasized if we are to evaluate the Meininger justly; for one cannot help thinking during the performances that with so much extraordinary care lavished on the staging, the mise-en-scène might restrain the unfolding of the poetic idea and deaden the full effect of the dramatic life, that it might become more or less an end in itself, thereby turning the drama into an extravaganza. The case here is just the opposite. With all the richness of staging, with all the fullness of detail, no production can justly be called an extravaganza less than one presented by the Meininger.[71]

No one was more aware than Georg that the scenery he put on the stage would do more than provide a setting for his theater reforms. For that he needed actors, and with great energy and intelligence he set out to forge a company of actors who could realize his goals.

FOUR

THE PLAYERS AND THEIR
DIRECTOR

𝔄s soon as Georg officially took over the Meiningen court theater, he began a systematic development of the company, which with the exception of the blind Josef Weilenbeck included no outstanding talents. Lacking the financial means to attract established actors, but even more, determined to build a company on his own principles, the duke sought out young and untried talents who were willing to submit to strict discipline and to subordinate individuality to ensemble playing. As the reputation of the theater grew, and especially after the first Berlin appearance, a place in the Meiningen court theater became the goal of every young actor.

On August 27, 1877, Josef Kainz jubilantly wrote his parents: "I am a ducal Meiningen Court Actor! . . . What has happened is almost beyond belief." After thirteen unsuccessful and unhappy months in Leipzig, Kainz broke his contract, obtained a referral from an agent, walked three days to Bad Liebenstein, where the Meiningen company was playing a summer season, and introduced himself to Ludwig Chronegk, whom he found a "very placid" man, a judgment he was sometimes to doubt in the years ahead. Assigned a tryout role in Schiller's *Kabale und Liebe*, he went to the first rehearsal with a "very heavy heart," for, he says, "I had already seen a production of *Clavigo*, and I knew into what an outstanding ensemble I was coming." The duke was present at his first performance, and Kainz was relieved to see that he "applauded like crazy." Chronegk assured him that he had done so well that the usual second tryout was not necessary, and welcomed him into the company. That night Kainz wrote his parents: "I can't write any more today: the happy events of the past few days and the great changes in my fate crowd on me so heavily that I don't have my wits about me." [1]

Established actors, too, were eager to become part of the new art movement, even at a financial loss. Marie Schanzer, then at the Hamburg Stadttheater, complained to her friend (and future husband) Hans von Bülow, conductor of the Meiningen court orchestra, about the lack of direction in her current position, and was offered a guest appearance in Meiningen at his intercession. In a letter of January 21, 1882, von Bülow tried to prepare her for the duke's ways. "The Meiningen principle," he wrote, "places the drama—the poet—over the individual. I freely admit that here they carry ensemble playing to the extreme, but the duke and his clever, warmhearted wife respect a towering individuality. In no way do they hinder the development of such talent, but instead seek to provide every opportunity for progress. . . . But since they have had up to now few really artistic individuals with whom to work, they have had little chance to put this into practice."[2] Marie took his advice, ingratiated herself with the ducal pair, performed Minna von Barnhelm effectively, and accepted a contract for a thousand marks less yearly than she had been receiving in Hamburg.*

Many of those who rushed to join the company in the early 1870's remained throughout the tours, but just as many left as soon as they had learned their profession. The genius of such artists as Anna Haverland and Josef Kainz lay precisely in their individuality; they were not ensemble players. Very few, however, left with anything but gratitude for the training they received, judging from the number who came back as guest artists or on festive occasions.

In casting his actors, the duke never referred to a Fach book. When he planned a production, he followed Laube's method of having the play read on stage to decide whether or not he had the personnel to cast it. Only after this practical test of his resident actors did he take any steps to engage a guest artist, who was never a "guest star," but merely an honorary member of the company, subject to the same rules as the contract actors. Then, disregarding tradition and considering only the personality and talent of his artists, he began to fill the roles with a "justice and accuracy that excited general admiration."[3] He waged an unending battle to prevent the actor of the large roles from becoming a "star." Thus the principal roles were usually shared. In *Die Räuber*, Leopold Teller and Franz Kober played Franz; Kainz and Emmerich Robert played Friedrich in *Der Prinz von Homburg*.[4] Even the honorary members of the company shared roles. If, in the course of the rehearsals, the duke found he had

---

* As an authoritarian conductor, von Bülow thoroughly approved of Georg's emphasis on the ensemble rather than the star, but Marie never became reconciled to the notion. It was for this reason that von Bülow finally left Meiningen.

Fig. 14 (left). Max Grube in Louis Napoleon Parker's *The Cardinal*. One of the "Old Meininger," Grube came to the court theater in 1873, at the age of 19, and stayed on to become the historian of the company. Fig. 15 (right). Josef Kainz joined the court theater in 1877 as a 19-year-old beginner and there learned the art that made him one of Germany's great actors. He is pictured here as Ferdinand in Schiller's *Kabale und Liebe*, the tryout role that earned him a place at Meiningen.

chosen the wrong actor, he freely admitted it. On rare occasion he even replaced a guest artist.

Georg raised to a general principle the casting of the despised "little roles" with artists of the first rank. The crowd, accustomed to standing silently and idly by, was given an important function in the stage action, and every actor in the company had crowd duty. The "hero" of today was almost unseen in the mob tomorrow. Thus Ludwig Barnay, already an important actor before he came to Meiningen as a guest, played Tell, Mark Antony, and Orestes, but he also carried a spear and cried "Fiesko, hoch!" with the lowliest beginner. The duke was fond of saying that great roles carried themselves, but good actors carried small roles. Every actor gave his all to the smallest role because he knew the duke's eye was on him as well as on the leading players. And because the company was not frozen in routine, the heroic figures of the classical dramas never appeared on the stage exactly alike.

Once the Fach system was disregarded and role monopoly discarded, Georg broke many other old molds. A talented actress no longer played both Viola and Sebastian, nor a gifted actor Karl and Franz Moor. The roles of Joan of Arc and Eboli, traditionally given to the often-aging "Heroine," became the parts of attractive young women. For Natalie in *Der Prinz von Homburg*, always the part of a Heroine, the young and pretty Adele Pauli was cast. Amanda Lindner was only seventeen when she played Joan in Schiller's *Die Jungfrau von Orleans*. When the smallest actress in the company, Augusta Prasch-Gravenberg, was given this role, the duke said: "It has always annoyed me that on the German stage Joan of Arc is portrayed by a large woman. There is a statue of Joan of Arc in the marketplace in Rouen that shows her as a small, attractive figure. It was not her herculean size that enabled the Maid to free her country from the yoke of the enemy."[5]

Like Laube, the duke seldom relied on the actor's estimation of his own capabilities. Frequently he astonished an actor with his casting. In his memoirs, Karl Weiser relates his own experiences as a beginner:

My first role was Uriel Acosta, my second Mark Antony in *Julius Caesar*. Strangely enough, I had never once had the opportunity to see this masterwork of Shakespeare. I therefore spoke to Chronegk and asked him to tell the duke. The duke replied: "All the better. Now I shall have the opportunity to see an original creation and something really fresh—then I'll be all the more able to judge Weiser's artistic being." The duke and his wife were present at the rehearsal, and after the first scene in the Curia of Pompey, I was invited to the ducal loge for tea. The duke said: "You are a born Meininger. We shall remain together for a long time. But on the tours you must play Brutus. That is really your part." And he turned out to be right, although at the time his statement flabbergasted me. A still more drastic judgment was made in the case of my old friend [Wilhelm] Arndt. For his tryout he had given a fiery young Karl Moor with the greatest success with the public. After the performance, the duke said to him: "You are a dandy actor. You must remain one of us. On the tours you will be a perfect Sir Andrew Aguecheek."[6]

Trained by Heinrich Marr to prize clarity of speech, the baroness undertook to pass the training along to the new Meiningen actors; but this was done at the duke's initiative. From the beginning of his theater activity, he entered into the closest association with the actors through reading rehearsals and discussions in order to win their understanding and at the same time measure their capabilities. Even after the baroness took up the work of schooling the beginners, the duke never lost his interest in the actor as an individual, as his training of Kainz proves. As Wolfgang Drews notes, "Josef Kainz went to the best school then in existence, the little cultural court theater of the clever duke of Meiningen. . . . The gifted actress Ellen Franz, called as the wife of the duke the baroness von Heldburg, assumed responsibility for his education. The duke demanded that the actor follow the poet and subordinate himself to the intent of the poet's words. He never wearied of stressing this."[7]

How well Georg impressed this principle on the actor is evident from a letter Kainz wrote some years later to an Englishman requesting information about his training and artistic principles. "I hate and despise most frightfully every kind of virtuosity in the art of acting as an ulcer of histrionic vanity and presumption that eats away at the work of the poet," he declared. "The ambition of the great actor is to become and to remain a well-polished stone in a beautiful mosaic. May God grant that the time is not distant in which I shall be permitted to work and create, not for me, but for the poet."[8]

One of the greatest favors the duke did Kainz was to identify his weakness in speech technique and devise a program for him in which Kainz worked until he became the powerful speaker whose delivery, Winterstein claims, set him apart from all other actors in Germany.[9] He learned to drive his voice in a furious tempo through every pitch without losing precision or clarity. Because of his unique ability to build up words and sentences, he was able, says Winterstein, "to unite the fire of Schiller's pathos with an almost naturalistic animation. With Kainz the 'tirade' never became an 'aria' as with so many other actors. . . . In short, he was in control of the basics of his art, he had learned his trade."[10] As Kainz himself acknowledged, it was his "three years of the most demanding, but in retrospect the most productive activity" in Meiningen, that made him the artist he was.[11]

It has been said that Kainz came to Meiningen a "street kid" (*Gassenbub*), and left it a prince. Although the duke probably saw in him an extraordinarily gifted beginner and one in whom he could well instill his own principles, other actors attested to the value of the education they received there.[12] On the stage, the actors were subjected to the most stringent discipline, but off it, they found both the duke and the baroness endlessly patient. In her private study, the baroness sought not to dominate the actors, but to awaken and develop their talent. Max Grube describes her wish to pass on to the novice what she had learned on Heinrich Marr's hard but fruitful stage: "The baroness von Heldburg devoted herself to her task as speech mistress. I do not say teacher, for it must be truly said that she never tried to turn an artistic personality into her own image; for that she was far too strong a personality herself. She could not— or rather would not—encroach on the individuality of a talent. She thought rather, as one might say, to make the pupil her speaking tube." *

Many artists credited their skills to the "spirited" and "amiable" baroness, who with each individual worked through the roles "word by word, syllable by syllable, with insight, patience, and perseverance, improving, advising, and training until the characterization was clearly formed." [13] Forty years after she had worked with Ellen, Amanda Lindner, then a celebrated actress, remembered her "lessons":

The baroness was the most ideal instructress, of admirable perseverance, mildness, patience. What these almost daily hours of study with my gifted and experienced teacher meant for me I did not realize until much later. In those days I was only too likely to come late, and the good woman often had to wait for me. Then she would meet me in a flowing morning gown with a watch in her hand and say, "Ah, child, dear Lindner, you are again so late that you are all out of breath. Now we'll have to wait to begin until you get hold of yourself, but then we must work and study hard." In spite of my tardiness, her goodness always remained the same. . . . The instruction took place in the fourth floor apartments of the ducal family. Often the duke appeared in our study room and asked if he might listen to something. I was then always so embarrassed at having the lord of the land, whose magnificent appearance always filled me with enormous respect, sit near me that the baroness usually asked him please to go, since he kept us from our study.[14]

This type of individual attention and work in what the baroness called "the school" was only a small part of an actor's training in Meiningen. The real learning went on onstage during the rehearsals. In order to extend the actor's range, everyone was cast in as many different kinds of roles as possible.[15] Performances were given three times a week, and in the early years Bodenstedt and Grabowsky were required to give the duke a plan every other week outlining the schedule for the next fourteen days, although this was occasionally altered. The company gave about seventy performances each season. Most of these were of what the duke termed

* Max Grube, *The Story of the Meininger*, tr. Ann Marie Koller (Coral Gables, Fla., 1965), p. 34. A good measure of her success is found in the praise the Meininger achieved for *Die Ahnfrau*. One reason Grillparzer's drama had not been heard on the stage for more than 50 years was that actors found it impossible to render the trochaic tetrameter verse intelligible. "What effort they must have made to prevail over the rattling cadences of the trochee!" wrote one critic. "How cleverly they concealed the rhythmic framework; and in those places that demand the broadest kind of declamation, they made everything clear to the audience by modulating the accent and moderating the tone." (Heinrich Bulthaupt, *Dramaturgie des Schauspiels*, Oldenburg-Leipzig, 1918, 3:25.)

bonbons, plays in which he took only a nominal interest. But at least once a week, usually on Sunday, a *Zugstück* was given—not, as the name might suggest, a drawing card, but rather an important work with which the duke was personally concerned. These performances had to be carefully spaced during the season for the benefit of the actors taking the heavy roles, who in between times participated in the other productions. It was for this reason that the duke required the schedule to which Bodenstedt so hotly objected (see above, pp. 62-63).

The daily rehearsals, which began early in the afternoon and lasted as long as necessary, extended over a long period and did not end when the play was put on stage.[16] There were six morning rehearsals for individuals or discussions led by the duke and five afternoon and evening rehearsals. Paul Lindau, speaking of the advantages of working in Meiningen, said that "above all, we had time."[17] Kainz wrote his mother that "the day before yesterday we gave *Die Räuber* newly staged in rococo as we will give it on the tours. Almost uncut. The whole week before we had frantic rehearsals that the duke conducted: for example, we rehearsed two scenes from 4:30 to 11:00 P.M. It was awful."[18] Weiser arrived in Meiningen at 10:00 P.M. and looked for his friend Arndt, only to learn that he was in rehearsal, "which could last until 2:00 A.M."; and Wohlmuth complained that the "rehearsals lasted endlessly."[19]

No one, no matter how important, was excused from the rehearsals. If Siegward Friedmann and Ludwig Dessoir had been dismayed over the monstrous size of the Meiningen toga when they appeared as guests in *Julius Caesar*, they were not a little put out about the rehearsal requirements, as Friedmann later related:

On March 30 [1870], we arrived in Meiningen; the performance was set for Monday, April 3. It came as an unpleasant shock to us to learn that we were expected to attend four general rehearsals. What did this little Meiningen think to teach Königliches Hoftheater actors? An old piece that we were well "up on"—two scene rehearsals were plenty! And now we were expected to spend our time in four endless rehearsals. . . . We went to the first rehearsal. The brilliant Dessoir, who was always in a happy mood, now looking as if he had drunk vinegar, peered tiredly around. . . . The duke sat in the auditorium and made his remarks in a loud, energetic voice. . . . With earnest and happy devotion the individuals as well as the crowds followed [his] instructions. And the duke was as untiring in his critical remarks as the artists who tried to carry out the intentions of the princely director. Each of his directions astonished us and earned our admiration. We had never even heard of any such well-thought-out instructions given to the actor on any stage. And all this was for a play that had been given countless rehearsals three years earlier and since had been a standing piece in the repertoire. We kept our mouths shut and were more and more astonished. After the first act, we looked at each other and shook our heads. We couldn't get one word out. It was just as if we had been seeing a piece of Lessing dramaturgy practiced. "Well, now,

Fig. 16 (above). Ludwig
Barnay in the lead role in
Schiller's *Wilhelm Tell*. The
duke's direction of Barnay as
an ordinary man called to extraordinary deeds caused a
controversy over the presentation of "heroic" figures on
stage.   Fig. 17 (above right).
Josef Weilenbeck as Argan in
Molière's *Le Malade imaginaire*. The blind Weilenbeck
joined the court company
while Georg was still crown
prince and remained a member until his death in 1885.
Fig. 18 (below right). Amanda
Lindner as Joan of Arc and
Alexander Barthel as Lionel in
Schiller's *Die Jungfrau von
Orleans*. Lindner was only 17
years old when she took this part.

that's what I call direction," Dessoir finally cried. "To me it's just as if we had come out of some backwater to the finest court theater." We could hardly wait for the next rehearsal; and we were really sorry that after four rehearsals we had to depart from such incomparable direction.[20]

The well-thought-out instructions of which Friedmann speaks were worked through before rehearsals began, but were constantly modified as the duke watched the play on stage. The preparation of just one scene—the execution in *Marino Faliero*—demonstrates the duke's method. The baroness von Heldburg asked the writer and artist Arthur Fitger to translate and adapt Byron's piece. In a letter of February 2, 1876, she reported to him how pleased she was with the casting: "Honored Friend! Do you know Faliero goes to the scaffold on March 7? I had the good idea—at least I think so—of offering the part to Max Grube, who took it with pleasure. So we are hoping for a worthy production. Weiser, Bertruccio; Teller, Calendaro; Barthel, the nephew; Arndt, Lioni; Richard, Benintende; Fräulein Lindner, a talented new acquisition, Angiolina; and Frau Berg, her woman friend. All the little roles are in trusted hands." [21]

The play was presented twice in Meiningen, but the duke was dissatisfied with the ending. On June 26, he wrote to Paul Richard, Chronegk's assistant, from the Bavarian Alps:

Dear Richard:

The actors will gather in Meiningen on the first of September. *Marino Faliero* would be better if the execution were more effectively staged. But that, I daresay, is not easily done. There must be a new set painted to present the great steps as they are in this sketch. If the procession came from the right to the left and climbed the stairs, the crowd could push in from the left. By the noise and the drumming a sinister effect could be achieved—as we experienced at *La Patrie* in Porte Saint-Martin, where the short drumming and short tolling of the bells were uncannily exchanged.[22]

Back in Meiningen on September 5, Georg wrote Richard again:

I have told Brückner in Coburg how the set for the execution is to be painted. All the canvas pieces [flats] are to be sent to Brückner. In the procession to the execution, the drumming of the six drummers will be exchanged with the tolling of the deep bell. The drummers are on stage:

        a. A roll of drums two seconds long (1, 2, and 3)
        b. Stronger beat of the drum on third second (4)
        c. Bell toll on fourth second (5) and so on
The numbering below shows how the beats are to be counted.

```
├────── (2 secs.) ──────┤ ├── (1 sec.) ┤ ├──(1 sec.)──┤
  1            2            3            4            5
├──────────────── (4 seconds) ───────────────┤
```

While this goes on, the *Gügelmänner* [hooded Franciscans who attended medieval executions] sing the Death Song.

Rehearsals continued, but Georg was still not satisfied with the last scene. On October 14 he wrote again:

In Saturday's rehearsal I shall see if the execution scene could be better and more effective if the procession moved from the left [stage right] to the right and then up the steps. I believe that the execution place should be empty until several armed soldiers with halberds enter and stand in front of the gate behind which the people have gathered. Some of these soldiers cannot move easily, for their calves are sheathed in armor—4 to 6 of these. If there is not a practicable gate, one must be constructed at once. Entrance to the procession: 30 men in Franciscan habit enter singing and go to (a) (see sketch). The *executioner* with two assistants: the executioner wears a black cloak carelessly thrown around him, like the four tuba players. The axe under the cloak. He takes off the cloak after he genuflects to the doge. He must do all this quickly if it is to be gracefully done. The assistants help him. The executioner and the assistants climb up the stairs and stand by the execution block.

Six drummers in two rows. . . . They take their place left of the steps.

A group of *Brabanten Dukes* in different garments. They climb up the steps and take their places on the balcony above the steps. There must be enough to fill the balcony.

    a. Bishop with two deacons
    b. Four trumpeters (can be women)
    c. Two *Signori della Notte*

a, b, and c climb the steps and wait on the second set of steps below the execution block.

The *doge* is under the canopy carried by four servants. (These can be women too.) If red garments can be quickly made, such as the doge's servants wear, these can all be clothed in red; I believe there were only three at first and one of those was Stoppenhagen. For the fourth servant we can use an extra. While the canopy remains at the bottom of the steps, the doge ascends to the execution block. The canopy will be placed by the servants at the left of the stage, somewhat folded. *The Judgment of the Ten*—while the president ascends the steps to the bishop, the others remain on the steps below the execution block. *The Six Members of the Great Council* remain between the gate and the steps. The procession includes a number (9) of *Gentlemen-at-arms*—enough so that the place between the proscenium and the trumpeters is filled. Before the procession begins, the litany is sung and at the same time the aforementioned drumming and intermittent tolling of the church bell. We hear the drumming first without seeing the drummers. At the rise of the curtain: enter the *Gügelmänner*. The drumming, the sound of the great bell, and the singing last until the first line is spoken. To strengthen the gentlemen-at-arms, extras can be garbed in the costumes of *Sixtus V*. (Do *not* use the costumes of the *Beefeaters* from *Maria Stuart*.)

After several more rehearsals, the duke was still not satisfied and on October 24 wrote:

I forgot this evening to direct that all those present should look at the doge, and that at the execution all must stretch their necks in order to see something of the execution. No one is excepted—trumpeters, drummers, no one!

Everyone must look at the doge when he comes on stage.

There are now six (6) more senators than before. With their long trailing garments, we need only ten on the steps; six can remain standing below left. Certainly, between those and the ones on the steps there can be NO space.

We must have a toller for a larger bell, but there isn't one! The tomtom is too shrill when struck hard, but when the stroke is held, then it is too soft.

In place of the twenty *Gügelmänner* there should be thirty. Costumes will have to be made for these.

Six drummers must go left [stage right] of the large steps and beat the drum when the procession accompanying the doge at the execution enters. While the drums roll and the bell of St. Mark's tolls, the *Gügelmänner* are singing. I have already written the directions for the drumming and the tolling.

The drums must be decorated with blue and red banners and not hang from the belts of the drummers, as in the case of the Meiningen 32d Regiment. The drums can hang from the waist on a leather strap. Whether it is practical to cover the drumskin with the material, we must see. A rehearsal must prove whether uncovered the tone is too strong; but the tone must be strong enough. The drumming must be done with greater pauses during which the singing is heard. Georg.

Otto must speak with a harsh, unsympathetic tone when he addresses the doge. Certainly not in a good-natured one! G.

Georg directed the movement of the individual actors with the same observant care he devoted to a crowd scene. Experience sharpened his eye. The directions for the second production of *The Merchant of Venice*, in 1886, twelve years after the first, reveal how much he had learned about integrating movement into the scenery. In the 1874 production, Act II was set in the narrow streets of a medieval ghetto where there was little room for movement. When he restaged the comedy, he brought the time forward to the Italian Renaissance and deepened the stage to allow actors to move in more interesting patterns. Further, he extended the use of the crowds from simply "atmosphere" to an integral part of the action, making their entrances and exits serve as a scene curtain. The Rialto Bridge now became the focal interest.[23]

Under a sketch of the ground plan and the rear elevation, Georg set out his directions:

THE MERCHANT OF VENICE, ACT II.

On this side of the dock is a beggar, who makes a profession of pulling the gondolas into the dock with a long stick with a nail in it. This is a well-known figure in Venice.[24] This beggar stays between the canal and the bridge and takes no part in the play. He does nothing to draw the public's attention to himself. He wishes only to earn money by helping pull in the gondolas and makes no movement of begging.

Not far from him, a woman beggar, and two children. The children are cowering. Farther upstage across the canal are a woman water-carrier, who moves

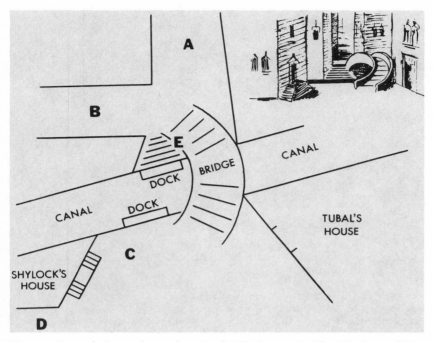

Fig. 19. Ground plan and rear elevation for Shakespeare's *The Merchant of Venice*. These appear as separate sketches on Georg's blocking instructions for Act II. (Adapted by Robert C. Johnson from the duke's originals.)

across the bridge from (b) to (d), and three citizens, who move from (b) through the street up to (a). Launcelot comes out of Shylock's home—monologue as he approaches the bridge. During the last sentence of Launcelot's speech, [Old] Gobbo enters at (a) and comes slowly to the middle of bridge. As he approaches it, it seems as if he does not know where to go. Gobbo says, "Master young man. . ." from the bridge to Launcelot, who is at the entrance of the bridge.

During the conversation Gobbo approaches Launcelot. Bassanio, Leonardo, and two servants from (d) to (c) by Shylock's house. A servant to (d). Launcelot and Gobbo walk between the bridge and Shylock's house and meet Bassanio and others, so that one sees Launcelot and Gobbo from the front, Bassanio 3/4 away.

Bassanio on his cue "See it done" goes with Leonardo and servant to the steps and speaks with Leonardo while Launce says, "Father, come. I'll take my leave of the Jew in the twinkling of an eye." Gobbo and Launce have approached Shylock's house during this speech and stand on the steps. Bassanio and his followers stand, after Launcelot has spoken, by (c) (bridge); Launcelot and Gobbo go into Shylock's house. Bassanio, "Hie thee, go," with Leonardo and companions up the steps to the bridge and speaks there with Leonardo, moving across the bridge as he does so. Leonardo returns over the bridge toward (d). Gratiano appears from the right [stage left], sitting in a gondola with a gondolier, and calls to Leonardo, who *at this moment* must be between the bridge and the corner of Shylock's house: "Where's your master?" After Leonardo has pointed out Bassanio, who in the meantime has moved up (a) a little, he says, "Yonder, sir, he walks." Gratiano, still waiting in the gondola, "Signior Bassanio!" Bassanio turns around and comes to the center (e) of the bridge, and from there he speaks to Gratiano, who sits with his back to Bassanio and therefore finds himself in an uncomfortable position to carry on a conversation. During the dialogue the beggar folk slowly gather around Bassanio without any commotion that would draw attention from the main action. Bassanio goes with his companions up (a), followed by the beggars, of whom 5 remain in the street in various places and three disappear with Bassanio. Gratiano disappears down right with the gondola.

Jessica, Launcelot, and Gobbo come from the Jew's house, Gobbo first, and go to the bridge, and Gobbo turns to his son, who follows. Jessica follows hesitantly after she has spoken timidly from the door: "I am sorry. . . . But fare thee well." She does not go far from the house. Launcelot and Gobbo exit up (a). Jessica goes back into the house.

The woman water-carrier from (d) to (a). An officer and a woman come singly from (a) and (b) to (d). Three women and two men from (d) to (a). Gratiano's gondola, meanwhile turned around backstage, now returns and stops on this side [downstage] of the canal.

Gratiano, Lorenzo, Solanio, and Salerio enter from (d) and go upstage to the gondola's dock. S and S step across Gratiano's gondola into one on the other side of it on the cue "and better in my mind not undertook."

Launce enters from (a) and Lorenzo speaks with him when he reaches the middle of the bridge (e). Lorenzo approaches him at the entrance of the bridge, so that he is separated from the others. Launcelot goes into Shylock's house and S and S go off right in the gondola. On the cue "Come," Gratiano and Lorenzo enter Gratiano's gondola and exit right. Instead of the words, "peruse this as thou *goest*," say "peruse this as thou ride." Shylock pushes Launcelot out of the house, comes out, and then Jessica comes out. During this scene it has become dark, and lights appear in the windows. Shylock with Launcelot ahead of him goes up (a). Jessica returns to the house and enters.

NIGHT: Masked people, accompanied by musicians playing on flutes and drums, enter at (b) and go to the middle, where another masked crowd from (d) meets them as they all turn and go out (a). If we have actors who can dance, it would make a fine picture when the group from (d) comes if Harlequin, Pierrot, Punchinello, and two Zerlinas, followed by watchers, stopped for a moment before the house of Shylock and with castanets and tambourines did a few turns. The masked group from (b) would then stand on the bridge and watch them. The children must not be wearing German smocks, but be dressed as beggars or Venetians.

Gratiano and Salerio enter in gondola from right [stage left] with a servant standing and carrying a torch. The gondola stops on the other side of the canal. When they get out of the gondola, they indicate a house on that side is the one they want to go to. As Lorenzo, holding a torch, enters from right in a gondola and stops on this side, the two friends cross the bridge and come to him. He gives the torch to his gondolier, and the servant of the others comes on to the stage with his torch.

Jessica's line (from window), "Here catch this casket; it is worth the pains," must be intelligible. She enters.

At this moment they all get into their gondolas, the friends first over Lorenzo's gondola, while the torch carrier from the other side gets into the gondola and the masked procession returns along (a).

The curtain falls before they are all in the gondola and the maskers have crossed the bridge.

THE MERCHANT OF VENICE, ACT II.

Venice, a street.

Solanio from (d) and Salerio from (b) meet at (c). The beggars who were in the former scene now stand at various places on the other side of the canal. "Now what news on the Rialto?" dare NOT be cut.

Shylock enters from (a) to a bench in front of the steps of his house, where he breaks down. Behind him runs a group of street boys. It must be carefully considered whether Shylock should *mumble* the following lines or *cry them out*: "My daughter . . . she hath the stones upon her, and the ducats!"

During this time the street urchins cry out, "The stones! The daughter! The ducats!"

(Even if one thought of Padua instead of Genoa as the place where Tubal has been seeking Jessica, enough time would still have elapsed since the elopement of the beautiful Jewess that this is NOT Shylock's first return home since her departure. He has moved heaven and earth to find his daughter and, as we can see from the text, has even been to the doge. All his steps have been futile. Therefore, the words that he speaks as he goes out are not to be spoken as if he has just learned that his daughter has gone, and that he has just now begun to look for her. Since the departure of his daughter, these words come much more involuntarily to his tongue—also, he does not notice the mocking of the street urchins. He does not become provoked.)

The street urchins do not follow Shylock farther than to this side of the bridge, where they still cry after him.

At the same time that Shylock sinks down on the bench, Tubal appears in a gondola with a shabby gondolier on the other side of the canal and walks over the bridge to his house. He has a stick in his hand and carries a bundle as a sign that he is returning from a journey. Gondola off left.

During the following speech, the street urchins slowly exit. On the cue "Gentlemen, my master Antonio is at his house," Shylock hurries to Tubal's house and fetches him out.

DO NOT CUT "We have been up and down to seek him." S and S and servant to (c) and exit.

The remainder is to be done as we have been doing it. G.

It has been asserted that Georg took his inspiration for the staging of the elopement scene in *The Merchant of Venice* from Haase's watercolor reproduction of the set used in Kean's 1858 production. But a comparison of the two sets (Figs. 19 and 20) indicates that he made important changes. By reducing the size of the buildings, moving the bridge downstage, and changing its direction, Georg centered the attention of the audience on the actors. The placement of the bridge, allowing a view of both sides of the canal, provided a variety of entrances. Shylock's house, as well as that of Tubal, is pushed downstage to the first border, thereby bringing important scenes as close as possible to the audience. If we apply Georg's directions to the sketch, we realize how the complex flow of movement provides contrast and at the same time complements the actions of the principal characters. Further, such movement provides an illusion of time passing beween the main events.

Chronegk and Richard would have received a copy of the directions before the first rehearsal. The Meiningen actors knew nothing of a blocking or, as Laube called it, a "placement" or "arranging" rehearsal. After a

Fig. 20. Reproduction by F. Lloyd of the carnival scene in Shakespeare's *The Merchant of Venice* as staged by Charles Kean in 1858. Compare this set with the ground plan in Figure 19 to see how little Georg's staging could have been influenced by Kean's, as is commonly asserted.

number of reading rehearsals in which they and the duke discussed and analyzed the drama, they appeared on stage with their lines learned.[25] To help them, he had a set prepared like the one in which they would finally play. All the furniture and properties were in place, and the actors were appropriately costumed from the first. They were to move in the scenery as if they had always lived in it and to feel totally at ease in their costumes.*

There was no *Regiebuch*, no book in which the action for the whole play had been set down. Each scene was rehearsed first as the duke had planned it, then in as many different ways as the baroness, Chronegk, or even the actors suggested. The most minute care was taken "step by step forward. No mistake was bypassed to get finished or cover more ground. Every tone, every movement, every expression, must reflect the intention of the poet. And even if we rehearsed one act hour on hour, the patience and energy of His Highness knew no limits."[26] On Barnay's first appearance in Meiningen, he thought the duke "was wasting my time on really minor things: on the louder or softer tone of every speech, on the bearing or placement of some silent player, on a tree or a bush—whether it was correctly or incorrectly placed, that is, pictorially placed or properly lighted—he gave the actors long explanations, whole exegeses about the mood of single scenes, about the significance of some dramatic incident—yes, even over the stress of an individual word; so the rehearsals went on forever."[27]

The duke interrupted the actors on important points, but other remarks he put into one of the small notebooks he carried to rehearsals.[28] In these he merely jotted down items he would discuss with his wife after rehearsals. A sampling reveals such remarks as these:

Wallensteins Tod: Penzinger isn't listening.
Jungfrau: 4th act, monologue too declamatory, false stressing, freshen costumes.
Winter's Tale: Get Florizel better hat—fountain terrible—clean jewelry—Görner keeps saying, "aaah aaah!"—scene change to "Time" and to Bohemia far too long—Richard not understandable—better chair for Leontes—the three court ladies should not have identical headdresses—the headdresses of everyone must fit the costumes better—streaks on the backdrop paint—the bear kicks over the set pieces every time he goes off.
Die Räuber: Too much noise at beginning—Grube laughs too much—too red in the distance, could be evening—Karl's and Schweitzer's boots too elegant—Franz more tempo—lighting far too red—Karl must be more disheveled, wild, sun-brown jacket—jabot of servant wrong—change Raven—Richard too soft—

---

* Such efforts did not go unnoticed. The London *Times* of June 23, 1881, reported: "Fräulein Haverland wore the chiton and the diploidion with natural ease, as if such garments were part of her everyday life."

locking of tower goes too fast—Stoppenhagen can't be heard—too much noise the whole scene—too many pauses and extensions—Felderer terrible make-up—everything terrible in silent acting. . . . Goreck much too calm after news of Karl's crime—libertines' beards and wigs?—Franz must not kiss Hermann—Werner not to lay his head on the breast of the old man until he is dying—scene change too long—extras terrible in movement and too far back—extras must not cover actors—Act III, Werner too shrill—must study with Nollet Act IV—Kober and Richard should not aim at each other a second time—table cover too dirty—scene change too long—actors are throwing shadows on the backdrop—see about the light on the first border—when all enter after the sleep the whole backdrop shakes—Kober often unintentionally funny—shirts too white—I can hear too much talking backstage.

From such jottings and her discussions with the duke about them, the baroness prepared a set of directions, which Chronegk and Richard were to carry out before the duke saw the play again.* Unmotivated movement—shuffling feet or awkward hand movements—were immediately reproved. Form pleasing to the eyes was the ideal, and any unrealistic pose was avoided. Franz Wallner recalled being chided by the duke for his posturing:

As the duke in Lindner's *Bluthochzeit*, I was in the foreground in a magnificent costume, standing on my left foot and balanced delicately on the toes of my right foot extended behind me (looking I thought very handsome and important). "Herr Wallner," came from the dark auditorium, "just look how you're standing there. That is the worst kind of 'tenor style.' Put your right foot down on the floor." Another time we were playing the scene at Caesar's bier. The dead Caesar lay on the bier; Mark Antony had just finished the funeral oration; I entered to bring Octavius's announcement. I was to see the body and fall to the floor with a cry. I fell (gracefully, I thought), allowing my feet to rise in the air. "Herr Wallner, don't wave your legs in the air. That is not artistic."[29]

In the same search for realism, the duke discontinued the beloved and common tableau vivant, in which a moment before the curtain fell, the actors arranged themselves in a "beautiful" picture. He abolished, too, the orchestral accompaniment to any songs in the drama, and with it, the custom of stopping all dramatic movement while a singer came to the footlights to sing his song as if it were an operatic aria; the duke incorporated all songs into the action. As we have seen, he also did away with the orchestra between acts: in his view, the music almost always destroyed the mood, for few conductors made any attempt to adapt the music to

* See Appendix B, doc. 4, for an example: the directions for *Der Prinz von Homburg*. More than 20 such sets of directions remain to testify how carefully the duke observed the staging and how astutely he worked to improve it. His remarks touch on everything: harmony in movement, grouping and placement, clarity of speech, accuracy of pronunciation and diction.

the tone of the drama; further, he felt the orchestra was a barrier between the audience and the actors.

The duke helped the actors by narrowing the acting area with trees, houses, columns, and other objects so that they were not dwarfed by space. He introduced step units, stairs, rocks, inclines—any device to vary the shape of the stage, add interest, and facilitate the actor's work. More realistic scene painting permitted actors a more realistic stage deportment. The performer could now, for instance, turn his back on the audience, something that had been frowned on since the time of Goethe.[30] Actors looked directly at one another, adding importance to the pivotal speaker. (But the duke was always alert to any actor who, by inching his way upstage, hoped to turn attention to himself. For habitual offenders, he had large crosses painted on the floor beyond which they might not move.) The artificiality of everything parallel was banished from the stage. The familiar straight line of actors across the front of the stage was never seen on the Meiningen stage, nor was the semicircle so dear to the Weimar School.

A more questionable device Georg used to heighten the effect of the acting was the quick curtain. Traditionally, after Antony's speech over Caesar's bier and the reading of the will, the crowd streamed off the stage. In Meiningen, the crowd was whipped up to a frenzy, which was cut off at the peak by a fast curtain. In *The Merchant of Venice*, as Jessica is about to elope, the duke's directions read: "The curtain falls before they are all in the gondolas."

Even the duke's staunchest supporter, Karl Frenzel, broke with him on the fast curtain in *Wilhelm Tell*. In his review in *Deutsche Rundschau* of May 19, 1876, he pointed out that because of this device scenes ended on too picturesque or dramatic a note. For example, he said, the fall of the curtain on the Rütli scene found the signal fires beginning to burn on the mountain while the leaders, still on their knees, repeated their vow to throw off Austria's yoke and establish Swiss freedom. Schiller did not have such an ending in mind, Frenzel argued. In his ending, the men leave the stage calmly to show the steadfastness of the leaders; the Meininger ending was too theatrical. Frenzel was right. The duke, in his effort to emphasize dramatic action, increased the drama in certain scenes and highlighted the actors, but too often at the expense of the author's desire to make a philosophical point.

What the ducal pair demanded above all was the active participation of everyone in the company. The actors rehearsed at all times in full voice; they never "indicated." They were to listen and react to what was going on even if they were not actively involved in the scene. Those not in the scene were to sit in the auditorium and watch. The duke liked to say that an actor never learned better than when attending a rehearsal. Many a young artist who began by leading a crowd and crying "Hail! Caesar, hail!," or "Fiesko, hoch!," studied, watched rehearsals, and finally advanced to a speaking role. Two beginners—later celebrated actors on the best German stages—Victor Kutchera and Alexander Otto, came to be known as "vultures" by others in the company. Initially assigned only silent roles, they studied and watched until they knew all the parts, then eagerly waited for someone to fall ill so they could jump into the role.[31]

That the duke was a ruling prince and thus the highest officer in the land gave him an authority no other director could command, but this was only a small part of the reason for his success with his actors. The consideration, respect, and genuine affection he showed to every member of the company, his own enthusiastic participation in the activity, and his skill and ability in theatrical matters elicited their admiration and devotion. In the telegrams he sent to the company on tour, he repeatedly thanked, commended, and encouraged the actors. When the critics in Berlin gave *Der Prinz von Homburg* unfavorable reviews, he wired Chronegk: "The critics will all be in the theater tonight. Heads high."[32] The baroness was equally supportive. One critic had been particularly hard on Josef Kainz, charging that his Prince Friedrich was more like "Little Fritzie." She instructed Chronegk to tell Kainz, who was only twenty years old, that his youth was his only fault, and time would take care of that.[33]

"I always put myself in the soul of my actors," the duke liked to say, "and I do not want their accomplishments judged by someone who does not have a full understanding of art."[34] His actors returned this consideration with an affection that made them give their best efforts to the company while they were in Meiningen and brought them back repeatedly for festive occasions.[35] It did not follow, though, that there was no jealousy, rivalry, or resentment in the company. Adele Sandrock left in a huff because the duke would not force a stiff-necked Kainz to play opposite her.[36] And Kainz himself complained so often to his parents that his mother advised him to thumb his nose at the duke and leave. "If His Highness does not give our Sepl [Josef] something after the tours, he should quote Götz's words on what to do with himself and show him his heels," she wrote.[37]

The duke looked at all players with equal interest; even the newest and least important could expect his praise for work well done and hope to be called out of the crowd. He would frequently say: "Yesterday you created a fine fellow on such-and-such folk scene. Now you will get a speaking part." Adele Sandrock, who came to Meiningen totally untrained, was typical of many young actors:

One day there was a rehearsal of *Julius Caesar* that we of course all had to attend. The duke himself conducted the rehearsal. I was called from the crowd and His Highness said to me, "You will do this next very well." It was the scene in which the murdered Caesar lay on his bier covered with a pall. I was to pull back the cloth and with a dramatic cry, an expression of despair, collapse on the bier. The duke played out the scene for me, and then I tried it. I heard the words, "Very good. Now try it once more." The scene was rehearsed over and over. My heart was beating so hard that I hardly knew how to go on. Anyone who knows the people who were standing there onstage will appreciate my feelings. They were all famous and accomplished actors.[38]

On the other hand, Georg was just as likely to say to an aspiring virtuoso, "The poet! He's the main one. Not you!"* Every actor heard over and over his favorite expression, "If this play's not a success, it's not Shakespeare's [or Schiller's or Kleist's] fault. It's yours and mine."[39] Occasionally, his interest went beyond the merely didactic. Once, when in a rehearsal of *Julius Caesar* the conspirators seemed too tepid, he leaped on the stage, seized a sword, and with a mighty thrust, shouted, "This is the way one brings down a tyrant."[40]

With the actors who had been with the company for a long time and whom he considered friends, his patience was endless. Such a one was Wilhelm Arndt, who seemed to take such pleasure in his own capriciousness that no one ever knew what he was going to do next. Assigned to play Mortimer in *Die Jungfrau von Orleans*, he raced through the part, throwing away lines in a different way each performance. When the duke threatened to take the part away from him, he promised to behave; and he behaved himself well enough for a while to be cast as Mellefont in *Miss Sara Sampson*, though he did not have the looks to make Sara's passionate attachment to him believable. Almost at once, he reverted to his old wild ways, and the baroness wanted him dropped from the role. Out of regard for his friend, the duke undertook such an intensive training

---

* Because Georg so consistently argued that it was the actor's duty to keep the attention of the audience on the poet's words, one criticism of the company by a London reviewer is unsettling: "There are a few unjustifiable errors of stage management, which should at once be set right. Mark Antony should not bow his acknowledgment to the public over the bier of Caesar. The artists should not be so eager to accept calls, and on no account should anyone after an exit in the middle of an act be allowed to return on stage to accept the congratulations of the audience." (*Life*, May 1881.) Such stage deportment would have been unthinkable in Meiningen. That Barnay, the worst kind of virtuoso at heart, should bow after his speech over Caesar's bier is not surprising, but that Chronegk should allow the others to return to the stage for applause in the middle of a scene is. This is one instance of the lack of sensitivity that Karl Grube regretted in Chronegk.

that Arndt became the best Mellefont she had seen.[41] Although Arndt remained the despair of the duke, he stayed with the company until the end of the tours.

But one did not have to be an old colleague to gain the duke's ear. Every actor was encouraged to express any opinion on any aspect of the staging, and Georg considered the remarks carefully. Then he called the speaker forward, explaining his own point of view and perhaps making a few rapid sketches on a piece of paper. He had always studied the play carefully, and if a contemporary work was involved, the baroness would have conferred with the author or translator. Georg thus had good reasons for his staging; yet he never hesitated to try something different when the actor had convincing arguments, especially if the question was one of interpretation. The duke had great respect for the intuition of the actor, who in Meiningen was urged to look into his own life for the understanding of a character. He was less impressed by the arguments of a purely literary expert, and so his arguments with von Bodenstedt, who found what he called the duke's "realism" too modern, were often heated.*

On occasion, the duke's passion for realism led him astray—as, for example, in the last act of *Wallensteins Tod* where Countess Terzky, grieving over Wallenstein's death, speaks with resignation to the conqueror, Piccolomini, "I close it all. And here deliver up the keys." At this point, Georg had her lay a large bunch of keys on the table. Few literary scholars believe that the countess, who has just taken poison, is here speaking literally, but see this rather as one of the figures of speech in which Schiller's poetry is so rich. Nearly all critics found the handing over of the keys a false and jarring note.[42] On the other hand, the duke sometimes failed to add a realistic touch when he could appropriately have done so. The absence of realism in Franz's suicide in *Die Räuber*, for example, disturbed a number of viewers, including Albert Lindner:

* Ernst von Possart remembered one that took place in 1868. The intendant, who belonged to the old heroic school, complained that newcomers to the theater were trying to force Schiller's larger-than-life figures into a realistic interpretation, which the "moderns" saw as more natural. Now, he charged, the duke was trying to do this with Wilhelm Tell. Georg replied that Schiller had let the hero Tell, the embodiment of the power of nature and the spirit of the people, fall out of that heroic role in the soliloquy at the mountain pass, for the sentimental philosophizing in his long monologue contradicts the description of a poor son of the mountains. "The modern actors are right," he said, "in trying to free the hero from the odium of Gessler's murder." Bodenstedt hotly replied that it had not been Schiller's intention to free Tell from the reproach of murder. He had thought of Tell's deed as that of a soldier who, in fighting for his country, aims at the breast of his enemy. (*Erstrebtes und Erlebtes*, Berlin, 1916, pp. 240-41.) At that early date, Georg was not certain enough of his ground to withstand Bodenstedt's arguments and acceded to his demand for symbolic acting. But he was not convinced, as his production 10 years later shows. At that time, many critics found Barnay's Tell too realistic.

Franz winds the rope 1-2-3 times around his neck and, before the audience real-izes what is happening, he falls suddenly into a corner and lies there as immobile as a stone. It really doesn't happen that fast. If realism has any right, let Franz show some signs on his face, let him bend his head down, gasping for air. Let him show despair of any relief on hearing the rising noise of the enemy's approach, and then fall with a convulsive twitching of his whole body. He may even make a convulsive movement when Schweitzer stands before him.[43]

The road to realistic staging was still an uncertain one, and Georg was not to tread it confidently until he approached more realistic drama. Un-til that time, he continued to experiment—not always successfully—and to rely on the power of his ensemble to support his sometimes less effec-tive principal actors.

How good these actors were has been a matter of some controversy. Many contemporary critics held that the Meininger players were at best mediocre, and that only the brilliance of their ensembles distinguished their work. To assess the justice of this, we must look at the standard then held for acting. At a time when "stars" acted by "inspiration" or "from the heart"—which too often meant reaching into a bag of tricks— it is not by chance that the most admired actor in the company was Lud-wig Barnay, a romantic, even florid actor, and that the rest of the Mein-inger seemed to underact or, in the view of many, not to act at all. Even when the duke forced Barnay into a realistic style, as he did in *Wilhelm Tell*,[44] the critics would not accept his interpretation. Nowhere was the dependence on "great tragic acting" more entrenched than in Russia, and much of the voluminous critical literature on the two visits of the Mein-inger to that country argues this question.[45]

As early as 1860, when Georg was working informally in the theater with von Stein, he was already building an ensemble; and when Ellen Franz joined the company in 1867 she brought with her Heinrich Marr's principle that close ensemble playing lay at the basis of all theatrical suc-cess. Almost at once, the duke found her experience and training valu-able.[46] By the time the company began to tour in 1874, the interplay of actors and crowds was developed in a mosaic, one complementing the other so closely that the audience experienced one single effect.

The duke went much farther in the use of crowds than Kean and Din-gelstedt, pioneers who employed crowds primarily for their own effect— who invented opportunities for processions or assemblies and even wrote dialogue for them in situations never hinted at by the playwright. Georg sought to make the crowds mirror the dramatic events and serve as a counterfoil for the principal actors. Their participation brought out psy-chological shadings of the dramatic composition and created a new ele-ment in staging. "How could so many points in a drama known to the

English public for generations be missed, and how could they be brought out?" asked an English critic after the Meininger production of *Julius Caesar* in London in 1881. "How could Mark Antony's speech, in itself always impressive, produce an effect which had never before been realized by the *habitué* of the theater and the Shakespeare scholar, while it appealed with a most thrilling intensity to the pit and gallery?" [47]

Five years earlier, Karl Frenzel had answered those questions in his description of the scene in *Deutsche Rundschau*:

The handling of the crowd is almost brought to perfection here. When Casca strikes the blow to Caesar, a single, heart-shattering cry runs through the mass of people gathered around the Curia. There follows a deathly silence; the murderers, the senators, the folk, stand a moment as if bewitched and frozen before the body of the mighty Caesar; then a storm breaks out, the movement of which one has to see, the roaring of which one has to hear, to realize how powerful, how high and how deep, the effect of dramatic art can go. In the scene following that in the Forum, one great and surprising moment excels the earlier one: as Antony is raised on the shoulders of the crowd and there, in the midst of the wildest movement, reads Caesar's will; as the enraged citizens grasp the bier with the corpse and others with torches mill about; and finally, as Cinna the poet, in the wildest turmoil, is murdered—as these scenes follow one on the other, a person could believe he was actually present at the beginning of a revolution. [48]

We can more easily understand the impression of this dynamic mass, whipped up from calm to frenzy, which made the "audience want to leave [its] place to make one with the howling, passionate crowd," [49] if we contrast it with the effect produced by the usual crowd scenes on the stage at that time. There were only a few German stages where large folk scenes, courtly ceremonials, or battles were not produced in a grotesque or ridiculous travesty. The uprising at Caesar's bier in the Forum by a crowd that wishes to "Seek! Burn! Fire! Kill! Slay!" was usually portrayed by about two dozen members of the opera chorus, known to everyone in the audience, assisted by a half-company of soldiers garrisoned in the town, all of whom were stuck in the most monstrous costumes. Everything appeared as a laughable farce. "There never was a performance of *Egmont* in which the public did not break out in riotous enjoyment as Alba's Watch strode through the streets and citizens crept into their homes." [50]

In Meiningen the crowds were made up of house extras and town extras. In the first group were the technical personnel; everyone served duty as an extra: stage crew, hairdressers, costumers, even office employees. They were supplemented by citizens of Meiningen, or when the company was on tour, by people employed temporarily in each city. These groups, built up by years of training, were divided into small units led by young actors, each responsible for a separate area of action. The duke considered the leaders as important to the success of the production as the leading players, and on occasion the whole crowd was made up of actors. In Ibsen's *The Pretenders*, the duke used, not extras, but young actors as well trained and as disciplined as the soldiers they portrayed. They fought with a skill and fire that brought the battle scenes to life. Aloys Prasch, in the role of Skalden Jatgeir, was so badly wounded in the cemetery scene that blood poured down over his face, but rather than shatter the illusion, he stayed on stage until the curtain fell fifteen minutes later.[51]

Grouping the crowd was a prime consideration on the Meiningen stage, and special attention was given to the harmonious line of the heads. Georg had been profoundly impressed by the Japanese prints that he had seen in Paris in the 1860's, and he experimented with their use of diagonal and broken lines.[52] He varied the line of a number of persons of equal heights by directing groups to sit or kneel, or by placing some on steps and risers. He found a diagonal line or even a broken semicircle preferable to the usual straight line. He advised the members of the crowd to watch their neighbors so as not to imitate their posture or position. When the crowd was used to remove "dead bodies" or the "wounded," the members should move not in a mass—something the duke found ridiculous—but rather in a way "to cover" the bodies from the audience and yet let the viewers see what was happening. To give the illusion that the crowd was massive, it should extend into the wings so the audience could not see where it ended.

The offstage sounds of the crowd were among the most admired of the Meininger's effects. The duke wanted the rhythm of the crowd noises to be varied, so he did not write out spoken parts for each group as Kean had done. Instead, about thirty people stood, sat, or lay backstage, each with a different newspaper or book, and read aloud. One would read, for example, "Emperor William, who is now in his eighty-fifth year, has not undertaken to accompany Bismarck"; another, "In addition to the earth a whole mass of comet families or isolated comets revolve around the sun"; still another, "But Jacob spoke to his mother, Rebecca, 'Esau is a hairy man'"; and so forth. Meanwhile, others chattered, laughed, joked—and the audience heard the rising excitement of an approaching mob in Paris or Genoa. The stage director modulated the sound by the wave of a hand.[53]

The Meininger introduced Berlin to the great offstage crowd sounds to give meaning and atmosphere in *Bluthochzeit*: "the ringing of the bells on Bartholomew's night, the noises of the mob, the shooting, the outcries of the victims, and finally the swelling, triumphant song of the Huguenots, 'A Mighty Fortress Is Our God,' rising, then falling away. All the terror and violence of the night contrasted with the happy dance music coming from the windows of the Louvre! This chaos of noises was nerve-racking. It helped picture all the terrors of that dreadful night, yet the performers were not drowned out or stifled." [54]

Quiet was as effective. Up to that time the Halli scene in *Die Hermannsschlacht* had been played in full voice, but in Meiningen the crowd spoke in whispers. "The Cherusci know that the Romans are sitting around their campfires," the duke said. "The resistance against the Roman yoke cannot take place in the open market; it must take place in secrecy." There were only whispers until the end of the scene, then three barely audible shouts rang out. "Revolt! Revenge! Freedom!" broke from a hundred throats as a single muted cry of rage. In rehearsal, when the company had not spoken softly enough, the duke had one performer after the other say the words, and he was not satisfied until he had heard all the actors murmur the words as he wished. [55]

If the voices were to come from afar, then the duke demanded even more from his people. "In several rehearsals of Ibsen's *The Pretenders*, there was a repeated effort to make the offstage voices of the besiegers sound as if they were coming from below. It was a comical sight when, after trying many ways, the duke brought in a number of mattresses, and the whole company, men and women, had to lie on the mattresses and shout into them. In this way, he got the effect he wanted, and it speaks for the discipline of the Meininger that on this occasion not a single person smiled at the comic situation." [56]

The composition of the crowd fell into five general forms according to use: the great masses, as in *Wilhelm Tell* and *Die Hermannsschlacht*, to reflect the spirit of a whole people; the tightly contained crowd in *Die Piccolomini* or the revolutionaries in *Fiesko* to perform one carefully delineated activity; the smaller groups, as in the banquet scene in *Die Piccolomini* or the trial scene in *The Merchant of Venice*, to emphasize the action as a sort of chorus; the background mass into which the leading characters were set, as in *Die Jungfrau von Orleans* or *Julius Caesar*; and the relatively disciplined ranks for parades and processions, as in the entrance of the Roman soldiers into the Teutoburg Forest in *Die Hermannsschlacht* or the coronation procession in *Die Jungfrau von Orleans*. Every person in the crowd was expected to participate as fully as the leading actors. Hans von Bülow was astonished at the depth and variety demanded of the personnel. "Have you seen the duke's troupe lately?" he wrote in 1878. "The virtuosity of the extras! Here they study every theater piece in a way I am sorry to say I have not studied all of Beethoven's sonatas." [57]

When Georg broke up the stage floor, he provided the crowds with a variety of ways to move. Very early he learned that movement downstage is more forceful than movement across it. His battles were fought against the audience. In Schiller's *Fiesko*, the storming of the Thomas Gate in the last act offered extraordinary staging problems, which were increased by the poet's adaptation. The scenic elements involved not only a harbor city ravaged by revolution, difficult enough to reproduce in any case, but also, for several situations in the act—above all the vital conversation between Fiesko and Verrina at the end of the act—an absolutely lonely street. If the street were to be filled with people before and after this scene, but empty during it, the staging would seem contrived.

The duke overcame these problems brilliantly by laying the scene inside the Thomas Gate, rather than outside, as it had been traditionally played. He cut the short first scene of Fiesko's warning to Doria and began the act with the conspirators' storming of the gate. This meant taking out Doria's house, which he had originally planned to place downstage left. "Otherwise, we'd have to storm it," he wrote.[58] In its place he put a small church. All of Act V played in this small courtyard, so that the sounds of the rising revolution came from outside the gate. A large fountain, raised on two steps, stood left center, and at the right were two narrow alleys. The background was closed in by a massive, slightly diagonally placed gate, which the conspirators did not entirely tear down, but literally broke through, stick by stick. The only light onstage came from lanterns carried by people crossing the stage. Soldiers lounged on the steps of the fountain, some asleep. Visible outside the gate was a set piece, the quay wall of the harbor, and the prospect showing Genoa lying in the moonlight (see Fig. 21).

From the distance could be heard the hum of the approaching crowd. Bells began to ring as soldiers came out of their guardhouse, and those by the fountain leaped up. Georg had ordered "in the storming of the gate scene, a door with three steps to the guard room. . . . At this door a fierce fight breaks out between the guards and the conspirators, while the gate to the street is torn down. . . . The little gate should be broken with little pieces of wood still hanging to the iron hinges. . . . I would recommend that at first only part of the door be broken in and the fight with the defenders, who are standing on the other side, can take place through the small opening."

As the gate splintered, the audience saw the Gulf of Genoa glittering through the holes. At first it seemed as if the gate would hold and the conspirators be repulsed. Then with a mighty explosion—"You may have to make a contrivance," Georg had written Max Brückner, "so that the

Fig. 21. Georg's sketch for the storming of the Thomas Gate in Schiller's *Fiesko*. The gate broke inward to allow the soldiers the forceful action of fighting toward the audience. The Bay of Genoa can be seen in the background.

gate crashes in violently"—the gate gave way, and the conspirators poured in. Through the sprung gate was seen the full expanse of the harbor, shining and sparkling. To clear the stage for the next scene without using a scene curtain, Georg had a number of monks enter with candles seeking the dead and the wounded, who were aided or carried off stage.*

For the Roman legions in *Die Hermannsschlacht*, Georg wanted to give a totally different effect. Now he had the soldiers marching to the Teutoburg Forest move diagonally upstage, away from the audience, as the people of the Cherusci stood silent and hostile, crowding the lanes and paths. Here was only a wave of armored, faceless power, a suggestion of the violence yet to come. To one Bavarian critic, the action of the crowds—the soldiers and the people watching them—seemed to reflect the very essence of the struggle:

In the foreground of a narrow path stands Hermann, bidding [the Roman] Varus welcome; on the rear of the stage rises an incline from which the German men

---

* In solving the difficulties of springing the gate, Georg created others for himself, the most important being that the drowning of Verrina had to take place far upstage. Further, the departure scene became awkward. Because the galley on which Fiesko planned to free the slaves lay out of sight, the new Duke had to reach the gondola in which he departed by crossing a plank leading through the quay wall. For Georg's instructions on this set, see Appendix B, doc. 3.

and women look toward the approaching legions, unable to give expression to their deep emotion. And now the Romans approach, armored for the march and bearing heavy packs, and turn sideways along the streets. In an endless line their march extends, and in the narrow space the boundless might of Rome reveals itself, threatening the destruction of all German life. One sees the picture and the available space, and wonders at the fine thought and gifted hand that knew how to create all this. At the same time that it gives us an all-powerful effect of Rome's might, it teaches us why the German Hermann had recourse to the weapon of cunning—the only weapon that could help the Germans to victory over such a force.[59]

The duke used this same device in *Die Räuber* for the attack of the robbers in the Bohemian forest. The upstage area was raised by huge practicable rock pieces, from which the robbers, their backs to the audience, shot upstage against the castle. Similarly, in *Der Prinz von Homburg*, Georg staged the battle behind a sharply rising hill, which covered the action from the audience. On transparencies in the prospect in the background was painted a village, which was burned by the use of light play. The sound of incessant firing was created by the explosion of small fireworks attached to the back of the set pieces.

The company's most famous use of the crowd as both a foil and a support for an actor was in the interplay between Mark Antony and the Roman citizens at Caesar's bier in *Julius Caesar* (see Fig. 22). But this was a device that Georg used often. The interplay between king and court in *Die Jungfrau von Orleans* made a powerful impression on Stanislavski:

The Meiningen players were able, by using purely stage direction methods, without the help of extraordinary stage talents, to show much in the creative work of the great poets. I can never forget a scene in *The Maid of Orleans*. A skinny, piteous, forlorn king sits upon a tremendous throne; his thin legs hang in the air and do not reach the floor. Around the throne is the confused court, which tries with all its strength to uphold the semblances of kingly ritual. But in the moments of loss of power, the deep bows of etiquette seem out of place. Into this picture of destruction of a king enter the English ambassadors, tall, stately, decisive, courageous, and impudent. It is impossible to hear the scorn and despising tone of the conquerors cold-bloodedly. When the unhappy king gives his demeaning order, which insults his own dignity, the courtier who receives it tries to bow before he leaves the King's presence. But hardly having begun the bow, he stops in indecision, straightens up, and stands with lowered eyes. Then the tears burst from his eyes and he runs in order not to lose control of himself before the entire court.

With him wept the spectators, and I wept also, for the ingenuity of the stage direction created a tremendous mood by itself and went down to the soul of the play. . . . The heavy atmosphere of the court artfully creates the moment of the appearance of Jeanne on it. The stage director thickened the atmosphere of the defeated court so that the spectator waits impatiently for the coming of the Maid.[60]

Fig. 22. One of the famous Meininger crowd scenes: the reading of the will in Shakespeare's *Julius Caesar*. (Sketch by J. Kleinmichel for the magazine *Die Gartenlaube* based on Georg's original.)

The duke used a similar method in Schiller's *Maria Stuart* to heighten the tension between the French and the English. On most stages the curtain rose on Elizabeth seated on her throne, surrounded by her court and awaiting the French ambassadors. Supported by Schiller's instructions, Georg staged the magnificently solemn entrance of the English court to reveal its heavy splendor in contrast to the light grace of the ambassadors, who entered after the queen had formally ascended her throne. The placement of the pages, the curtseys, the bows—all this was polished to the finest point. The conferring of the Order of the Garter reproduced a ceremony Georg had seen at the English court.

The action of the crowds brought urgency to scenes usually cut for lack of personnel. One such was the banquet scene after the murder in *Wallensteins Tod*, where all the servants run about aimlessly. The duke directed it with the greatest precision in order to raise the tension, which spoke directly to the audience. Similarly, in *Die Jungfrau von Orleans* the entrance of the battle-weary English soldiers pushing without much luck a wagon of provisions told the whole story of the state of the army. The commander's order, "Station a good watch," only increased the viewer's awareness of how unable these soldiers were to guard anything.

In 1857, after Georg saw Charles Kean's *Richard II* with one of the most magnificent processions ever staged, he deprecated such display as "*pompös.*" When he staged processions, his effort was not to emphasize the procession as such, but to heighten the effect it made on those watching it or those appearing in it. In *Die Jungfrau von Orleans* the audience saw not the usual sparsely covered stage, but one filled with people, packing the lane in front of the cathedral, standing on walls and fountains, on the church steps, on balconies (see Fig. 23). The procession pushed through the crowded mass, shouting with jubilation.[61] The music and the fanfare solemnly sounded. The enthusiasm reached a peak with the appearance of the king and Joan of Arc.*

The duke composed the crowds, decided how they were to be used, and in Meiningen worked carefully with them, but on the tours Chronegk had charge of all extras. Aloys Prasch always remembered Chronegk, "the little man, standing on a chair, a huge bell in hand, directing extras like a field marshal." In Meiningen as well as in other German cities, soldiers could always be used for extras, but in Austria and Hungary the military was forbidden to appear on stage. Prasch recounts one occasion in Budapest when Chronegk was trying to turn a group of rude, unemployed baker boys into Roman citizens, but all to no avail. Finally, he jumped from his chair, rushed into the group, and shouted, "If you don't learn this instant, I'll beat you!" The German actors were terrified, certain that a catastrophe would result. Quite the contrary. Chronegk had hit on the one direction his extras understood. At the next rehearsal, one of them marched up to the director with a huge stick in his hand and said, "*Tesek* [please], give it to 'em good if the dumb crew doesn't listen." [62]

Such hastily prepared crowds seldom reached the artistic goal at which the duke aimed, but he had to learn many things about their use, too. In 1874, during the first appearance of his company in Berlin, Paul Lindau's review of *Sixtus V*, although bad tempered in tone, was right in pointing out that there were refinements the duke needed to make:

The repetition of the same nuance must be avoided. Only one example: Sixtus raises his crucifix against the revolutionary masses and forces them, one after the other, to their knees. It is so arranged that at first a few women sink to the ground

---

* The duke complied with Schiller's instructions for a procession composed of one hundred and one persons. "Well, almost," he confessed to Gotthilf Weisstein. "To tell the truth, I've added four persons; the bishop will be accompanied by four deacons." (Weisstein, *Meininger Erinnerungen*, Berlin, 1906, p. 14.)

Fig. 23: Georg's blocking sketch for the coronation scene in front of the cathedral at Rheims in Schiller's *Die Jungfrau von Orleans*. The duke's emphasis here was not on the magnificence of the procession, but on the crowd's reaction to it. The actors spilled over into the wings to give the impression that there was no end to the crowd or to the procession.

under the gaze of the cross-bearer, while the others remain standing and by silent action reprove and mock them. The first time this was extremely effective, but it was repeated three or four times on both sides of the stage. The second time it seemed superfluous, the third laughable.[63]

Another respected and influential critic, Ludwig Speidel, wrote on September 29, 1875, that he found the crowd scenes unbearable: "The Meininger Shakespearean crowd is a monster in which no nerve sleeps, no limb is motionless. It pounces upon a person and then withdraws; it gnashes and bellows. But it is also a half-dumb, inarticulate element for whose movement there is no artistic principle."[64]

By the time Georg restaged *The Merchant of Venice* (1886), however, he had learned much about the effective use of crowds in the intervening years. The variety of movement, the gathering and dispersing of large and small groups, and the continuity of these groups appearing and disappearing reflected a noticeable advance over his early use of large—and sometimes unwieldy—masses. Further, he had learned to use crowds more sparingly. Often only a few individuals acted symbolically for the whole, as a Bavarian critic noted in *Die Jungfrau von Orleans* near the end of the tours: "How effective it is, for example, when in the first act of *Jungfrau* before king and court, in the midst of the shimmer of weapons and ornaments, the Maid in simple but gripping words reveals her heavenly message, and at the end the raw warriors, full of inspired belief and self-sacrifice, fall at her feet. With this one fact how simply and yet how strikingly motivated is the storm of enthusiasm that now breaks forth over the Savior of France."[65]

In *The Winter's Tale*, the duke used only a few court ladies to set the tone of Hermione's life and contrast it with her fate. In one of the most memorable scenes in the drama, the queen sat in a deep window niche in her room playing with her boy, while some of her ladies sat listening to a lute and others were busy with embroidery. Here the scene of homelike trust, soon to be shattered by the words of the jealous husband, prepared a contrast for the struggle of Leontes and Paulina over the infant Perdita. Through the richly open hall the audience looked out on the blue sea and the rocky beach, purple in the setting sun. In the shadowy palace itself there was only a dim light to reinforce the glittering beauty of the sea without.

Folk scenes in *Die Hermannsschlacht* were handled in a masterly fashion without great crowds: for example, the ancient Germanic rites performed at the Wotan Oak and the choir of bards, moving behind the warlike masses in the last act. One of the dramatic high points comes when Hermann, surrounded by the fighters, commands the father of a dead maiden who had been abused by the Romans to dismember the girl and send the parts to the German tribes to stir them to revenge. This dreadful idea Kleist took from the Book of Judges; the miming of the crowd in the Meininger production gave it a horrifying life.[66]

The use of crowds became one of the most admired and imitated of all the Meininger accomplishments, but there were also two common and sometimes valid pieces of criticism aimed at the practice; namely, that the crowd scenes often diverted attention away from the principal actors, destroying the thread of the plot, and that the interjections of the crowd sometimes broke the flow of the poetry. Alois Wohlmuth, who played Friar Lawrence in Meiningen, complained that "while Romeo spoke of Rosalind—that is, while he spoke of the soft arrows, which should prepare us psychologically for a mighty passion—the Meininger market women offered him apples and oranges to buy." [67] Critics found that the repeated "Ja!" of the crowd in *Wilhelm Tell* during Stauffacher's speech in the Rütli scene or during Tell's speech in the apple-shooting scene, and the continual interruptions in the trial scene in *The Merchant of Venice*, worked to the disadvantage of the poetical essence of the plays.

No one knew better than the duke that the final test of the effectiveness of the crowd, like that of the scenery and acting, had to be made in the theater. Once the curtain went up, there was only one judge, the audience. Georg was clearly willing to put his company to that test, since he allowed audiences in thirty-six cities to make their judgment on more than two thousand separate occasions over a period of more than seventeen years.

FIVE

THE FIRST BERLIN
APPEARANCE

𝕱or the first Berlin appearance, May 1–June 16, 1874, the duke and the baroness chose the Meiningen company's program with great care.[1] They knew that the first impression would be decisive, but they took something of a chance in opening with *Julius Caesar*. Although no German manager would say that Shakespeare spelled ruin, his work, as well as that of other foreign writers, was being badly scorched by the fires of nationalism raging through Germany after the Franco-Prussian War. Only six weeks before the company arrived in Berlin, Cosima Wagner wrote in her diary that "a veritable school has risen against Shakespeare,"[2] and a few days earlier she and Wagner had been "appalled" to find an essay that was a "defamation of *Romeo and Juliet*." Despite this hostility toward foreign literature, the duke not only sent *Caesar* to the capital, but had also selected *Twelfth Night*, *The Merchant of Venice*, Björnson's *Between the Battles*, and Molière's *Le Malade imaginaire* for the first appearance. Only two German dramas, Julius Minding's *Papst Sixtus V* and Albert Lindner's *Bluthochzeit*, were scheduled.

Ludwig Barnay, who had acceded to Ludwig Chronegk's invitation to "join the party," was playing Henry VIII in Rudolf von Gottschall's *Katharina Howard* in Frankfurt am Main on April 24 and did not join the company until the evening of April 26. He found everything in disorder and the company in near panic: Chronegk attempting to turn inexperienced soldiers into Roman citizens; the music conductor in despair over the additional musicians engaged in Berlin; the crew trying to fit the scenery on a strange stage; the cast rehearsing now together, now with the newly trained extras; and in the midst of it all, Karl Grabowsky stalking

147

about like some oldtime theater hero "representing His Highness." Barnay had to pay the obligatory visits to the newspaper critics, rehearse with the extras, and finish his costume fittings. Not until he had done all that did he fully accept the magnitude of what they were attempting, and he trembled at their audacity. Only Grabowsky, out of a lack of imagination, and Chronegk, out of wisdom, were certain of success. A born Berliner, Chronegk knew his fellow citizens, and he knew too that success lay not in individual performances, but in the ensemble.[3]

Finally everything was in place, and before the curtain rose, Chronegk came on stage with a telegram from the duke: "Remind the actors that in the conspiracy scene not one loud word. Cover the wings right and left; no harsh moonlight. Don't let Pfutz suffer too long. Fight on the middle ground until you can take the hill. Cinna scene short and meaningful. Courage. Georg."[4]

For his *cheval de bataille*, as the critics came to call *Julius Caesar*, the duke used the Tieck-Schlegel translation, strongly influenced by the Laube stage text. He restored the scene in which the poet Cinna is murdered by the mob; this had been cut by Laube and subsequently by all other German theater managers. In order to lessen the shifting, Georg reduced the number of set changes to eight: Act I was played in the Roman Forum, Act II at Brutus's and Caesar's houses, Act III before the Capitol and in the Roman Forum, Act IV at Antony's house and in Brutus's tent, and Act V on the Plain of Philippi. This arrangement did not require any alteration of lines.*

Originally, the sets had been made by a Weimar painter, Ernst Händel, whose sketches, based on those of Pietro Ercole Visconti, a member of the Papal Archaeological Academy and director of the Vatican Collection, had pleased the duke; but when the work arrived in Meiningen, Georg found the pale colors insipid and old-fashioned. He sent them to Max Brückner with instructions to repaint them and at the same time make corrections.[5] The Forum scene was to be painted according to a photograph enclosed, and raised higher than it was in Caesar's time. Among other things the Plain of Philippi was to be widened. Further, he wanted the floors of the inner rooms painted as mosaics.[6]

The duke cast *Julius Caesar* with his usual original thinking. For the principal roles he engaged three nearly unknown actors, who were to travel throughout Europe with the company and would come to call

---

* However, two of the four scenes in Act II, iii and iv, were transferred to Act III, probably because ending on the ironic scene between Caesar and the conspirators provided an effective second act curtain. The meeting of Antony, Octavius, and Lepidus at Antony's house (IV, i) was cut after the 1874 Berlin appearances.

themselves "Old Meininger." Caesar had always been played on the German stage by an older character actor, but Georg felt that as a central character, Caesar should present an imposing appearance, and cast Joseph Nesper, whose Fach was the Hero, in the role. The young, highly intelligent Leopold Teller came from the Leipzig Stadttheater to play Cassius, and Wilhelm Hellmuth-Bräm was Brutus. The only well-known actor in the company was Ludwig Barnay, who played Mark Antony.

The curtain rose promptly at seven o'clock to reveal the Roman Forum lying in the blazing sun. "The sets in *Julius Caesar* made me forget that I was in our cold capital; I could have believed myself back in ancient Rome," the Grand Duke Constantine said later, when the company played in St. Petersburg.[7] Properly attired Romans, individualized by their garments, footwear, and headdresses, crowded the Forum and moved naturally amid the sounds of those gathered to rejoice in the festive advent of Caesar.* Among them moved soldiers armored according to rank and company. Already in progress was the stormy scene between the citizens wanting to view the ceremonial procession and the republican-minded Tribunes determined to clear them from the Forum. As, in the midst of all this commotion, the trumpets signaled Caesar's approach, men and boys clambered to rooftops, women jostled for position on porches, and fathers held children aloft. The audience was impressed enough to break into applause before a word could be understood. To the shouts of the populace, Caesar moved in state across the stage attended by his soldiers, their armor clanking and their weapons glittering, with a great crowd trailing after.[8]

Georg's set was designed to reflect the might of Rome (see Fig. 24). It was also practical to permit the crowds to move realistically, yet artistically. The entire floor upstage from the first wing was raised two steps. On the left was the Basilica Julia, which continued from the backdrop; in front of it was a practicable bench with a frieze that Brückner had to repaint because he first used the Arch of Titus as a model. On the right, no houses but instead a column with an awning (which Georg thought "if put in the right spot [would] enliven the decoration of the Forum"[9]) and the outline of the holy fig tree. The numerous openings in the heavens on

---

* Karl Weiss, author of two important books on costuming, was responsible for some of the significant changes in the company's attire. Up to that time, for example, designs had been sewn onto stage togas, making them difficult to drape. Weiss had the designs painted on, then had long sessions with the actors showing them how to wear the mantle, the toga, the tunic, and the peplum. And instead of making the women's garments in the customary two parts, a long skirt with a separate blouse, Weiss used a one-piece garment, longer than the length from shoulder to floor, then bloused the upper part over a belt so that the garment fell in natural folds.

Fig. 24. Georg's sketch of the set for the Forum scene in Shakespeare's *Julius Cae-sar*. Note the large statue of Pompey in the center, placed where he could over-look the death of his bitter enemy.

the backdrop helped create a frighteningly real storm as the clouds dark-ened, the thunder rolled, and the rain beat down on the conspirators.

Act II opened on a view of Brutus's house bathed in soft moonlight. To allow the set for the Forum to remain up, a shallow "Meininger" décor, a house prospect with columns, provided the background for the conspira-tors to whisper their plans.* Before the house lay a small garden, and dimly seen in the background rose the Temple of Zeus on the Capitoline Hill. As the clock struck three, the conspirators prepared to depart, and dawn gradually washed over the scene. Backlighted through gauze-covered openings high in the background, the "cold raw morning" slowly warmed as the rays of light struck first a temple roof, then the corner of a wall and the tips of the cypresses.

The walls in Caesar's palace, a shallow room, were painted almost black up to a frieze displaying hovering figures. Two niches in the back-ground were painted according to Pompeian models. Prominently draped across a marble stand was Caesar's purple mantle, the same he wore the

---

* "Not one loud word in the conspiracy scene," the duke had warned. "Conspirators don't shout their intentions." (Telegram, Georg to Chronegk, Meiningen Theater Museum, Meiningen, May 1, 1874.) Brückner had to repaint the prospects later. The first had too many openings—"too modern," said the duke. (Georg to M. Brückner, COL, Meiningen, Sept. 2, 1880.)

day "he overcame the Nervii," the same that Antony would raise to the crowd.

For the climactic moment of the production—the assassination of Caesar and the speeches of Brutus and Antony—the stage was richly dressed with an imposing statue of Pompey, positioned in such a way that he might watch as his bitter adversary met his end.[10] The base alone was almost four feet high, the figure about seven-and-a-half feet. Eight columns stood in a semicircle, before one of which, in the right foreground, Caesar was assassinated.[11] Framing the scene were drapery wings.

As the curtain rose on what was both the theatrical and the dramatic high point of the production, the audience saw Caesar sitting alone on a high elevation at the back of the stage, surrounded by the senators seated in a half circle at his feet, while the folk milled about in the foreground. Close in front of the great man, who in no way suspected his fall, knelt Metellus Cimber. By so disposing the conspirators, the duke suggested to the audience that here, around "The Master of the World," was a ring through which he could not escape. For the actual murder, Georg went back to Plutarch and added to Shakespeare's words the Roman historian's "Cursed Casca, what are you doing?" and "Help, brothers!" Caesar grasped Casca by the arm and wounded him with a stylus; then, recognizing the members of the conspiracy—Brutus among them—he fell. At that moment the crowd let out a terrible cry, and amid the tumult in the marketplace came the speeches of Brutus and Antony. Accompanied by a thick swarm of Roman citizens, the corpse was brought in and placed in a conspicuous spot close by the speakers. Caesar, dead, was still the center of the action—a departure from traditional staging, in which his body was shunted to one side of the stage.

The swelling of the tumult; the raising of Antony by the people; the torches, their dusty-red glow lighting the dead, the defeated, and the victorious; the demands of the debauched mob—the terrifying fascination of all these events prepared the audience for the next shocking deed, the murder of the innocent poet Cinna by a mob gone out of control. "The elements of the Meininger staging of this scene should be a model," said one critic. "It is unsurpassable."[12]

For the first Berlin appearance the duke set the scene with Octavius, Antony, and Lepidus (IV, i) in Antony's house, but later, on Frenzel's advice, he dropped the scene and played all of Act IV in Brutus's tent.[13] The shallow décor of the tent, placed far downstage to permit the scenery for Act V to be set up behind it, offered nothing unusual, but the appearance of Caesar's ghost, effected by the use of a spotlight, caused a sensation.

The duke hit on an admirable plan to permit all five battle scenes of Act

V to play on one set. He thought of the downstage area as the Plain of Philippi with a rocky height rising on stage right. In the middle of the stage was a gully over which arched a high bridge. Behind the gully, the terrain covered with the gravestones of long-dead Philippians ascended toward the towers and battlements of the besieged city lying on the heights. While Octavius and Antony with their armies marched from stage right into the valley, Brutus and Cassius with their legions began a slow descent from the heights: the one above, the other below, the opponents carried on the angry dialogue that ended in battle. During the fighting, individual soldiers and leading characters of the republican army covered the heights. The armies moved, fighting, to stage right. Sharply delineated actions individualized the scenes: just before the death of Cassius, Titinius could be seen hurrying through the gully to find out whether the approaching soldiers were friend or foe, Pindarus remained on the heights, and Cassius, already determined on suicide, slowly descended. The duke provided an extraordinarily poetic picture, said one critic, when Brutus, driven with the miserable remnants of his comrades between the overhanging rocks and the arched bridge, rested wearily while the moonlight fell softly on his helmet, armor, and white garments. And finally, as the curtain fell, the audience saw the chilling picture of the victorious commanders standing high on the bridge, lighted only by torches, looking down on their defeated enemy lying in the shadows.[14] At this, the audience broke into tumultuous applause, the kind of outburst, says Max Grube, "that erupts just as the curtain starts descending, 'the desire to praise long held in check,' which releases the emotion of the audience. Then followed that other, more thoughtful applause, which begins only after a pause filled with tense emotion."[15]

The following evening there was only a partly filled house. Not until the notices appeared would the general public hear of the Meiningen company. When they did appear, a storm of controversy swirled through Berlin: on the one side admiration and enthusiasm; on the other rejection and biting scorn. No one talked about anything else; "even political events receded into the background. For weeks the mighty city breathed the thoroughly artistic atmosphere originating in the grandiose Forum scenes and the exciting crowd scenes, which up to that time no one had even imagined."[16]

Critics of the new staging fell into three groups: those who out of professional and artistic conviction believed that the emphasis on decoration would destroy the drama; those who were dramatists as well as critics and had no wish to offend the managements of the theaters that staged their works; and those who merely opposed anything that ran against the accepted practice. The most outspoken and determined enemies of the duke's company were Oscar Blumenthal, Hans Hopfen, and Paul Lindau, all respected and influential critics. Hopfen set the tone in the first of many scathing reviews:

I admit that nothing would move me to write a review on the accomplishments of this company if the matter did not concern a battle over principle that has divided all Berlin into two camps, if a dramatic crusade was not here in a position to win its first battle to conquer all Germany for its method of staging, if the followers of this principle were not already trumpeting . . . to the world that this guest appearance marks a dramatic revolution, a new era in the German theater. . . . In the crowd scenes singing, screaming, shoving, shrieking, shifting, shuffling, shouting. . . . What then is the purpose of tragedy? To arouse pity and terror. When there is so much on the stage, then my pity is for the actors, and my terror for the degeneration of art.[17]

Hopfen admitted that "no one who attended the performance, not even resolute opponents, could fail to recognize the power of an unusual director's talent," but he believed that filling the stage with "fripperies" would end in the "excesses seen on the English stage." Karl Frenzel led the praise for Georg's methods, and in general the public agreed with him; but whatever people thought, no one could deny that here was something totally revolutionary.

Those who opposed the "revolution" believed themselves vindicated when the second production, Julius Minding's *Papst Sixtus V*, failed. The drama, though much admired by intellectuals in Switzerland and Germany, was unsuccessful as a piece of theater. There is one imposing scene in which the protagonist, Cardinal Montalto, to all public appearances a sick weakling, having been raised to the papal throne thrusts his crutches from him and reveals his true character in a thundering speech. Weilenbeck gave a masterly reading of this scene, but the rest of the play was so weak that his performance could not save it. The play was dropped after four performances. A fortune in costumes and scenery was lost, and thirty long rehearsals.

Caesar pictured the Rome of antiquity, *Sixtus V* the Rome of the Renaissance. The first prospect showed Castel Sant' Angelo with the bridge before it so cunningly painted that it seemed to extend nearly out to the footlights. The impression was strengthened by soldiers stationed behind barricade set pieces as guards. But the greatest effort was expended on the scene in the Sala Regia, through which the audience saw an elevated portal to the Sistine Chapel and therein, the high altar, the papal throne, the paintings, indeed even Michelangelo's *Last Judgment*. In order to keep audience attention on the action rather than on the magnificence of the chapel, Georg told Max Brückner that "the audience need get only a suspicion of the respective paintings." *

This failure suggested to the duke that in light of the success of *Julius Caesar*, Shakespeare was the man for Berlin. *Twelfth Night* proved him right. This work was known to German audiences only in the mangled version of Johann Ludwig Deinhardstein, *Viola*, which was introduced at the Burgtheater in 1839 and soon made its way into all theaters. The adapter revised the plot by returning to the original novel to make Viola already in love with the duke when she enters his service, so that she has come to his court with the intention of winning him. The ending was changed to allow one actress to play Viola and Sebastian; the dialogue was trivialized; and the comic situations were eliminated. Georg went back to Shakespeare's text and made only a few alterations in words, none in scenes.

The production was a triumph of simplicity, confounding those who said that the Meiningen company could succeed only with crowds, elaborate staging, and colorful decorations. Even Hopfen was forced to say that "the arrangement of the stage and above all, the arrangement of the text [were] to be recommended to every theater." [18] All the action took place on a unit set; only twice was a shallow room inserted, once for a room in the duke's palace and once for a room in Olivia's house. On stage left stood Olivia's house; a flight of nine descending steps ending in a narrow veranda led into a garden in the back, set off from the street by a fence. The backdrop showed a garden landscape and a half-hidden building. In front of the house were a bench and garden set pieces. Doors and windows were practicable, the windows transparent to allow the candlelight inside to fall into the garden and mix with the moonlight. This touch particularly appealed to one reviewer, who thought it endowed the poetic scene with an indescribable magic. He also liked the liveliness of the comic scenes, where "one forgot he had actors before him and believed that he had wandered into a madly merry party." [19] For the first time in Germany the actors in *Twelfth Night* wore Elizabethan dress, and Georg designed costumes that made the resemblance between Viola and Sebastian even more striking.

---

* Georg to M. Brückner, COL, Meiningen, Jan. 3, 1874. Paul Lindau attacked the play, the production, and the performance; but he found the realistic touch of the burning incense on stage especially offensive. "The whole theater was full of the odor," he wrote. "Good heavens, think what would happen if the drama played in a stockyard! Then what wouldn't we have to smell!" ("Papst Sixtus V," in *Die Gegenwart*, 5.21, May 23, 1874: 331-33.)

For the fourth production the duke had yet another surprise. After the great success of the simply designed *Twelfth Night*, he brought out Albert Lindner's *Bluthochzeit*, which offered the Meiningen players opportunities to display all their specialities, and gave their opponents fuel for fire in all the magnificence of the court of Charles IX. In a drama with little substance, the scenic splendor had nothing to illuminate and therefore became an end in itself.[20] But even Lindau had to admit, somewhat sourly, that he had never seen such an artistic, true, and effective setting.[21] This production again foreshadowed the odors of smelly hallways and cooking cabbage that would permeate the naturalistic stage. As with the incense used in *Sixtus V*, here a substance was put into some "poisoned" candles, and during the scene the audience smelled the "deadly poison" as it worked on stage.

This drama of bloody events in Paris was followed by a double bill, Molière's *Le Malade imaginaire* and Björnson's *Between the Battles*. True to the French tradition, Georg staged the Molière as one uninterrupted piece. The setting, costumes, and outfitting were of the greatest simplicity, yet true to the period of Louis XIV: a box set with a sort of alcove in which Argan's bed stood, a table with medicine bottles, a few chairs. Karl Frenzel pronounced it the company's best production:

The production of *Le Malade imaginaire* by Molière has refuted the objection—if any impartial person still needed proof—that only the externals made the success of the Meiningen company. . . . Our guests presented Molière's comedy with so much truth, merriment, freshness, and humor that . . . the public did not cease its happy laughter. The magic of this performance lies in its harmonic development in which [the actors] provide body and color to the spirit of the poetry. As they present in *Julius Caesar* the revolutionary elements of the poem; in *Twelfth Night* the moon-drenched, musical, mad elements; in *Bluthochzeit* the mournfully fantastic, dissolutely sensuous, and melodramatic elements; so here in Molière's comedy they present an incomparable embodiment of the ridiculing of doctors, and of the burlesqued but intrinsically still so tragic game of illness and death. Of all their productions, this is the most complete.[22]

Another fan of the production was Theodor Fontane, who found the Königliches Schauspielhaus's production of *Tartuffe* lacking next to the visitors' *Malade*. Though the Meiningen sets and costumes were nothing, he said, the ensemble resulting from a continued study of the piece allowed the actors to grow into their characters as well as into their costumes. "When I saw these plays by the Meininger," he wrote later, "I had the feeling that I had moved among people of another land and of another time, and yet I could hear them talking without any feeling of strangeness. This is as it should be. We should feel the 'old-fashionedness' of these plays, but in a way we find pleasurable, not disturbing."[23]

The second half of the program, *Between the Battles*, by Björnstjerne Björnson, who was then almost unknown outside the Scandinavian countries, did not fare so well. Georg had asked Max Brückner for a "low blockhouse, with narrow doors, and a floor covered with reeds."[24] He gave great care to the setting: a comfortable fire of great logs burned on the hearth, fir boughs covered the floor, the wind whistled and raged every time the door opened. Georg tried by every detail to individualize the Scandinavians so that they would not seem to be German peasants living in another land. The public and most of the press found the heavy northern darkness too strange to accept, but Björnson remained one of the duke's favorite writers, and many of his plays made their first appearance on the Meiningen stage.

The final production, *The Merchant of Venice*, proved something of a disappointment. The run in Berlin, planned for a month, had to be extended two weeks, and the third Shakespearean play closed the engagement on June 15 and 16. The weather had grown hot, and the actors, accustomed to repertory work, were tired after playing in a series of long runs. Because of the heavy scenery and complicated machinery, it was nearly impossible to vary the plays often; *Julius Caesar*, for example, was given nineteen times in succession, something unheard of in Germany at the time. These elements, however, were only partly responsible for the failure. Cuts had not been judiciously made,[25] the stage design—not new, but refurbished old sets—did not provide for a flow of movement, and much of the action had not been thoroughly enough rehearsed to integrate the parts.*

Set in the medieval ghetto in view of St. Mark's Square, the stage was so cramped that the movement seemed excessive, and much of it irrelevant. At the beginning of Act I, beggars and children crowded the stage with hands outstretched, a street musician strummed a mandolin, a party of foreigners—Greek sightseers—put on such a show that the entrance of Antonio and his friends went almost unnoticed, and the important conversation between Antonio and Lorenzo unheard.[26] Scene-curtain changes were so numerous that the play dragged on interminably. Further, the duke had not shown his usual skill in casting. Only Adele Pauli as Nerissa came out with a whole skin; the other actors were much criticized. Josef Weilenbeck—gentle, good-hearted—was completely miscast as Shylock, and Marie Moser-Sperner made an ineffective Portia.[27]

Rudolf Genée, whose editions the Meininger used for several productions, wrote in the *Deutsche Rundschau* that the scenery was excellent,

---

*By the time Georg restaged *The Merchant of Venice* in 1886, experience had taught him how to solve many of these problems. See the account of his design for Act II on pp. 124-27, above.

especially the low medieval ghetto and the exact replica of the doge's palace. He deplored the immoderate use of the scene curtain as breaking the mood of the play. "Give this company a piece," he quipped, "and it will soon be in pieces." Although he was concerned about the effect the emphasis on externals might have on the German theater, he "had to admit that these productions have given a lively and entirely new stimulation to the important questions of art." [28] Confident that they had indeed stimulated the German theater, the Meiningen players were ready to go home.

Before the month of May was out, newspapers from the provinces were entering the controversy. A Bavarian newspaper, after commenting on the artistry of the Italian tragedian Ernesto Rossi's powerful interpretation of Othello and King Lear at the Victoria-Theater in Berlin, reported that the entire theater world was divided between his style and that of the Meiningen players. In a review of the company's *Julius Caesar*, the writer stated:

We must say at once that the individual artists of the Meiningen court theater are not of the first rank. . . . Yet the accomplishment of these artists is most pleasing and . . . we assert that the performances are worthy of great dramatic art. . . . There is no movement, no placement, no step, no accent of the mood, that is not suited to the spiritual content of the scene; and the conspiracy scene in Brutus's garden (in which two or three subordinate figures with only a few words to say appear) was a masterpiece of miming. Of greater effect were the crowd scenes . . . , which shattered the audience by their reality and pleased it at the same time by the beauty of the pictorial groups. . . . All in all, in spite of its weaknesses, the Meiningen company has offered us more artistic excitement than Rossi with his magnificent skill (of his co-workers we do not care to speak—they were not worthy of the most insignificant itinerant troupe). [29]

So in the first month of the company's appearance outside Meiningen the critical principles by which it would be measured for the next seventeen years were enunciated: praise for the crowd scenes, for the fidelity to the author's intent, for the ensemble playing, and for the accuracy of the setting; but deprecation of the individual acting, and fear of the excesses to which the visual and sound effects might lead. By its very success the company made some powerful enemies. The Königliches Schauspielhaus soon felt the effect of the Meiningen company's success. A day after Crown Prince Friedrich's first visit to the Friedrich Wilhelmstädtisches Theater, General Intendant Count Botho von Hülsen received a sharply worded letter from the Royal Palace, along with a copy of Karl Weiss's book on antique costumes. Mincing no words, His Royal Highness indicated that since the Königliches Schauspielhaus had greater financial resources than the court company of a small duchy, he thought it should be able to provide better scenery and costumes than that provincial theater. [30]

Von Hülsen, in thanking the prince for the book, was heedless enough to remark that the Meiningen company did not know "the ABC's" of costuming, for "the Romans had never worn sandals with high heels as the Meiningen actors did in *Julius Caesar*, and it would never have occurred to the Romans to wear colored or black bands around the knee." There was no response from the palace to this impertinence; but on the day the crown prince received the letter, he took his son, Wilhelm, to see the visiting company. And the emperor came in from his summer residence in Babelsberg twice to attend performances. To further show his displeasure, the prince went to the Royal Opera for a ballet but ostentatiously left just after the dancers began.

The *Berlin Tribüne* printed an account of this controversy on June 4, 1874; three days later, in a long letter published in the *Berliner-Börsen Zeitung*, von Hülsen hotly defended himself and his theater management. The crown prince remained silent, and the matter disappeared from the newspapers, but von Hülsen blamed the Meiningen company for what he considered a personal attack. When the duke announced Kleist's *Die Hermannsschlacht* as one of the dramas to be brought to Berlin the following year, von Hülsen rushed the play into production to forestall the company's bringing a new piece to the capital. He followed this pattern for years, until the duke learned never to refer to a new drama by name.

Ludwig Barnay said that after the first performance of *Julius Caesar*, he could have written, as Lord Byron had, "I awoke one morning to find myself famous." The entire company could have said the same thing. No one spoke any longer of the duke of Meiningen's company; now it was the "Meininger," a name given to the troupe by the magazine *Kladderadatsch*, a play on the word Meiningen, but also, said the magazine, on the month of May when the company gave its first performance.[31] The Berlin appearance was a financial as well as an artistic success. The duke had figured on a cost of 500 thalers a day while the company was on tour, a sum that included not only room and board for the troupe, travel, theater rental, and general expenses, but double pay as well.* By May 20 enough money had been made to pay all expenses; the profits from the sold-out houses from May 20 to June 16 allowed the duke to set his sights even higher. He decided to bring the company back to Berlin the following year and to extend the tour to Vienna and Budapest. So began the plans that set the Meininger on a string of tours that were to extend farther and last longer each year.

*Translated into dollars, the daily costs came to about $460, a considerable sum for 1874.

SIX

THE MEININGER ON TOUR

$\mathfrak{A}$s soon as Georg announced the repertoire for the 1875 tour—Schiller's *Fiesko*, Molière's *Les Femmes savantes*, Kleist's *Die Hermannsschlacht*, and Grillparzer's fragment *Esther*—the intendant of the Königliches Schauspielhaus rushed a production of *Die Hermannsschlacht* onto the stage.[1] If he could not rob the Meininger of success, at least he could deprive them of the charm of novelty. The production got bad reviews, but the play was successful with the public, and the Meininger returned to Berlin with a drama that had already been on the boards for three months.

The play itself was not a popular one. Written in 1807-8, when Germany was occupied by the French and many people advocated making a pact with Napoleon to ward off further assaults, the play reviewed the current situation in terms of the Romans' assaults against the ancient tribes. Kleist made the romantic but barbaric hero, Hermann, a knightly figure representing the Germans who were standing firm against the French; and in his characterization of Thusnelda, who takes a Roman lover, Kleist poured his scorn on the German women who consorted with the French. The Meininger used Rudolf Genée's adaptation, but at the most important parts returned to Kleist's original text. They restored the frightful bear scene in which Thusnelda, learning of her lover's perfidy, entices him into the bear cage to be crushed by the beast, a shockingly realistic scene for the German stage.

Die Hermannsschlacht was followed by the double bill of *Les Femmes savantes* and *Esther*. Berliners had never seen the Molière piece, and even in Ludwig Fulda's fine translation, they did not care for it. The duke then repeated the previous year's successful *Le Malade imaginaire*, which was enthusiastically received, but the public would still not accept its com-

Fig. 25. Georg's sketch of the set and blocking for the battlefield scene in the Teutoburg Forest in Heinrich von Kleist's *Die Hermannsschlacht*. The detail shows the positioning of the fallen soldiers and horses.

panion piece, Björnson's *Between the Battles*. Out of necessity, then, there was forged one of the company's most successful programs, the combination of Molière's *Le Malade imaginaire* and Grillparzer's *Esther*. The Grillparzer especially astonished the audience with its oriental luxury, splendid wall paintings, and heavy costumes worked with gold—all the majestic antiquity and brilliance of the East.

During this season a second unifying thread of the tours appeared: an emphasis on the dramas of Schiller. Throughout the next fifteen years, the works of Shakespeare and Schiller formed the core of the Meininger repertoire and accounted in good measure for the impact the company made on the thirty-six cities they visited. *Die Verschwörung des Fiesko zu Genua* was the first of the Schiller series. Stamped by the splendor of the Renaissance, the production made an enormous impression, surpassing, in the words of Paul Lindau, "everything that we have seen from the Meininger."[2] Generally considered the weakest of Schiller's plays, it had never been a popular item among the German theater managers. For that reason, its novelty was one factor in the Meininger success. Act III brought gasps of amazement from the audience as the curtain rose on a view of Genoa lying on the sea with the Maritime Alps in the background. The lighting gradually changed from foggy sunrise to gleaming sunlight, until the mighty city lay completely extended and colorful before the count's eyes, giving added emphasis to his opening speech in praise of his fatherland.[3]

Later that year, when the Meininger made their first visit outside Germany—to Vienna—they received a mixed reception. Some of the critics were lukewarm at best. In part this was because Franz Dingelstedt had been at the Burgtheater since 1871, so elaborate scenery was no novelty to the Viennese; those who could not see beyond the stage furnishings recognized nothing revolutionary in the Meininger productions. Beyond this, the Burgtheater had viewed itself as the preeminent German-speaking stage for so long that the notion of a small ducal company's being able to teach the Viennese theater anything was simply unacceptable. But among the public and with most of the press the Meininger succeeded. The Berlin *Theater-Figaro* published a wire from its Vienna correspondent, written after the opening performance on September 25, 1875: "Meininger success absolutely decisive. Storms of applause of the most unusual sort. After third act, *Julius Caesar*, eight curtain calls."

One of the severest critics was Heinrich Laube, then at the Stadttheater. He attacked the company's work with the same words he had used for Dingelstedt's, condemning it as "wallpaper direction" as opposed to the "lean means" he himself worked with. When reporters asked him which Meininger productions he had seen, he replied, "None, thank God!" The *Wiener Punch* exacerbated the situation by noting on October 23 that the duke of Meiningen had attended a matinee at the Stadttheater that week and had remained to the end of the performance. "This," wrote the satirical magazine, "should keep Laube from complaining." Georg, however, was a true admirer of Laube and never failed to acknowledge his debt to him.*

A far more serious if less sarcastic attack came from the influential Ludwig Speidel, one of those critics in the view of the theater historian Robert F. Arnold "with an outspoken aversion to everything new, progressive, and original, and with an equally outspoken sympathy for the mediocre, the traditional, and the accepted."[4] To begin with, Speidel thought it offensive that the Meininger should even come to Vienna. On September 29, he wrote: "The Meininger in Meiningen and the Viennese in Vienna seem to me the right thing." He complained about the scenery and the costumes, and found the specialty of the company "merely exter-

---

* This was one of the three times the duke visited the Meininger on tour. On these occasions there was what Josef Kainz called a "general panic" backstage as the news ran through the company that His Highness was in the audience (Heinz Isterheil, "Die Bühnendekorationen bei den Meiningern," Ph.D. dissertation, University of Cologne, 1938, p. 98).

nals." The Meininger had only one good actor, he said, and that was a guest from Dresden. "He is a good actor and speaker; therefore, among the Meininger, a giant." The low comedy in *Twelfth Night* was good: "since they are actors in a small town and have little to do but frequent the taverns, they are wonderfully suited to their tasks."[5]

But the public paid little heed to Laube and Speidel, and at the end of the tour the Meininger were firmly established throughout the German-speaking lands. It was not long before the first notice of them appeared in England. In April 1876, *The Academy* took stock of the company's accomplishments and told its readers that it was in the spirit of Goethe and Lessing that "the duke of Meiningen labors with untiring energy and earnestness to attain artistic perfection in the theatre. Recognized in Germany as the enlightened protector of dramatic art, he is a true artist in every sense of the word, and he enters into every detail himself, chooses the pieces and the actors, designs the costumes and scenery, and superintends the rehearsals with minute care."[6]

Invitations came from all over Europe for guest appearances, but 1876 saw the Meininger only in Berlin, Breslau, and Dresden. For this tour, Georg had scheduled five new productions: *Macbeth*, Kleist's *Das Käthchen von Heilbronn*, Otto Ludwig's *Der Erbförster*, Schiller's *Wilhelm Tell*, and Ibsen's *The Pretenders*.

"One can say," wrote Karl Frenzel, "that for the first time Kleist's poetic *Das Käthchen von Heilbronn*, that chivalric drama of the time of Maximilian, 'the Last Knight,' attained complete realization."[7] Although Laube and Dingelstedt had both made steps toward breaking with the bowdlerized text, the Meininger were the first to dare to present the drama without any major changes. Scenes traditionally dropped because of their "vulgarity" were played in all their realistic ugliness. Yet the skill of the staging gave an unsuspected pictorial charm to the drama.

Max Brückner, given short notice, could not complete the sets for this play, so some were the work of a Budapest painter by the name of Lehmann. The landscape decorations showed the usual tree arches, and the set was made realistic through the use of practicable stones, bushes, and the like. A masterly touch was the burning of the castle in Act III, during which the battlement and balcony fell burning to the ground. The transparent prospect allowed for a complicated lightplay backstage, made the more effective by a totally dark stage. The crowd scenes were notable: the secret court, the ball at Worms, the grouping at a forest inn. The knights and heroes, wearing the garments of the noblemen of the fifteenth century, impressed the historical artist Hans Makart, who found the settings worthy of "the finest art"; and Max Grube said "everything clattered of iron armor."[8]

Following the Kleist piece, Georg sent up *Der Erbförster*, one of his favorite plays, for which he had ordered from Brückner a forester's hut, only the simplest of rooms with painted paneling. All sorts of hunters' equipment and booty were not to be painted, but to be the real thing.[9] Again Georg resorted to odors to heighten the effect of the setting. Critics praised the earthy smell of the drama, the odor of the Thuringian pines, and found the whole production more impressive and "true" than the highly artistic Burgtheater performance; but the Berlin public found it unsophisticated and provincial. After the second performance it was replaced by another new production, *Wilhelm Tell*.

Departing from the old romantic tradition, the duke presented Schiller's masterpiece as a realistic drama, thereby bringing in a production as controversial as anything he ever directed. Barnay's interpretation of the hero Tell was especially disputed. To get away from the old declamatory style of acting, Georg had made Barnay's Tell an ordinary hunter. Schiller, the critics said, was thinking of the Tell of song and story, the hero to whom a chapel was dedicated. In Barnay's performance the idealistic and "superman" element was lost.[10]

The staging also departed from tradition in many respects, especially in the scene in which Melchtal, first played by Aloys Prasch, later by Josef Kainz, listened to the account of his father's blinding. Here we find an excellent example of the duke's use of scenery to assist the actor. Georg had a long ramp fashioned across the back of the room leading to the attic where Melchtal was hiding. As he heard his father's name, he gradually began to descend the ramp, unseen by those on stage. His reactions were then gradually integrated into the action on stage, something that had been impossible when he traditionally rushed into the room on hearing the tragic news.

The apple-shooting scene was entirely framed by painted scenery; only the apple tree and a linden tree were three-dimensional. To lessen the unnatural effect of the painted scenery, the apple seemed to be picked from the side away from the audience. In the pause between Acts III and IV, a four-step-high platform, sloping forward sharply, was built up and remained standing until the end of the play for the mountain defile near Küssnacht. Here and also on Lake Lucerne, the stones and rocks scattered over the stage were of molded material, not painted set pieces.

"*Wilhelm Tell!* What a hit for the Meininger," Ludwig Speidel now conceded when it played in Vienna.[11] "They are certainly masters in han-

Fig. 26. Georg's sketch for the backdrop of a fjord landscape for Ibsen's *The Pretenders*. The duke had made many sketches and drawings in Norway during his visits there, and used them for this 1876 production, which introduced Ibsen to Berlin.

dling crowd scenes. . . . No wonder that *Wilhelm Tell* is one of the most complete productions of the Meininger. No less than Schiller himself has pointed the way for them when he wrote his scenic instructions." The play was extraordinarily popular in Berlin, where the emperor is said to have told Chronegk, "If Schiller could only have seen that." [12]

On June 3 the Meininger gave Ibsen his first Berlin appearance with *The Pretenders*. Georg carefully designed both the costumes and the scenery from first-hand source materials he had gathered on his journeys to Norway in 1849 and 1875, striving to illuminate for the Berlin audience the foreign aspects of the cold, thirteenth-century Nordic life. The sketches still extant reveal the solemn and powerful effect he achieved through the use of massive gray scenery and of deep blues, grays, and dark reds for the heavy costumes. The drama provided the Meininger with an opportunity to display all their specialities: artistic grouping and crowd movement, realistic battle scenes, effective offstage sounds, all rehearsed to perfection.

Ibsen came up from Munich for the première and later visited the duke and the baroness in Bad Liebenstein. After the first performance, Chronegk wired the duke: "Hurrah! Greatest success of the season. . . . Ibsen called up three times. Bowed from his seat. Press throwing laurel wreaths.

Ibsen absolutely entranced." But when the reviews appeared and the public had made its judgment, even Ibsen's most enthusiastic supporters had to admit the play had not been greatly successful.[13]

The final production of the 1876 Berlin engagement was *Macbeth*, which opened June 12. It was an unlucky day for the Meininger, for two years earlier *The Merchant of Venice* had failed on that date. The "worthy setting" of Bodenstedt's 1867 production was now completely replaced.[14] After his successful staging of *Twelfth Night* on a unit set, Georg again designed scenery that would lessen shifting and at the same time heighten what Frenzel called the extraordinary unity of tone and atmosphere. Using the Tieck translation, he reduced Shakespeare's twenty-eight scene changes to eight and played all of them on one set with shallow Meininger insets. The first four scenes of Act I played on a rocky heath, which rose sharply to a height on the left. On the right was an elevation of rocks. This set remained on stage through the play and became in turn the castles of Inverness, Forres, and Dunsinane. Critics found that the narrowness of the castle courtyard added truth to Act V, where all the Macbeth-Macduff scenes played, for with followers standing on the steps and terraces, Macbeth and Macduff did not appear to be alone on a large battlefield as they usually were in earlier stagings of these scenes.

Two shallow insets were notable. One for the banquet scene was placed far downstage (see Fig. 6, p. 99), with the ghost of Banquo appearing behind heavily painted transparent curtains when a strong spotlight caught him. The murderers appeared from a trap on the left. Macbeth leaned over the railing to hide them from the guests. A second inset provided the room in which Lady Macduff speaks to her son. The murderers entered above and crept silently down the steps as mother and child spoke together. "As a production," said Ernst von Stahl, "it had one of the most poetic of all the great classics in the Meininger repertoire—the uncanny, terrible feeling of the tragedy was extraordinarily well realized."[15] Georg understood exactly what was wanted. The witches were no longer the comics of the English stage or the gigantic bubble-like characters of Schiller's version: they were simply ghastly old women hovering near the earth, seemingly appearing and disappearing into the mist of the rocky heath. Banquo's murderer, whose intrusion into a banquet is always hard to justify, came through the trap downstage while the banquet took place farther up.

Berlin supported the play for just five performances. Reliance on the setting and fidelity to the poet's intention resulted only in bitter failure. *Macbeth* played only five other times, in Breslau, but at least one performance made a powerful impression. Gerhart Hauptmann was an un-happy boy of fourteen when he saw *Julius Caesar* and *Macbeth* in 1876-77, and fifty-five years later he remembered what these performances had meant to him:

Theater history knows the Meininger. They played in a really grand style, un-known up to then. . . . No word can describe the worth of these experiences for my empty, hungry soul. No word can measure the extent of the spiritual wealth that these few evenings provided me for my whole life. *Julius Caesar* followed *Wallenstein*. . . . *Macbeth*, great in cowardice, sublime in cowardice, finished the series. The high point of this was Banquo's ghost. How could this ascent into murderous rage, into murderous madness, work this cleansing, liberating, inspir-ing effect on me, elevating my soul to sublimity. I believe it was so because it raised my spirit for all time over the flatness and lifelessness, over the hateful or-dinariness, of everyday life and made it fit for a greater discernment [which] from that time on did not let me overestimate so much as before the power of my mis-ery and my general surroundings.[16]

In a study of Hauptmann, Felix Voight says that the boy was deeply struck by the mythic elements of the witches' scenes in *Macbeth*. For the first time he felt the power of tragic catharsis. More than that, in those hours were formed his lifelong appreciation for the greatness and power of Shakespeare.[17] The huge sums of money and time spent on a *Macbeth* that played only ten times were not totally lost if the tragedy laid the groundwork for the spiritual and artistic life of a great German dramatist.

In 1877 the Meininger bypassed Berlin but broadened the tours to take in two new cities, Cologne and Frankfurt am Main; and that year Josef Kainz came to the company as a nineteen-year-old beginner. The duke, recognizing his extraordinary but untrained talent, cast him in large and small roles. To examine the plays given during the three years Kainz was in Meiningen is to suspect that the duke chose them with the young actor in mind. The first of these was Schiller's *Die Räuber*, which the Mein-inger took on tour the following year.

Die Räuber had long since fallen into disrepute on German stages and was played only by stars who had turned the role of Franz into a com-bination of Iago and Richard III. The theater world was astonished when the Meininger brought it to Berlin on May 1, 1878. For the first time the play was set in the eighteenth century, the poet's own time. In general, the arrangement of the scenes was based on Schiller's 1781 text with few changes. The first scene of Act IV was cut, thereby losing Karl's beautiful soliloquy on his homeland, but strengthening the dramatic qualities of the act. Because Georg was persuaded that the old Count Moor lived in an original castle, not a restored one, he designed the interiors in the pe-riod of the Renaissance. The crowd scenes were wonderfully staged. University students had always considered the play their own. During Schiller's lifetime it was a tradition for them to break into the "Song of the Robbers" before launching into "Gaudeamus Igitur."[18] On the evening the Meininger opened in Berlin the students sang so jubilantly that the safety of the old house was feared for.

Theodor Fontane reflected the public's generally favorable reaction to *Die Räuber* in his review of May 3, 1878. "A poetical magic lay over the production from beginning to end," he wrote. "In Meiningen the actor has at his disposal that which raises and ennobles weak talents, interest, and love. Added to these are appreciation and fine training. It is really to be deplored that every year in the beautiful month of May we must be shown by a little German capital how . . . to achieve success."[19]

The duke made an even more surprising choice than *Die Räuber* that year in presenting Grillparzer's gothic tale *Die Ahnfrau*, a work that had not been played for fifty years. The story of a doomed family, a lost son raised among robbers and becoming one himself, an innocent daughter loving a robber she does not recognize as a brother, the ghost of an ancestress unable to find peace until the last of the family is dead—such a plot did not seem to lend itself to a company dedicated to Shakespeare and Schiller. Perhaps it was chosen because its simple setting contrasted with the richness of the other plays (and of course, as we have seen, the duke had been attracted to the eerie and the mysterious from his childhood).

Four of the five acts took place in a single room, a Gothic arched hall, architecturally beautiful and designed to emphasize the irony that the hand of Fate should fall on a family who, from all appearances, had lived in comfortable well-being for generations. Karl Frenzel wrote in the *Deutsche Rundschau*:

One has to see the second act of the Meininger production of *Die Ahnfrau* in the uncanny, chilly hall, half-dark, lighted only by the moonlight that falls through panes and by the glowing coals, to form a clear perception of the heights to which terror and ghostly fright can mount on the stage. On the adherence to this mood rests the art of this production. Nothing disturbing, no false tone, no preeminence of the actors—everything carefully in tune so that once we step into the magic circle, we cannot leave it until the curtain falls.[20]

Georg succeeded in producing a ghost story in exact balance; there was not too little or too much. The effective entrance of the ancestress accompanied by a shrill tone like a drawn-out sigh was made more eerie as she stepped into the light, then withdrew into the shadows and disappeared into the darkness. The duke proceeded with the finest sensitivity and care to prevent the final act, played among the coffins in the castle crypt, from

Fig. 27. This sketch for the castle and grounds that figure in Franz Grillparzer's *Die Ahnfrau* was one of many Georg did merely to give his scenic artists and actors a feeling for the milieu of a play. All the acts in this drama were actually staged inside the castle.

Fig. 28. The unit set for *Die Ahnfrau*, converted in Act V from the great castle hall, where the first four acts took place, to the castle crypt filled with the coffins of the family's long-dead ancestors.

descending into the ridiculous, especially in the scene where the ancestress slowly raises the coffin lid, steps before the long-lost son, has a long conversation with him, and then returns to her grave.

The third play of the 1878 tour, Kleist's *Der Prinz von Homburg*, was notable primarily for the splendid production. The play had not been popular on the stage, but at a time when German patriotism was at a high point, this "work of the Fatherland" was received with considerable enthusiasm in Prussia. Even so, a sleep-walking hero, a prince who begs abjectly for his life at any price, is a difficult character to present sympathetically. In trying to overcome the plot difficulties, the duke sometimes allowed the staging to become more important than the actors.

The authenticity of the settings—the Berlin Castle constructed from plans and views of the original, the castle at Fehrbellin built in the French style with interiors true to the German late Renaissance, the Dutch room based on a picture that Georg sent Max Brückner "because the grand duke [who built the castle] loved the Dutch style," the battlefield with a village burning in the background, the flare of weapons produced by little fireworks attached to the back of set pieces, the beautiful June landscape, the columned hall "that formerly stood before the main entrance of the castle," the prince's prison with its practicable barred windows—could not breathe life into the play. It was a failure in every city except Berlin.[21]

On the other hand, *The Winter's Tale*, the fourth production of 1878, was one of the most successful of all the Meininger productions. Georg rescued it completely from the operetta form devised by Dingelstedt, for which von Flotow had written the musical score and in which all the action took place without any lapse of time. Dingelstedt had dropped the comedy's many contradictory elements and turned the plot into a retelling of the Hermione story, but Georg believed that Shakespeare intended the play to be what he named it—a tale in which an incredible plot demands an incredible world—and that to remove the geographical and historical caprices was to deprive the tale of its charm. If Leontes in the presence of a saint's image could call on the Oracle of Delphi, if Polixenes could return to his landlocked kingdom in a ship, if the poetry uncritically and naïvely overlooked the limits of time and space, Georg thought that we should accept those improbabilities in the same spirit.*

Act I played in an interior of Leontes's palace before a prospect of Mount Etna looming above the ruins of Taormina. The duke later found the foreground too bare and ordered playing fountains installed.[22] The

---

* If nothing else, Georg was consistent. More than 30 years later, when *A Midsummer Night's Dream* was being prepared for the new theater, he wrote: "It's a dream, not a lecture on the correctness of style" (Georg to Max Brückner, COL, Meiningen, n.d. 1909).

beautiful scenery, the grouping of the principals and the crowds, produced an effect that prompted a grudging admission from Speidel in Vienna that "everything [was] clear and absolutely convincing." But he would concede no more than that. He found Shakespeare's humor inferior to that of his fellow countryman Ferdinand Raimund and believed that only the extravagant outfitting saved the play. It was meant as a poor compliment to both Shakespeare and the Meininger when he said, "They deserve each other." *Die Neue Freie Presse* agreed that the Meininger had made a serious error in returning to Tieck's translation instead of using Dingelstedt's "improvements." Shakespeare was "full of superfluous talk." [23]

Again the public begged to differ. *The Winter's Tale* charmed a whole generation, becoming the theatrical wonder of its time. "With its artistic atmosphere, which set the tone and color of both the tragic and the happy, it enchanted many tens of thousands throughout all Europe and won for the still controversial and much undervalued work a place in the German repertoire." [24] The French actor and theater manager André Antoine was delighted with the production when he saw it in Brussels on a later tour, as was Stanislavski in Moscow.[25]

When the company visited Prague in 1878, the whole city became Meininger-mad. Kainz wrote to his parents on September 17: "24 curtain calls. . . . In the evening after the first performance the hawkers came into the restaurant and offered us 'Caesar cigarettes' and 'Meininger' ties and gloves." [26]

The next year Josef Lewinsky, the tragedian of the Burgtheater and an adherent of the Laube school, who in the 1850's had shaken his head over the display in Kean's planned production of *Richard II*, saw the Meininger and noted in his diary:

The duke is the greatest director in Germany. The costumes and decorations disappear for me before a deep understanding of the poet. The duke joins with the boldest ingenuity all the ingenuity of the poet—he executes everything with a sureness that is overpoweringly effective, and to me it is clear that in many, many things he surpasses Dingelstedt. Dingelstedt is theatrical, if also remarkably clever, but the duke is a great, true artist, who presents the idea with a puritanical strength that gives full power to the poet—far more than Dingelstedt, who makes more noise with less splendor.[27]

Christmas 1880 saw something unusual on the Meiningen stage. It was Georg's custom to present a special program during the holiday season when the company was at home and there were usually guests at the castle, that year visitors from England. Ordinarily, this was a concert or some other musical offering, but in 1880 events took a dramatic form.

First, Georg presented *Julius Caesar* in the newly refurbished setting to be taken to England the following spring, then *The Taming of the Shrew*, in a staging that resulted from his long interest in arranging two parts of *Faust* to be played together with the Walpurgis Night scenes. In 1875, when he and the baroness had dined in Munich with Richard and Cosima Wagner, the two men had spent the evening discussing the problems and possible solutions of staging Goethe's poem; but in May 1876 Georg saw Otto Devrient's Weimar production of *Faust*,[28] which set his mind in another direction. Devrient played Goethe's work on two nights in succession on what he termed a "medieval mystery stage." Bypassing the rules of contemporary staging, Devrient's acting areas, representing Heaven, Earth, and Hell—one above the other—were visible at all times. Karl Frenzel enthusiastically predicted that this staging with no shifting of scenery would prove as revolutionary as the Meiningen productions of 1874. He was wrong, at least for the near future, but Devrient's production turned Georg's mind to the Tieck productions of Shakespeare he had seen as a young man and to the antique Greek stage he himself had used thirteen years earlier for the Oedipus trilogy.

The Taming of the Shrew was given on what Georg believed to be an Elizabethan stage. This consisted of a bare stage with one large door upstage and a small balcony against the backstage wall. The comedy was given uncut, with the same attention to costumes and staging devoted to the plays prepared for the tours. On December 26, 1880, Hans von Bülow wrote to a friend: "Pity you did not stay a few days longer. *The Taming of the Shrew* with the old English stage, the never performed prologue, the original clown, etc., was a very remarkable treat."[29] Why Georg did not take this production on tour was never explained. Max Grube described the one that did tour as 'frightful." At that time, Georg went back to the text of Johann Ludwig Deinhardstein, the only sin, Stahl says, that the Meininger ever committed against Shakespeare.

By this time plans were complete for the English engagement, a two-month run at the Drury Lane Theatre from late May to late July. Two new plays were prepared: Goethe's *Iphigenie* and, at the request of the prince of Wales, under whose patronage the Meininger were appearing in England, Wolff's *Preciosa*. On May 5, 1881, Georg wired Chronegk in Bremen, "I have written Harris [their business manager in England] that it is high time to begin some basic advertising."[30] On May 27 the London *Times* ran a long story on the Meiningen court theater and pointed out it was not a new idea for "actors of Italy, Holland, and France" to appear on the London stage;[31] and on May 28 the *Morning Post* carried a review of the Meininger's aims and methods. Other newspaper accounts followed, so that on their first appearance, on May 30, the Meininger played to a full house. Among those present, according to *The Stage* (June 3, 1881), were the prince and princess of Wales, the king of Sweden and his suite, Prince Edward of Saxe-Weimar, and the duke of Mecklenberg-Strelitz.

The company opened with *Julius Caesar*, given in German, as were the other plays. It was the best possible choice, the *Times* said, for several reasons: the play had not, within living memory, been associated with a great actor, English or foreign; it was not a "one-actor" play, with Brutus, Antony, and Cassius dividing the honors; and there were many difficult minor parts, such as Casca, Trebonius, Octavius, and the poet Cinna. The *Times* had nothing but praise for the scenery, the costumes, and the crowd, but it was less enthusiastic about the principal actors, reserving its kudos for Barnay alone.

Julius Caesar and *The Winter's Tale* were much admired in London; *Twelfth Night* and Schiller's *Fiesko* and *Wilhelm Tell* less so. *Die Ahnfrau* was praised for its atmosphere and mood, but the play was dismissed as worthless. Neither Kleist's *Käthchen von Heilbronn* nor Schiller's *Die Räuber* found much favor. Two unusual successes came toward the end of the engagement. The *Times* pronounced Goethe's *Iphigenie in Tauris*, presented on June 23, the "greatest intellectual triumph. . . . Only five persons . . . no change of scene . . . no chorus, action and plot almost nil . . . long serious speeches in beautiful German, devoid of exciting or sentimental features. . . . Yet Goethe's drama was received with every mark of approval by the numerous audience, which listened with rapt attention, frequently rising to vociferous enthusiasm. [This was] a performance which with regard to purity of style has certainly never been surpassed at a London theater." *

Equally successful was the final attraction, Wolff's gypsy drama *Preciosa*, a musical that subsequently proved to be one of the greatest box-office draws of the tours. Fräulein Schweighofer as Preciosa could not sing and did not even pretend to. A double, standing in the wings, sang von Weber's music, while the actress danced on stage. The use of every sort of effect—illumination by gas, a practicable fountain with electrically lighted jets of water, a generous use of pedestals and broad practica-

* Ludwig Barnay, *Erinnerungen* (Berlin, 1903), p. 215. Later, when the Meininger could find no audiences in Germany willing to listen to Goethe's words, Barnay wondered if the English had really found the performance so enthralling or had merely been impressed by the name of the great poet. For lack of an audience the play was performed only 12 more times after the 2 London performances. But the duke maintained that no German theater had the right to tour without at least one work by Germany's greatest literary figure, and kept it in the repertoire. It was performed in Odessa in 1890, the troupe's last engagement.

ble stairways, rapid changes through sets one within the other—charmed the audience. The *Times* (July 1) called this play "one of the best stage pictures presented by the Meininger," and *The Stage* (July 11) found this last production of the Meininger as exciting as the first.[32]

Although the company played to good houses in London, the expenses were so heavy that the tour was not a financial success, and the Meininger did not return to England. But they left their mark on a number of men who would determine the direction of the English theater. Frank R. Benson and Henry Irving, two of the most prominent actors in England, both claimed to be adherents of the Meininger method. Many years later, Benson's brother wrote: "The Meiningen performance of *Julius Caesar* had powerfully impressed my brother, and the Meiningen system took a prominent place in the theory of his art."[33] Henry Irving attended many of the performances, invited the Meininger players to his theater, and formed a friendship with Ludwig Barnay. He took up the externals of the Meininger method to such an extent that six years later the duke and the baroness thought his *Faust* was glittering but a "burlesque."[34] The actor-manager William Poel, founder of the Elizabethan Stage Society, called the Meininger production of *Julius Caesar* "astonishing" and as late as 1913 found no troupe in Germany to compare with the Meininger he had seen in 1881.[35] J. T. Grein, drama critic and theater reformer, wrote in 1899: "Whenever cosmopolitan students of the drama meet and exchange their memories of glorious bygone days, three names never fail to arise and to arouse enthusiasm among the speakers, for the Meininger, Chronegk, and Barnay have been to the continental drama what Wagner, Ludwig II, and Bayreuth have been to the world of music."[36]

The 1883 tour saw another daring play for a court theater, Arthur Fitger's *Die Hexe*.[37] Centering on a young woman caught in the middle of a struggle between Catholic fanatics and Protestant bigots, the plot had raised a storm over its "free thought" when it was given a few years earlier in Vienna. Georg softened only one scene of the drama, that in which the heroine tears the Bible to pieces and cries out, "I love these noble pages, the most splendid the human spirit has ever received; but if you want to make them chains for me, I rend the chains." It would have been unthinkable to destroy a Bible on stage. Georg had her merely fling the Bible away.

In 1884 Otto Franz Gensichen's *Lydia*, a light and pretty folk play, became the curtain raiser for Molière's *Le Malade imaginaire*; and the Meininger introduced Ludwig Ganghofer's *Der Herrgottschnitzer von Oberammergau*, a product of the *Bauerntheater* (Peasant Theater) in Bavaria.[38] All three parts of Schiller's *Wallenstein* were also given that year, still another astonishing move by the duke. The second part, *Die Piccolomini*, had been out of the German theater for years and was nearly forgotten; and *Wallensteins Lager* was played only now and then on festive occasions. *Wallensteins Tod* alone was current on all stages. Because the entire trilogy was too long for one evening and the individual parts too short for three separate performances, the Meininger gave *Wallensteins Lager* and *Die Piccolomini* on one night and *Wallensteins Tod* on the next.

The *Lager* was a mass of sound and activity.[39] Noise rolled unceasingly from the far background, matched by the cries and street brawls of the crowds crammed onstage—a commotion of such naturalistic compactness that the realism was portrayed to the last shout.[40] *Die Piccolomini* was distinguished by surprisingly beautiful and stylish settings: the Gothic hall in Pilsen authentically and tastefully furnished with flags and implements of war in accordance with Schiller's instructions; the splendid room in Wallenstein's house; the magnificent banquet hall and the intimate rooms in the Piccolomini home. The banquet scene, one of the most difficult in Schiller to stage—he instructs that everyone should be constantly in movement, yet the conspiracy must be carefully enunciated to the audience—was skillfully set. The Questenberg scenes were realistic and true.*

Of *Wallensteins Tod* Theodor Fontane wrote: "In addition to the new settings—one cannot think of the old anymore—are new costumes of corresponding magnificence and completeness: the iron armor of the Pappenheimer, the rich mail in which Wallenstein, as well as Octavio and Max Piccolomini, appear, the dragoon and page costumes. The furnishings with the Renaissance chests with figures in relief, the heavy doors with polished locks, hasps, and mountings, are living riches. But all this is not dead ballast. There is not a trace of overdressing as was so feared; in fact, all this elevates the soul of the viewer. The great transformation that the new art of staging all externals has made, the heightening of the audience's understanding and interest, is never more apparent than in Act III with the storming of the Pappenheimer troops and in Act IV in the prelude to the murder of Wallenstein and then the murder itself."[41]

In 1885 the company moved east, to perform in Warsaw, St. Peters-

---

* In the Franco-Prussian War Georg, as a general in the 22d Division, was ordered to shell Chartres. He wanted to spare the essentially defenseless city with its priceless cathedral and accepted the mayor's offer to surrender without a struggle. Georg's second son, Prince Ernst, later wrote: "Some of the officers were dissatisfied with this. They sat about the room complaining and treated the mayor very rudely. My father used their behavior as a model for the behavior of Wallenstein's generals toward Questenberg." (Cited in Heinz Isterheil, "Die Bühnendekorationen bei den Meiningern," Ph.D. dissertation, University of Cologne, 1938, p. 51.)

burg, and Moscow, using plays in their existing repertoire. That year the baroness was stricken with meningitis; for weeks her life was in danger, and the duke was not involved in the theater at all. When it was possible to move her to the mountains—it was thought the mountain air would be beneficial—he remained there much of the time. Her recovery was slow—"snail-like," the duke said. During that time Chronegk carried on alone, and no new productions were prepared for the next season. For that reason, the company visited only three cities, all in Germany, in 1886.

The next year, however, brought a splendid new production. Schiller's *Maria Stuart* became a specialty of the Meininger, though the crowd scenes were limited to the celebrated "murmur" offstage. Georg's brilliant, absolutely correct historical staging overreached its limits in this production. The research he had done earlier in the British Museum on the castle at Fotheringhay yielded so much material that Schiller's tragedy was often drowned in detail. Everything was designed to contrast the luxury of Elizabeth's court with Maria's unhappy surroundings. The play was enormously popular, but the *Allgemeine Zeitung* of Munich reflected the general critical reaction in its review of July 23, 1887: "The great and merited recognition that the Meininger have earned everywhere . . . for their incontestably beneficial effect on the slovenly direction of many court theaters cannot blind us to the results of too much in this case."

Byron's *Marino Faliero*, on which the duke and the baroness had lavished much care and which had been enthusiastically received in Düsseldorf the year before, failed completely in Berlin. The piece did not have enough dramatic power, and the audiences had learned too well from the Meininger to be satisfied with beautifully prepared pictures alone. As was his custom, the duke said nothing about the play's unfavorable reception, but the baroness was angered by the attack critics launched on the stark realism of the execution scene. On April 16, 1887, she wrote Max Grube, who was playing the title role:

From our point of view, Berlin certainly has not shown itself a city of intelligence in respect to *Marino Faliero*. The great aesthetic indignation shown over the execution scene is scarcely believable in view of the manner of death usually seen on the German stage: to speak, for example, of Othello, where Rossi plays on for several minutes with the knife in his slit throat, of a smothered Desdemona, of a Franz Moor hanging himself, of the coughed-out spirit of Marie Beaumarchais, not to mention all the ladies of the *demimonde*, who "pass out" (Pardon!) slowly from consumption or poison.[42]

For some time the duke and the baroness had been considering extending the Meininger repertoire to include modern dramas. In 1886 the baroness had told Karl Frenzel they had in mind three new plays that had made a deep impression on them and in which they had great hopes: Paul Lindau's translation from the Spanish of José Echegaray's Ibsen-inspired *El Gran galeoto*; *Alexandra*, a realistic drama by their good friend Richard Voss; and a new translation of Ibsen's *Ghosts*. They planned to present the three dramas at Meiningen as the annual Christmas event and then add them to the tour repertoire. Frenzel was not enthusiastic. On December 6 he wrote to the baroness:

My long-standing interest in your theater gives me the courage to beg you not to build too strongly on the success of the new pieces you have named. Ibsen's *Ghosts* is a sticky piece, which seems to me more likely to be in the end a complete failure—like his *Nora*—than to be even the smallest success. I hope you have prepared one or two poems of our great dramatists. I always come back to *Die Jungfrau von Orleans* or the first act of *Demetrius*. These would be the surest mainstay for the Meininger. A fixed theater that plays three hundred evenings in succession can very well mount an experiment—should, probably, in order to awake the interest of some of the literary epicures. A theater that tours does best to stick to its specialty.[43]

The ducal pair took Frenzel's advice and began work on Schiller's *Die Jungfrau von Orleans*. But they also proceeded with the modern dramas, which were given on three successive evenings shortly before Christmas. Ibsen's *Ghosts*, at the time banned on all public stages, was the center of interest. Writing thirty years later, Lindau said of the play: "Everyone who saw the Ibsen drama on that evening has agreed that never again on any stage has this dreadful yet beautiful work so approached what we mean when we say 'Ibsenism.' The poet himself had just one word to describe the presentation, 'Unsurpassable.'"[44] *Ghosts* afforded the Meininger no opportunity to exhibit any of the spectacular effects for which they were famous. Everything depended on the duke's direction and the interpretation of the small cast, which was made up of his most experienced actors, Marie Berg, Max Grube, Alexander Barthel, and Karl Weiser. For the role of Regine an actress from the Munich court theater was engaged.

When the residents of Meiningen learned that a "play so indecent and immoral" as *Ghosts* was to be presented on their stage, those who had no tickets resolved to buy none, and those who had tickets planned to make a furor in the theater. It would have been extremely embarrassing if the house had been empty, for all literary Germany had been invited, and the drama was to be played in the presence of the author. The most important critics were expected: Karl Frenzel, Hans Hopfen, Gotthilf Weisstein, Isadore Landau, Richard Voss, and Paul Lindau. When the duke was apprised of the plot, he merely smiled and said: "The house will be full as never before." The tickets were given away to anyone who would apply for them at the office of the court chamberlain. Hints were given to all court employees that such tickets were available.

Georg was right. The theater was completely full on December 21, when *Ghosts*, the second of the three plays, was performed. There prevailed, says Voss, a ghostly atmosphere on the stage, a ghostly atmosphere in the theater, and a full understanding in the audience of that passionately controversial drama—a drama so little understood in those days.[45] For that understanding the audience could thank the duke, who illuminated the meaning of the play, and the baroness von Heldburg, who had worked through the parts with the actors. From act to act, from scene to scene, the enthrallment grew. When the curtain fell for the last time, a heavy silence fell over the audience for a moment. Then a frenzy of applause broke out. Ibsen had to bow again and again from the railing of the ducal loge, then again from the stage with the actors. After the excitement, it was a relief for the guests to go out into the cold air and head for the castle, where a reception had been prepared in honor of the three authors.

The court chamberlain, staff in hand, met the company. The duke, as usual in civilian clothes with only one ribbon as a decoration, greeted his guests in his simple, friendly manner. Present were senior officers, court officials, and friends of the ducal family. The outstanding artists of the Meiningen court theater were present, including those who had just appeared in *Ghosts*, barely out of makeup and obviously relieved that the tensions of the day were over. Georg's son, Crown Prince Bernhard, and his wife, Charlotte, sister of the German emperor, had arrived on the last train to get through from Berlin.[46] Others, including Otto Brahm, one of Ibsen's greatest champions,[47] were on a later train that had to turn back because of the heavy snow. The crown prince and his wife received the guests with the baroness von Heldburg—Berlin critics, writers, and artists, all gathered to honor the new drama.

Despite this glittering occasion, Frenzel was proved right. The duke was to have no success with the new pieces. *Ghosts* was repeated without incident in Meiningen on December 28, 1886, and was announced for the Berlin appearance that spring. But because the company played in a public theater in the capital city, the repertoire had to be submitted to the censor, and both *Ghosts* and *Alexandra* were banned. After permission for a performance in Breslau was denied, Chronegk urged the duke to try again; but Georg had had enough of censorship. "I'll take no more steps in that direction," he wired Chronegk on October 14, 1887. But he seems to have changed his mind, for on December 17 of the same year the

Meininger succeeded in giving one performance of *Ghosts* in Dresden. They bowed to police pressure, however, and cancelled a second one, which Ibsen was expected to attend.[48] *Ghosts* would not be repeated, Chronegk announced; Marie Berg was "too hoarse to play Mrs. Alving." Not until 1889 did the Meininger give another performance of *Ghosts*, and then they played it in Copenhagen.

In 1887 plans were at their height for a tour of the United States, but they came to naught. Chronegk spoke no English and demanded one guarantee after another of the American agents,[49] but his continued poor health was probably what ruled out the ocean crossing. He had broken down in Düsseldorf in the summer of 1886. His health did not greatly improve, and the duke would not allow him to exert himself in any way. "Conduct only the most necessary rehearsals," he wired repeatedly. By the end of 1887, when it was clear Chronegk was still ailing, Georg decided not to undertake the American tour.

That year saw the last Meininger appearance in Berlin—and one of their greatest artistic and popular successes, Schiller's *Die Jungfrau von Orleans*. It played fifty-five straight nights to an acclaim unlike any they had experienced in their seven previous appearances. It was as if they had come for the first time. Scalpers got 300 marks for a ticket, and crowds were turned away every evening. "They surpassed even themselves," said Max Grube.[50] For the first time, the duke had reached the goal he had always strived for: to wed Laube's pure speech to a suitably furnished background. Critics agreed that the fresh staging and careful attention to detail unified all elements of the drama and gave new life to Schiller's tragedy. It had the effect of a new play.

The scenery united with the costumes to form an extraordinarily atmospheric stage. The coronation in Act IV was the high point of the staging. As the curtain rose on the beautiful setting of the square before the cathedral at Rheims, the audience never failed to break into spontaneous applause, which, added to the cheers onstage, created an unforgettable effect. One critic wrote: "It is to be deplored that this picture composed by the finest artistic talent cannot be held fast in some way." Similarly impressive were the scenes of the arrival of the knight of Lorraine at the court of the king, the Maid's entrance before the court, the death of Talbot on the battlefield, and the final scene. The *Dresdener Nachrichten* critic thought that it was "as if Schiller had written [the play] just for the Meininger"; and Stanislavski, who admired this production especially, wrote of it, "The spirit of Schiller, Shakespeare, and Molière lived in the Meininger players."[51]

In 1888 the Meininger gave twenty-nine performances in Brussels.

Fig. 29. Newspaper advertisement, *Pester-Lloyd* (Budapest), Oct. 20, 1888. Many of the actors listed (including Max Grube, Richard, Arndt, Teller, and Weiser) had toured with the company since the first Berlin appearance 14 years earlier.

Twelve of these were seen by André Antoine, who was then formulating his own ideas on the theater.* This followed runs of thirty performances in Rotterdam and twenty-nine in Antwerp. In the fall the troupe returned to Graz, Budapest, Prague, and Leipzig.

The following year, after a month in Stettin in April, the Meininger moved on to Scandinavia. The tour began badly with thirty unsuccessful evenings in Copenhagen, but on the next stop, Stockholm, the company was well received. On June 30 the baroness wrote Max Grube from Weggis on the Lake of Lucerne, where the couple had gone to consult a Swiss specialist about the duke's loss of hearing: "That the public in Stockholm is not so chauvinistic as in Copenhagen, and that it went very well for the Meininger there you have probably already heard. I think from now on the theater will have a more auspicious season." After describing the duke's treatment, "which has done much good, but how long will it last?," she concluded the letter with prophetic words: "Oh, if the tours weren't so extensive and so expensive! It would suit me best if the tours could—at least for a few years—be given up." [52]

In 1890 the Meininger made their second tour to Russia. In 1885 they had given sixty-eight successful performances in St. Petersburg and Moscow, which had aroused great interest in both artistic and intellectual circles. [53] Now they extended their tour to Kiev and Odessa. It was in Odessa that the company received the surprising news that the duke had decided to discontinue the tours. The final performance was Shakespeare's *Twelfth Night* on July 1. On August 31 the baroness von Heldburg explained the move to Arthur Fitger:

Yes, the Meininger as "Meininger" are no more. The principal reason for the discontinuance was Chronegk's health. . . . In addition, the duke and I begin to feel the preparing of great things and the constant educating of the actors more and more of a load. We had all the work and others had all the pleasure; and in the last three years the work has cost the duke a good deal of money, for only in the first *Jungfrau* year did the theater pay for itself in spite of longer and longer tours. It became important for us to allow Chronegk a long-deserved rest and ourselves some enjoyment of the theater. [54]

Still, in the preceding month some consideration had been given to making one farewell tour. Chronegk clearly liked the idea:

I regard the idea of a farewell tour very positively and not for Berlin alone. . . . Yet I consider *two* months too long for the old pieces; therefore, from the pieces

* For his reactions, see his letter to the French critic Francisque Sarcey in Appendix C. Antoine's subsequent work at the Théâtre Libre reveals that he "appropriated" many of the Meininger's innovations in developing his own individual methods. (See Samuel Montefiore Waxman, *Antoine and the Théâtre Libre*, Cambridge, Mass., 1926.)

proposed by His Highness, I suggest these: *Jungfrau*, certainly! about 6-8 times, perhaps 10. *Caesar*, certainly, but 6 times at the most, especially since Barnay [intendant of the Berliner Theater] has given it so often. . . . *Wallenstein*, no! It has been at the Hoftheater [Königliches Schauspielhaus] too often and well done with a splendid production. At most, it could be given twice for devoted partisans, that is, if we can cast it well. *The Winter's Tale*, no! L'Arronge [Deutsches Theater] begins September 1 with it—the main point is—why? Barnay will begin his season with it too, but, in Dingelstedt's adaptation. *Merchant*, 2 or 3 times. Probably *Maria Stuart* too, if [Amanda] Lindner makes a good Maria, but who for Leicester? The piece has too few crowd scenes, something everyone wants to see the Meininger do—only such pieces are good box office. Experience has taught us that the repertoire has to be broad. My view of a farewell tour is simply a great alternating repertoire of all our pieces; otherwise the farewell will have no real appeal for the public, since some will want to see this, others that.[55]

In the same letter Chronegk again stated the basic principle of all Meininger staging: "The Berliner Theater, Hochberg, Barnay, L'Arronge, all follow *one* principle; they give *our* repertoire to hinder us. But they are indifferent about *how* they give it, only glittering décor and costumes with which they think, or thought, they could carry it off. Many better individual talents are at their disposal, but His Highness and you will understand me [when I say] that the heart and soul of the attraction lies in the ensemble and the spirit of the whole, and to protect that has always been my concern."[56]

The Deutsches Theater, founded in 1883, took over the Meininger method and repertoire but put more stock in general in the quality of its individual actors. In the *Vossische Zeitung* of September 9, 1884, Otto Brahm wrote, "The Meininger have passed their zenith; the Deutsches Theater has surpassed them." He was proved wrong three years later when the Meininger brought *Die Jungfrau von Orleans* to Berlin; but each season a greater effort had to be made. Other theaters, too, had adopted the duke's reforms, thus putting pressure on him to keep preparing new works season after season to attract an audience.[57] Georg could say to Max Grube, when the actor urged him to such an undertaking: "No, what the German theater had to learn, it has learned." He recognized that the illusionistic stage had reached its artistic limits.

Other reasons, too, entered into the decision. The long tours were wearing on the company. Between 1874 and 1890 the actors spent almost half the year on the road (the average over the period was 162 days). In each city they played every evening, and between engagements they had only two or three days for travel and rest.[58] Meanwhile, the duke's hearing continued to deteriorate, and he suffered from arthritis. The year 1888 was not a good one for him. His mother died in January, and during the course of the year he lost two very old friends, first Emperor Wilhelm I and then a short time later the Crown Prince, on whom great hopes had been laid by the liberal elements of Germany. The policies of the new emperor, Wilhelm II, disturbed the duke. Much of the old optimism had disappeared in the middle classes; there was a whole new feeling abroad in Germany. In 1890, twenty-three years before the outbreak of the First World War, Georg wrote Carl Werder, professor of the aesthetics of dramatic poetry at the University of Berlin:

It is really questionable whether we can keep the peace that has prevailed since the Franco-Prussian War, or whether we are not instead facing a colossal storm, which may break even during my reign. It seems to me that among us everyone in high places becomes more and more chauvinistic—perhaps because we realize that the armed peace is gradually ruining us, but perhaps also because the general view of a great German army strengthens the trust in our own power. In the best circumstances, what would we accomplish if we explode? Holding the status quo! But we have that today. But what if the affair goes wrong, what then? [59]

Georg was ready to bring his troupe home. Those who wished to leave the company could consider themselves free; for those who wished to stay there was a place. When Georg recalled his company in 1890 to the little ducal Residence, he could look back on twenty-five years of work that had influenced every theater in Western Europe. He had come into the theater when the drama was debased, the acting profession demoralized, and the theater arts nearly forgotten. Now he saw the theater standing at the beginning of a new era, and he knew that part of the progress was the result of his own accomplishments. He had, first of all, built a sound classical repertoire. By resting his reforms on the great dramatists—notably Shakespeare and Schiller—he had demonstrated the shabbiness of the trivia passing as dramatic literature. But more than that, his company rescued the great poets from many of the "improvements" to which they had been subjected.

To set the poet again as the most important element on the stage, he brought about reforms in staging and directing. The director was for the first time a real director, whose imagination and skill could mold a production into one entity. He banned for all time on his stage the tyranny of role monopoly and its attendant evil, "the star system." Balance with harmony was the goal of a Meininger production. The close, flexible playing of groups and masses, the skillful acting in subordinate roles, the artistic placing of "supers"—all these reinforced the work of the principal actors and contributed to the ideal of the unified whole. The Meininger gave life, movement, and artistic grouping to the ensemble, and then subordinated these to the intention of the dramatist. "Works such as Schiller's and Kleist's were proudly staged by the Meininger. What Schiller dreamed of one hundred years before and perhaps without any hope of fulfillment, the Meininger reached. . . . The basic plan of their mass direction has remained as a model."[60]

The Meininger showed what could and should be added to the poetry in color and life, in depth and atmosphere, through the use of the sister arts. If, to the eye of a later generation, the magnificence, the "historical accuracy," and the "realism" seem overdone, even false, we do well to recall that Georg's company was speaking to the public in the idiom of its own day.[61] Building on his artistic training and on the theater he had been seeing from boyhood, he fashioned for the drama a frame through which the public might look until it learned to value the drama itself. There he reached back to Marr, Immermann, Klingemann, and Laube. He educated the public by presenting the greatest theater literature, and he made the productions enticing enough for the public to want to see those works. He was willing to send his company into every kind of theater in every kind of town, large and small, east and west, so that everyone might participate in the theater as he saw it. He elevated the taste of a generation by the purity of his repertoire, the completeness of his productions, and the beauty, charm, and magic the Meininger brought back into the theater.

If Georg was a man of his time and one who looked back in history, he was also a man who saw clearly what lay ahead for the theater. He was one of the first to see the direction the new writers were taking. He gave many of them their first hearing, and some saw their names become famous as the Meininger carried their work throughout Europe. The Meininger served also as a model for a number of men who were dissatisfied with the condition of the theater in their own countries and were groping their way to new things. It has been pointed out that it was not an accident that around 1890 three directors of the new era simultaneously emerged in widely separated cities of Europe: André Antoine in Paris, Otto Brahm in Berlin, and Constantin Stanislavski in Moscow. Each of these men took his departure from the reforms of Georg of Meiningen, and each has noted that seeing the Meininger was a turning point in his thinking. The significant impact of the Meininger principle was that with its promise of authenticity and historical realism it awakened a vital desire—what Brahm called "ferment"—for the formation of a contemporary stage in a true-to-life way. Stanislavski wrote: "I value the good which the Meininger brought us, that is, their director's methods for showing the spiritual content of the drama. For this they deserve great thanks. My gratitude to them is unbounded and will always live in my soul."[62]

Just as the duke of Meiningen did not invent any staging methods but merely assembled the ideas current in his time, synthesized them with the best in tradition, and put the stamp of his artistic and spiritual personality on them, those who followed him did not invent the methods they used. Directors like Antoine and Stanislavski would have worked reforms in the theater even if they had never seen the Meininger, but the reforms they did effect were influenced by what they saw in the German company. They, not the slavish imitators piling more furniture on the stage and more lavish costumes on the actors, were the heirs of Georg. Like him, they realized that the body of the staging—all the scenery, costumes, apparatus, in short, the externals—had no valuable place in the new theater. Few would question that it was the spirit of the Meininger—the constant effort to find ways to illuminate the soul of the drama—that animated their work.

EPILOGUE

━━━━━━━━━━━◆━━━━━━━━━━━

𝖂hen the duke recalled his company to Meiningen, the Meininger ceased to be, but the Meiningen court theater did not. Less than three weeks after the company gave its last performance in Odessa, the duke telegraphed Chronegk, "Rehearsals will begin on September 1." In March and April of that year the duke and baroness, accompanied by Prince Ernst, had made an extended trip through Italy, Greece, and the Ottoman Empire, but by July, as the baroness wrote her brother, they were ready to go back to work.

They began the new season with Hermann Sudermann's *Die Ehre*, written the previous year. The drama of middle-class family life required none of the famous Meininger effects, but proved popular. The duke and Chronegk gave it all the attention they accorded the classics, but the play itself stood between the old and the new. Later that year they did Lessing's *Nathan der Weise*. Before the visit of Professor Carl Werder of the University of Berlin that fall, the baroness wrote Max Grube in Berlin: "Please order German translations of *War and Peace*, *Anna Karenina*, and Strindberg's dramas for me, because Professor Werder is going to read them with me."[1]

After this visit, she and Georg prepared Tolstoy's *The Power of Darkness*, which was given on the Meiningen stage that winter. "Tolstoy stands for me next to Ibsen and Björnson," the baroness told Grube; "then comes Anzengruber and not to forget Sudermann and Wildenbruch." They followed *The Power of Darkness* with Voss's *Schuldig* and Paul Heyse's *Kolberg*. New plays deserved new equipment, the duke decided, with the result that by the end of the year many of the sets and costumes from the tours had been sold.[2]

185

Chronegk stayed on as stage manager until his death on July 9, 1891. By that time, the members of the original company were in theaters all over Germany, and there were only two "Old Meininger," Paul Richard and Anna Schwenke, in Meiningen to see his casket laid in the stone sarcophagus on which the duke had inscribed: "Georg, Duke of Saxe-Meiningen, and Helene, Baroness von Heldburg, to their friend."

In 1894 the duke read *Der Andere*, a new play by Paul Lindau, his severest critic in the early days of the Meininger, which interested him enough to invite Lindau to Meiningen for its first performance. *Le Figaro* sent a reviewer at Antoine's request, the play was a success, and Lindau remained in Meiningen as intendant. There followed five years of intensive theater work. Many of the "Old Meininger" returned as guest artists: Amanda Lindner in Paul Heyse's *Vanina Vanini*, Joseph Nesper in *Rabbi David*,[3] and Kainz in Voss's *König*. Lindau gave Ibsen's *The Wild Duck* and *John Gabriel Borkman*.

In 1891 Georg celebrated his silver anniversary as duke of Saxe-Meiningen, Hildburghausen, and Saalfeld, and in 1898 the silver anniversary of his marriage to Ellen Franz. This event drew all the "Old Meininger" except Josef Kainz, who was playing in the north, back to Meiningen for a surprise performance of *The Merchant of Venice*. In 1899 a simple ceremony, led by Max Grube, marked the silver anniversary of the first Berlin appearance, but the ducal couple were in the south. The duke and the baroness had made their last trip to England in 1897. There the duke dined at the Beefsteak Club with Irving, who gave him a promptbook and sketches for *Romeo and Juliet*. In turn, the duke upgraded the class of the Ernestine Order he had bestowed on Irving in 1887. The duke personally participated less and less in the theater as his hearing became increasingly impaired, and by 1909 he was no longer attending any productions. His interest continued strong, however. The theater burned in 1908, and two days later he began to draw up plans for a new one. Over the great portal he had carved the words: DEM VOLKE ZUR FREUDE UND ERHEBUNG (For the pleasure and elevation of the people).

On January 1, 1909, the baroness wrote to Felix Dahn, who had inquired about sending a beginner to Meiningen for training: "We continue to take an active interest in our theater, although we don't do much ourselves. No one who does not please us is engaged. I still consider the Meiningen school one of the best."[4] Kainz sent his stepdaughter there for experience, writing to Intendant Lindau: "I know there is no one who can work with her better than you."[5]

In 1912, at the age of eighty-six, the duke returned to active participation in his beloved theater by directing what was to be his last play, George Bernard Shaw's *Caesar and Cleopatra*. The baroness entered into the preparation with all her old enthusiasm, and long letters arguing details, especially over Caesar's age, went back and forth between her and Max Grube. Max Brückner did the scenery, and the play was well received.

In old age, the duke worked on his scientific studies and read widely. He sketched landscapes but no costumes or scenery. It was as if these were an inherent part of his directing. Once he stopped being a director, he had no interest in the outfitting.* By 1914 he was entirely deaf and endured silence impatiently. He and the baroness lived quietly, but not uneventfully, until his death on June 25, 1914, three months after his eighty-eighth birthday. Three days later he was buried in the public cemetery as he had willed, for only there could his middle-class wife lie beside him.

The little duchy had known only three rulers in one hundred and eleven years, and its citizens could not believe that His Highness was no longer there as they joined the long funeral procession of writers, actors, theater people, and nobility. The "Old Meininger" talked of the past and of their colleagues, no longer living: of Weilenbeck, Barthel, Prasch, Teller, Kainz, and especially Chronegk. Now they were burying the last German prince who had stood in the Hall of Mirrors at the founding of a united Germany. As they came down the steep hill past the Jewish cemetery where Chronegk's sarcophagus stood, they told each other that this was the end of an era. They did not know how right they were until they came to the Hotel Sächsicher-Hof to wait for trains to Berlin, or Munich, or Dresden. There an army officer waited with the announcement that the Grand Duke Franz Ferdinand and his wife had been assassinated that morning in Sarajevo.

The war put an end to the court—and, of course, to the court theater as such. When the Meiningen theater opened again, it was as a *Landestheater*, a theater for the people of the land. But during the reign of Georg II, it had always been that. He had proclaimed it over the entrance to the theater: FOR THE PLEASURE AND ELEVATION OF THE PEOPLE. And he had shown it in every action of his life as ruling duke.

---

* When he did return to directing for one last time, in 1912, he also returned to sketching costumes. See his drawing for *Caesar and Cleopatra*, Fig. 11, p. 109, above.

APPENDIXES

APPENDIX A

THE GUEST APPEARANCES OF THE MEININGER, 1874-1890

1. Dates of Appearances and Names of Theaters

Date	Theater	City
1874		
May 1-June 16	Friedrich-Wilhelmstädtisches Theater	Berlin
1875		
April 16-June 15	Friedrich-Wilhelmstädtisches Theater	Berlin
Sept. 25-Oct. 31	Theater an der Wien	Vienna
Nov. 3-Nov. 19	Deutsches Theater	Budapest
1876		
May 1-June 16	Friedrich-Wilhelmstädtisches Theater	Berlin
Sept. 16-Oct. 10	Königliches Hoftheater in der Neustadt	Dresden
Oct. 15-Nov. 16	Lobetheater	Breslau
1877		
May 1-June 10	Stadttheater	Cologne
June 15-July 8	Altes Stadttheater	Frankfurt
Sept. 20-Oct. 15	Residenztheater	Dresden
Oct. 18-Nov. 25	Stadttheater	Breslau
1878		
May 1-June 15	Friedrich-Wilhelmstädtisches Theater	Berlin
June 20-July 9	Altes Stadttheater	Frankfurt
Sept. 15-Oct. 11	Neustädter Theater	Prague
Oct. 15-Nov. 15	Altes Stadttheater	Leipzig
Nov. 18-Dec. 19	Lobetheater	Breslau
1879		
May 1-June 3	Stadttheater	Cologne
June 7-July 15	Stadttheater	Hamburg
Sept. 10-Oct. 10	Neustädter Theater	Prague
Oct. 15-Nov. 23	Ringtheater	Vienna
Nov. 26-Dec. 18	Deutsches Theater	Budapest
1880		
May 4-June 11	Grosse Schouwburg Theater	Amsterdam
June 15-Aug. 1	Stadttheater	Düsseldorf
Sept. 15-Oct. 24	Carola-Theater	Leipzig
Oct. 29-Nov. 29	Stadttheater	Graz

191

Date	Theater	City
1881		
April 28-May 23	Stadttheater	Bremen
May 30-July 23	Drury Lane Theatre	London
Sept. 1-Sept. 30	Stadttheater	Breslau
Oct. 4-Oct. 31	Deutsches Theater	Budapest
Nov. 3-Dec. 2	Stadttheater	Graz
1882		
April 22-May 31	Friedrich-Wilhelmstädtisches Theater	Berlin
June 3-July 1	Stadttheater	Nürnberg
July 4-July 24	Carola-Theater	Leipzig
Sept. 7-Oct. 15	Victoria-Theater	Berlin
Oct. 18-Nov. 19	Lobetheater	Breslau
Nov. 22-Dec. 18	Residenztheater	Dresden
1883		
April 4-April 29	Stadttheater	Barmen
May 2-May 29	Stadttheater	Bremen
June 1-June 27	Stadttheater	Magdeburg
July 1-July 31	Königliches Theater am Gärtnerplatz	Munich
Sept. 15-Oct. 9	Neustädter Theater	Prague
Oct. 13-Nov. 15	Carltheater	Vienna
Nov. 18-Dec. 18	Residenztheater	Dresden
1884		
April 20-May 15	Stadttheater	Mainz
May 18-June 15	Stadttheater	Strassburg (Baden-Baden, Metz)
June 17-July 14	Stadttheater	Basel
Aug. 31-Oct. 12	Victoria-Theater	Berlin
Oct. 15-Nov. 17	Lobetheater	Breslau
Nov. 19-Dec. 18	Residenztheater	Dresden
1885		
Feb. 22-March 27	Imperial Alexandra Theater	St. Petersburg
April 6-May 3	Lentowsky Theater	Moscow
May 8-May 29	Imperial Grobes Theater	Warsaw
June 2-June 30	Stadttheater	Königsberg
Oct. 1-Oct. 28	Stadttheater	Graz
Nov. 1-Nov. 29	Politeama Rossetti	Trieste
1886		
April 8-May 2	Stadttheater	Barmen
May 5-May 31	Stadttheater	Mainz
June 2-July 4	Stadttheater	Düsseldorf
1887		
Feb. 1-April 4	Victoria-Theater	Berlin
April 10-May 10	Stadttheater	Strassburg
May 14-June 28	Stadttheater	Basel
July 4-July 31	Königliches Theater am Gärtnerplatz	Munich
Oct. 10-Nov. 12	Lobetheater	Breslau
Nov. 16-Dec. 19	Residenztheater	Dresden
1888		
April 1-April 29	Theater Royal	Antwerp
May 2-May 31	Stads Schouwburg	Rotterdam
June 2-July 2	Théâtre Royale de la Monnaie	Brussels
Sept. 9-Sept. 26	Stadttheater	Graz

The Meininger's Guest Appearances

Date	Theater	City
Sept. 30-Oct. 29	Deutsches Theater	Budapest
Nov. 1-Nov. 27	Königliches Deutsches Theater	Prague
Dec. 1-Jan. 1	Carola-Theater	Leipzig
1889		
Feb. 19-Feb. 20	Herzogliches Hoftheater	Gotha
April 2-April 29	Stadttheater	Stettin
May 2-May 31	Casino Theater	Copenhagen
June 3-July 2	Svenska Theater	Stockholm
Sept. 21-Oct. 22	Lobetheater	Breslau
Oct. 25-Nov. 29	Carola-Theater	Leipzig
1890		
March 2-April 4	Imperial Alexandra Theater	St. Petersburg
April 14-May 11	Korsch Theater	Moscow
May 16-May 29	State Theater	Kiev
June 1-July 1	State Theater	Odessa

SOURCE: Paul Richard, *Chronik Sämmtlicher Gastspiele des Herzoglich Sachsen-Meiningen'schen Hoftheaters während der Jahre 1874-1890* (Leipzig, 1891), n.p.

2. Number of Performances in Each City in Each Year

City	1874	1875	1876	1877	1878	1879	1880	1881	1882	1883	1884	1885	1886	1887	1888	1889	1890
Berlin	47	60	48	—	46	40	—	78	—	43	—	—	63	—	—	—	—
Vienna	—	37	—	—	—	—	—	—	—	35	—	—	—	—	—	—	—
Budapest	—	17	—	—	—	29	—	21	—	—	—	—	30	—	—	—	—
Dresden	—	—	—	30	—	23	—	21	30	30	29	—	—	33	—	—	—
Breslau	—	—	25	26	32	34	31	33	—	—	34	—	35	—	—	—	—
Cologne	—	33	39	41	—	—	—	—	—	—	—	—	—	—	—	—	—
Frankfurt/Main	—	—	41	24	—	—	—	—	—	—	—	—	—	—	—	—	—
Prague	—	—	24	20	31	—	—	25	25	—	—	—	27	31	—	—	—
Leipzig	—	—	32	31	40	—	—	21	—	—	—	—	31	35	—	—	—
Hamburg	—	—	—	—	39	—	—	—	—	—	—	—	—	—	—	—	—
Amsterdam	—	—	—	—	39	—	—	—	—	—	—	—	—	—	—	—	—
Duesseldorf	—	—	—	—	48	32	—	—	—	—	—	—	—	—	—	—	—
Graz	—	—	—	—	32	—	—	28	—	34	—	18	—	—	—	—	—
Bremen	—	—	—	—	30	—	—	—	—	24	—	—	—	—	—	—	—
London	—	—	—	—	26	—	—	—	—	—	—	—	—	—	—	—	—
Nuernberg	—	—	—	—	56	29	—	—	—	—	—	—	—	—	—	—	—
Barmen	—	—	—	—	—	26	—	—	—	24	—	—	—	—	—	—	—
Magdeburg	—	—	—	—	—	27	—	—	—	—	—	—	—	—	—	—	—
Munich	—	—	—	—	—	31	—	—	28	—	—	—	—	—	—	—	—
Mainz	—	—	—	—	—	—	—	—	28	28	—	—	—	—	—	—	—
Strasbourg, Baden, Metz	—	—	—	—	—	—	—	—	34	—	—	—	31	—	—	—	—
Basel	—	—	—	—	—	—	—	—	28	—	—	—	45	—	—	—	—
St. Petersburg	—	—	—	—	—	—	—	—	—	39	—	—	—	38	—	—	—
Moscow	—	—	—	—	—	—	—	—	—	29	—	—	—	28	—	—	—
Warsaw	—	—	—	—	—	—	—	—	—	24	—	—	—	—	—	—	—
Königsberg	—	—	—	—	—	—	—	—	—	29	—	—	—	—	—	—	—
Trieste	—	—	—	—	—	—	—	—	—	29	—	—	—	—	—	—	—
Antwerp	—	—	—	—	—	—	—	—	—	—	—	—	29	—	—	—	—
Rotterdam	—	—	—	—	—	—	—	—	—	—	—	—	30	—	—	—	—
Brussels	—	—	—	—	—	—	—	—	—	—	—	—	29	—	—	—	—
Gotha	—	—	—	—	—	—	—	—	—	—	—	—	2	—	—	—	—
Stettin	—	—	—	—	—	—	—	—	—	—	—	—	27	—	—	—	—
Copenhagen	—	—	—	—	—	—	—	—	—	—	—	—	—	30	—	—	—
Stockholm	—	—	—	—	—	—	—	—	—	—	—	—	—	30	—	—	—
Kiev	—	—	—	—	—	—	—	—	—	—	—	—	—	—	14	—	—
Odessa	—	—	—	—	—	—	—	—	—	—	—	—	—	—	30	—	—
Number Of Performances During Each Year	**47**	**114**	**106**	**130**	**157**	**167**	**159**	**172**	**182**	**202**	**196**	**178**	**86**	**235**	**194**	**156**	**110**

Number of Performances in the Individual Cities

Berlin	385 in 8 Appearances
Breslau	269 in 8 Appearances
Dresden	164 in 6 Appearances
Leipzig	159 in 5 Appearances
Vienna	112 in 3 Appearances
Prague	110 in 4 Appearances
Graz	108 in 4 Appearances
Budapest	99 in 4 Appearances
Duesseldorf	82 in 2 Appearances
St. Petersburg	77 in 2 Appearances
Cologne	75 in 2 Appearances
Basel	73 in 2 Appearances
Strasbourg	65 in 2 Appearances
Munich	59 in 2 Appearances
Moscow	57 in 2 Appearances
London	56 in 1 Appearance
Mainz	56 in 2 Appearances
Bremen	54 in 2 Appearances
Barmen	50 in 2 Appearances
Frankfurt/Main	44 in 2 Appearances
Hamburg	39 in 1 Appearance
Amsterdam	39 in 1 Appearance
Rotterdam	30 in 1 Appearance
Copenhagen	30 in 1 Appearance
Stockholm	30 in 1 Appearance
Odessa	30 in 1 Appearance
Nuernberg	29 in 1 Appearance
Königsberg	29 in 1 Appearance
Trieste	29 in 1 Appearance
Antwerp	29 in 1 Appearance
Brussels	29 in 1 Appearance
Magdeburg	27 in 1 Appearance
Stettin	27 in 1 Appearance
Warsaw	24 in 1 Appearance
Kiev	14 in 1 Appearance
Gotha	2 in 1 Appearance
	2591 in 81 Appearances

Total number of performances during each year: 2591

SOURCE: Same as Table I, p. 7.

3. Number of Performances of Each Play in Each City

City	Julius Caesar	Pope Sixtus V	Twelfth Night	Massacre of St. Bartholomew	Between the Battles	Imaginary Invalid	Merchant of Venice	Battle of Arminius	Esther	The Learned Ladies	Fiesko	Kathy of Heilbronn	Hereditary Forester	William Tell	The Pretenders	Macbeth	The Huntsmen	The Robbers	Prince of Homburg	The Winter's Tale	The Ancestress	Wallenstein's Camp	Iphigenia in Tauris	Preziosa	Taming of the Shrew	Piccolomini	Wallenstein's Death	The Witch	Lydia	The Crucifix Carver	Maria Stuart	Miss Sara Sampson	Bride of Messina	Marino Faliero	The Maid of Orleans	The Great Galeoto	Alexandra	Ghosts	Rose of Tyburn	Frau Lucrezia	's Nuliel
Berlin	52	4	6	11	6	11	5	15	15	10	29	16	2	21	7	5	—	13	10	27	6	24	1	6	1	24	21	13	—	—	9	—	—	3	3	—	—	—	—	—	—
Vienna	16	—	6	7	—	1	5	17	15	3	—	2	—	8	—	5	—	5	2	10	10	6	6	—	6	6	6	7	7	—	3	—	—	3	—	5	3	—	—	2	—
Budapest	9	—	9	2	1	—	2	4	6	3	5	4	—	10	8	—	—	2	4	10	4	7	4	4	—	8	6	10	5	—	3	—	—	2	5	5	2	1	2	—	—
Dresden	10	—	7	2	—	6	6	10	10	3	5	10	—	7	—	—	—	4	4	10	6	7	3	3	6	8	8	10	4	—	8	—	—	—	13	—	—	1	—	—	—
Breslau	35	—	20	11	5	12	8	8	10	3	9	10	—	19	—	5	2	8	4	17	7	16	4	8	9	12	10	—	—	—	10	—	2	2	14	—	—	—	—	—	—
Cologne	14	—	5	3	1	3	3	10	3	3	12	6	—	12	—	—	—	5	4	9	4	7	3	3	6	7	7	3	—	—	—	—	3	—	4	—	—	—	—	—	—
Frankfurt/Main	8	—	5	2	—	3	3	4	3	1	4	4	—	3	—	—	—	5	5	7	6	6	—	3	3	6	6	—	—	—	4	—	—	3	3	—	—	—	2	—	—
Prague	10	—	5	3	2	2	4	4	3	—	4	7	—	11	—	5	—	8	5	14	5	8	2	5	2	6	6	—	2	—	3	—	—	1	5	—	—	—	—	—	—
Leipzig	19	—	10	2	1	4	6	8	7	2	12	5	—	5	—	—	—	8	3	11	5	5	1	2	2	7	5	—	—	—	3	—	—	—	11	—	—	—	—	—	—
Hamburg	4	—	8	7	2	2	4	8	2	2	5	4	—	7	—	—	—	4	5	5	5	8	2	5	2	6	6	—	—	2	—	—	—	—	—	—	—	—	—	—	—
Amsterdam	6	—	4	3	—	—	3	5	3	3	4	5	—	5	—	—	—	4	3	9	5	3	1	2	—	6	6	3	2	2	4	—	—	2	10	3	—	—	—	—	—
Duesseldorf	11	—	3	2	—	—	3	6	2	2	4	5	—	4	—	—	—	3	2	5	3	8	1	3	3	7	6	3	4	1	4	—	2	2	9	—	—	—	—	2	—
Graz	7	—	6	3	1	1	2	4	3	—	5	5	—	13	—	—	—	3	2	11	6	2	—	2	3	5	5	4	2	—	5	—	—	2	5	—	—	—	2	—	—
Bremen	7	—	4	1	—	—	2	4	2	2	6	3	—	8	—	—	—	3	1	6	6	2	—	2	2	6	6	1	4	2	4	—	—	1	6	—	—	—	2	—	—
London	16	—	2	—	—	—	4	—	—	—	5	3	—	4	—	—	—	2	1	7	—	3	—	—	3	3	2	—	1	—	3	—	—	—	5	—	—	—	1	—	—
Nürnberg	6	—	3	—	—	2	—	4	2	—	3	3	—	5	—	—	—	2	2	5	4	4	—	2	2	4	4	2	2	—	3	—	—	—	—	—	—	—	—	—	—
Barmen	6	—	3	3	—	—	2	6	—	2	3	3	—	5	—	—	—	—	2	6	4	2	2	3	—	6	6	—	—	—	4	—	—	2	6	—	—	—	—	—	—
Magdeburg	4	—	2	2	—	2	4	4	2	—	3	3	—	3	—	—	—	2	2	4	1	3	2	—	2	4	4	—	—	—	4	—	2	2	7	—	—	—	—	—	—
Munich	7	—	3	1	1	2	4	8	4	2	3	3	—	4	—	—	—	2	2	6	5	6	6	2	2	7	7	—	—	—	4	—	—	—	6	—	—	—	—	—	—
Mainz	7	—	3	2	1	2	4	7	3	2	3	3	—	4	—	—	—	2	3	4	2	3	3	3	2	6	6	2	3	—	4	—	1	2	5	—	—	—	—	—	—
Strasbourg, Baden, Metz	6	—	4	3	—	1	3	4	3	—	3	3	—	3	—	—	—	3	4	6	3	6	—	2	2	6	6	2	4	2	3	—	2	—	7	—	—	—	—	—	—
Basel	10	—	1	1	—	—	4	4	3	2	5	2	—	9	—	—	—	3	3	5	2	4	—	2	—	6	6	2	4	—	4	—	—	1	4	—	—	1	—	—	—
St. Petersburg	12	—	5	3	—	—	3	3	—	—	2	1	1	6	—	—	—	2	—	4	2	7	1	2	—	7	7	—	3	—	5	—	2	—	9	—	—	—	2	—	—
Moscow	7	—	3	—	—	—	—	—	—	—	2	—	—	6	—	—	—	—	—	3	1	6	—	—	—	6	5	2	—	—	4	—	—	—	5	—	—	—	1	—	—
Warsaw	4	—	1	—	—	1	1	—	—	—	1	1	—	4	—	—	—	2	—	6	—	6	—	—	—	3	3	—	—	—	4	—	—	—	—	—	—	—	—	—	—
Königsberg	4	—	2	2	—	2	2	—	2	—	2	—	—	4	—	—	—	—	1	7	1	3	—	—	—	4	3	—	—	—	3	—	—	—	—	—	—	—	—	—	—
Trieste	4	—	1	—	—	—	3	—	—	—	3	—	—	3	3	—	—	—	—	4	—	3	—	—	—	3	3	—	—	—	3	—	—	—	7	—	—	—	—	—	—
Antwerp	3	—	3	—	—	—	3	—	1	—	2	—	—	2	2	—	—	—	—	3	—	3	1	—	—	4	4	—	—	—	4	—	—	—	6	—	—	—	2	—	—
Rotterdam	3	—	2	1	—	—	4	—	—	—	1	—	—	2	2	—	—	2	—	—	1	2	—	—	—	3	3	—	—	—	4	—	—	—	5	—	—	—	—	—	—
Brussels	3	—	1	2	—	1	—	—	—	—	—	—	—	3	—	—	—	1	—	2	2	3	—	—	—	3	2	—	1	—	—	—	—	—	—	—	—	—	—	—	—
Gotha	1	—	1	—	—	—	—	—	1	1	1	—	—	—	—	—	—	—	—	—	—	—	—	1	—	2	1	—	2	—	—	—	—	—	—	—	—	—	—	—	—
Stettin	4	—	3	1	—	2	3	—	1	2	1	—	—	—	—	—	—	3	—	4	—	3	—	—	—	3	3	2	—	—	4	—	—	—	5	6	—	—	—	—	1
Copenhagen	3	—	3	1	—	—	1	—	1	—	1	—	—	3	2	—	—	—	—	3	3	4	—	—	—	4	2	—	2	—	4	—	—	—	6	7	—	—	—	—	—
Stockholm	2	—	2	—	—	1	4	—	—	—	1	—	—	2	1	—	—	1	—	2	—	3	—	3	—	3	3	1	2	—	3	—	—	2	5	—	—	—	—	—	—
Kiev	2	—	1	2	—	1	4	—	1	1	1	—	—	—	—	—	—	3	—	2	—	4	—	1	3	3	3	—	1	2	—	—	—	2	7	—	—	—	—	—	—
Odessa	1	—	3	—	—	—	2	—	—	—	2	—	—	—	—	—	—	—	—	3	—	2	—	—	—	4	3	—	2	—	—	—	—	2	4	—	—	—	—	—	1
Total	**330**	**4**	**132**	**85**	**21**	**83**	**94**	**101**	**74**	**29**	**152**	**83**	**2**	**223**	**7**	**10**	**2**	**104**	**38**	**233**	**79**	**176**	**14**	**54**	**21**	**161**	**140**	**56**	**25**	**11**	**89**	**7**	**11**	**19**	**194**	**7**	**5**	**2**	**5**	**2**	**2**

SOURCE: Same as Table 1, p. 7.

APPENDIX B

GEORG II AS DIRECTOR: DOCUMENTS

1. *Letters to Carl von Stein, January 1864, and Friedrich Bodenstedt, February 1867*

LETTER TO VON STEIN

Concerning the opera, *Margarete [Faust]*, allow me to make some observations that I wish you to refer to the stage manager.

1. The appearance of Margarete in the first act: her left arm rests on a little table with slender legs. From a distance, the arm seems to be floating on air. It would be better if this little table were covered with the dark blue cloth that I presented to the property room. If this were done, the effect would be more attractive.

2. Crowd scene: it is a pity that at the performance the business of placing the actors at the tables as the director ordered in rehearsal before the first performance was omitted. In that manner the group on the left, especially, would attract the attention of the audience.

3. The first entrance of Margarete: she would appear more maidenly if she did not remain standing near Faust, but crossed the stage without delay. Her solo is so short that this is practical. Faust must walk backwards before her, and then move away from her up to the wings.

4. Scene with the jewel casket: a more beautiful case, and within it a mirror to be taken out. In place of a gentleman's golden chain, a lady's necklace—such a one is in the property room.

5. Moonlight: this must begin the very moment that Mephisto orders Nature "to breath voluptuousness"—in Berlin, if I remember correctly, a magical moonlight spell suffused the landscape. If there are some blue silk lampshades available, these could be drawn in front of the lamps to produce a blue luster, which must also be visible in the background.

I believe that the garden scene would be more effective if Margarete's house were standing back behind the next border and the light of the moon came from the other side. Then not only would it strike the walls of the house, but more importantly, Margarete's face would not be constantly in the shadow, as is now the case.

6. The arrangement of the war scene is certainly a horror—at least, to my taste. The much discussed goose step is quite out of place here. I think it would be more effective to alter the whole scene. As it is now, one gets the idea that the medieval soldiers who sing in the Soldiers' Chorus are modern soldiers. Let sixteen soldiers be put in brown uniforms (Wallenstein) and the singers in medieval battle apparel of different kinds, using coats of armor and both open-faced and spiked helmets. Three tall underofficers should be in sets of armor from the property room. One might look like Dr. Locher when he played Götz [hero of Goethe's *Götz von Berlichingen*, 1773].

At the beginning of the scene before the soldiers appear, women and children should be seen running across the stage, in and out, expressing joyful expectation. Then the soldiers appear, singing; the women and children run ahead of them, gathering and grouping on both sides of the stage. The singing warriors march in quickly to martial tempo, but not in rank and file; instead, they enter in a crowd with joyful gestures—by this, I mean swinging weapons, and here and there, hats. The soldiers, joined by the three knights, move to the right side of the stage and stand so closely together that the audience can see past them to the left. After this crowd has arranged itself, the sixteen soldiers march in. The leader himself stops near the wings and commands: "Halt!" "Front!" (softly) when the last row of the company has entered.

This group, in two ranks, must march in so that the left group stands somewhat to the rear of those at the right. (See drawing.) After the soldiers, who enter with their lances up, stand at ease, they bring their lances "to foot." In this way, they move so that they open ranks a little.

By this means the scene would become an excellent one. That it is possible to do this can hardly be doubted—all the more so, since now there is only a chorus rehearsal. The warrior chorus could be provided with battle-axes, maces, and the like. Such weapons as the two-handed sword can be obtained from the Henneberger collection—shields and spears, too. The stage manager should direct the entrances from behind the scene. It would be best if he were costumed as a knight *à la* Götz. If the soldiers stood in the hallway in front of the property room before the scene began, they could march on stage with a "right face," while the Soldiers' Chorus marched on with a "left face."

7. Mephisto ought not to be compelled to stand beside the organ in order to sing; he should be able to project the song even if the organ is on the opposite side of the stage. Then the praying people, instead of kneeling with their faces to the side altar where Margarete is kneeling, could be turned in the opposite direction and always see the choirmaster merely by turning their heads. They should enter from the opposite side and kneel, if possible, farther in the background. In this scene the stage is lighted too brightly. There is enough light if the audience can see Margarete's features clearly. If the stage is dim, all the better. If the praying congregation is arranged as I suggest, the members would not observe the shocking expression of Gretchen and not be aware when she falls into a faint. She would then lie there unnoticed by the congregation; this would make a stronger impression on the audience.

8. The prison scene: a flat mattress covered with straw would be better than the present wooden-plank bed. The mattress can be dragged off, leaving the straw lying there, so that it will not disturb the last scene, the apotheosis. With our present means, this last scene is not successful.

9. The apotheosis: the group in the background may be too symmetrical. The audience cannot see the angel's wings because they are too white. If they were painted in dark rainbow colors, they would stand out from the background.[1]

LETTER TO BODENSTEDT

Can you not arrange a special correspondence in the local daily newspaper about the *Caesar* performance and in it explain what the three new sets really represent? The Weimar scene painter still has the Visconti sketch.[2] I'll have to send for it, because in it are named the various buildings of the Roman Forum. The local public must be prepared for the next performance of *Caesar*.

First set: the Capitol as seen from the Forum. The substructure of the middle building still stands today, as does the tower. Above to the right there stands the temple of Zeus Capitolinis. The Via Sacra leads under the outside staircase to an arch on the left and down to the left side of the Capitoline middle building.

Second set: legislative assembly of Pompey, where the Senate sat in conference in the year of Caesar's death because the Senators' Assembly Hall in the Forum had been burned during the civil wars. In the foreground is an open space with the Curia opening into it. The assemblies of the Senate take place outside before the people. Caesar's throne stands between the curial benches, in front of which is the recently restored statue of Pompey. This statue is a copy of the one in Rome, which was excavated in the Curia of Pompey and is therefore the one that stood in the Curia. The original is marble, over three feet high. . . .[3] An addition to Shakespeare's text: "Cursed Casca, what are you doing?" and "Brothers, help!" according to Plutarch. Caesar grasps Casca by the arm and wounds him with a stylus. (Caesar's costume according to the Roman authors.) (Make-up of Caesar and Brutus from coins.)

Third setting for the Roman Forum (the designation of the building according to Visconti drawings). Place the Rostrum with the front facing the Curia, the narrow side to the crowd. (The byplay of the crowd is produced through the actors and the extras.)

Fourth and fifth acts: the javelins, weapons invented for use against Pyrrhus, with which the Romans won their victories, just as Prussians with their needle-guns, etc., etc.[4]

2. Discussions with Actors, 1872

The duke expected the directors and the actors to pay the strictest attention to the remarks he made in the theater or conveyed through the baroness. The stage directors were invited to visit him in the castle and make any objections to his instructions. The actors were encouraged to do the same in the theater. When this happened, he usually called the actor over to him and in a few swift lines sketched the scene as he saw it, at the same time explaining his reasons. But he would listen to the actors' objections and frequently acted on them, as can be seen from Ludwig Barnay's account of two incidents during the rehearsals of *Hamlet* in 1872.

The first scene of the Watch with its extraordinarily effective appearance of the ghost was over, and the court was about to enter the royal hall. Already formed behind the wings was a festive procession, and the entrance of the king was to be accompanied by a mighty fanfare. As the music sounded, the call of "Halt" was heard from the auditorium. Scarcely had the word sounded when all the actors standing about whispered to each other, "His Highness!" Intendant Grabowsky, the stage director Chronegk, the stage manager, the orchestra conductor—all hurried to the footlights to hear the duke's command. Actors, extras, stage crew, all stuck their heads out of the wings anxious to hear what would be called from the auditorium. The duke began to speak. . . . It was incorrect to have fanfares sounded at this place; one must have a solemn Danish march here. Also it was wrong that Hamlet and the king enter together; each must come from an opposite side. Hamlet has just come home. Had they already spoken, then the speech of the king in which he says he has married the queen is superfluous. Grabowsky greeted each remark with a bow and a stereotyped, "At your command, Highness!" and started at once to prepare everything as the duke had commanded.

During this speech of the duke's, I was standing in the wings eagerly listening and becoming more excited with every word, for I believed that something impossible was being planned. Imprudent hothead that I was in those days and completely immersed in my role of Hamlet, the crown prince of Denmark forgot completely that he was speaking to the ruling duke of Meiningen, who was giving these dramatic hints. I ran out onto the stage and said loudly, "But that's wrong; it's nonsense!" Scarcely had I reached the ramp and said these words when I saw a ring of frightened eyes staring at me, and I saw on the faces around me the enormity of what I had said. I myself was terrified by then, but I could not undo what I had done. Everyone listened breathlessly for what the duke would say. After a little pause, the duke's voice came out of the darkness. "Well, the German language is not so poor. What do you mean that it's nonsense, Herr Barnay?"

Now I stammered out my reasoning. Hamlet's father has been dead two months, as we know from the soliloquy, "Oh, that this too too solid flesh." That could not have been spoken if Hamlet had just returned home. This is merely the *official* announcement that the king slyly gives in the presence of Hamlet because he knows that the prince would never embarrass his mother in front of the court. The king must enter with Hamlet.

An unearthly stillness followed my words. Then after a long silence, the duke said, "Herr Grabowsky, prepare the scene as Herr Barnay has described it. He is right, and I am wrong."

A second incident came in the scene where Hamlet orders the player to prove his art by "giving the pathetic speech of Aeneas to Dido." Hamlet speaks the first lines and then says, "Proceed you." I spoke the lines gropingly, slowly, quoting as I thought the prince would do, seeking the lines out of his memory and correcting himself with the words, "'Tis not so; it begins with Pyrrhus." The duke's voice interrupted me, "I think, Herr Barnay, that this speech cannot be spoken so lightly, so incidentally, so *parlando*, but it must be spoken very beautifully." "Your Highness," I replied, "the prince is only an amateur, a patron of the arts, not himself an artist; a dilettante, not an actor." "Yes, but Polonius praises the speech extraordinarily, calls it well spoken with good grace and tone."

Then without thinking and wishing only to defend my point of view, I said hastily, "Yes, Your Highness, but Polonius is a courtier and such people find everything the prince does wonderful." A hearty loud laugh out of the darkness was my only answer.[5]

3. *Instructions for the Set for 'Fiesko,' 1874*

A good example of the duke's methods appears in his instructions to Max Brückner concerning the *Fiesko* sets. On December 22, 1874, he returned the sketches to Brückner and directed him "to reconsider the designs with the following remarks in mind":

1. The street L is only 4' wide. It would be advisable to widen it so that Fiesko carrying the body of his wife and the crowd can exit here. Two exits are needed on the left. Both are possible if the palace of Doria is widened to the curtain and the door placed there. . . . I have had the house of Duke Albrecht placed diagonally up to the curtain, where it looks good. The door can be covered partly by the front curtain. Sianette enters here and Doria enters and exits here.

2. The Thomas Gate could stand a little more on the diagonal. Then the gate opening could be wider. . . . I am afraid that those on the side of the auditorium will see too little of the backdrop and the death of Fiesko (which takes place on the other side of the quay) if the gate opening is not wider than 10'—it must be at least 12' wide.

3. The lions bearing the columns on the church must be shown lying down and can project a little more.

4. If the room between Doria's palace and the first wing of the church is widened, the profile of the church receding into the wings on the right will have to be widened.

5. The garden wall R could be made practicable in front of the first wing and could be pushed up (like Doria's palace) as far as the front curtain. The tree would then come forward too.

6. At the indicated spot between the first and second wing, the fountain on two steps, practicable. The fountain so: [sketch] consists of four pieces, foreview and innerview. The knight's statue in the so-called gothic armor to be fastened between the two long walls of the fountain trough. The side walls to be painted in perspective.

7. In the storming of the gate scene, a door with three steps leading to the guard room. The door: 3½' higher than a man's height. At this door a fierce fight between the guard and the conspirators will take place while the door to the street is torn down.

8. The wooden gate should be broken in with little pieces of wood hanging to the iron hinges. You may therefore have to make some kind of contrivance so that the wooden door crashes violently. It would really be enough if a canvas flat fell and *at the same time* beams from right, left, and above. These beams must be made of canvas sacking and filled with wool or bran. They must be long enough so that the whole thing seems plausible. I would recommend that at first only part of the door be broken in and the fight with the defenders, who are standing on the other side [downstage], can take place through the small opening.

9. The moon must not be visible because it is too hard to give the proper direction with the electric light. The moon must be thought to be high above. You must be very careful of the cut-outs (gauze insets) on the water; as they recede they must become very small.

10. The wings on the right don't seem to cover properly, but the sketch may be deceiving.

11. The fruit-shop wing in *The Merchant of Venice* will have to be practicable, so it will not do here as the second wing L.

12. I believe it will be possible to have a 2' high parallel on this side of the gate, diagonal to the quay, and on that to have a little wall 1' high, so that Fiesko will fall three feet into the water. The parallel must be covered with canvas painted in perspective with paving stones.

13. You must paint, too, the little skiff, which moves on rollers when Verrina arrives on it. It must naturally be about 1 foot above the little wall and must consist of an outer and inner piece. It must be broad enough (sketch) so that three persons can sit in it, one behind the other, 1-2-3, namely Verrina and two boatmen. This whole contrivance requires room between the gate and the backdrop. I would recommend that at an early date you give Schaefer [the stage manager] instructions concerning which step units and parallels must be acquired, also how long and how wide the skiff must be. Also send Schaefer directions of what you wish for the elevation and the steps for the set in the "Orange Court."

With the highest regards, Duke Georg of Meiningen

If you don't understand this, please ask.[6]

4. Instructions for Improving a Performance, 1878

During the rehearsals the duke, sitting in the audience, interrupted the action on stage only when necessary, but he took careful notes on the changes he wanted made. These he discussed with his wife, who expanded them into a full set of instructions to be sent to the stage director, who was to put them into effect before the duke saw the next rehearsal. Following is such a set of instructions made after a rehearsal of *Der Prinz von Homburg*, with Josef Kainz, Leopold Teller, Joseph Nesper, Paul Richard, Hermann Nissen, Aloys Prasch, Marie Berg, and Adele Pauli in the leading roles.

1. Kainz is too well dressed. The duke wishes him to appear first without a sash; this, however, must be fitted with hooks, so that during the scene it can be quickly put on.

2. Kainz must do more with the wreath—it would be better if some branches lay near him on the bank—doesn't really need to be much.

3. Be very careful of Richard's pronunciation of *eu* and *au*, especially in such verses as "Und sich erst *heute* wieder atemlos," "Der ganze Flecken könnt *Feuer-auf*," [and] "Wie eine . . . *Haube auf*probieren."

4. When Richard wakes him, Kainz is too quickly wide awake. He must say the words, "indeed, love," as if still half-asleep, while he rubs his eyes. And the next three speeches, (1) "Quick, my helmet, my armor," (2) ". . . Heinz," (3) "yes . . . I think," *still drunk with sleep*. Then he must realize he is not in his own room; he becomes excited, wild, so, "Ho, Franz! That rascal was to have awakened me!" The acting here is really very poorly done. The longer Kainz is not fully awake, not clearly himself, not obviously oriented, the easier it will be for him to project the meaning of the scenes. I was not at all satisfied with that part—he must rub his eyes, or indicate in some way that he is not fully himself—he must look at Richard; then at the garden as he says, "Not to be, etc."

5. He must remain so after Richard's searching tone—at least until "Forgive! I know already! You know the beat."

6. After Richard's words, "Now, so speak," Kainz should make no pause for acting.

7. The great speech: "Raise high the wreath, etc., etc.," must be said with an

undertone of astonishment, indicating he does not grasp the situation—yes, not too loud and rising at the end.

8. The "What! to me? by my love—!" must be more meaningful.

9. As they exit, let Richard lay his arm over the prince's shoulder—naturally let the prince walk on the side of the public.

Scene 2

1. The notebook used here is not good; at least try to find a larger one. In this scene the prince tears a page to write on it, and the notebook seems to me ridiculously small. At the performance I saw some officers smiling at it.

2. I have already spoken with Frau Berg [the grand duchess]—here she must not be too tearful—at first, concerned, but composed. Historically, this grand duchess always traveled in the wars with the grand duke; therefore, battles are nothing new to her. Naturally she could not allow herself to be indifferent. At the very end of the scene, she might wipe away a tear, but she must not weep. Right here, I'd like to remark that the tiny handkerchiefs of the two leading ladies, which in their grief they roll in their hands, are a real torture. Such little handkerchiefs for general use were not the mode until recently; they were used by court belles or with the most formal dress, never on journeys. Frau Berg and Fräulein Pauli should have simple batiste handkerchiefs—in the second scene, with so much crying, those tiny "hankies" look silly.

3. Nesper should say, "Kamin will lead my dear Luise," not "Elisa" as it stands in the text. The first grand duchess, whom Kleist incorrectly shows to be still alive, was named Luise, something every Prussian knows today. (The second was named Dorothea.)

4. Teller makes the mistake in this scene of saying everything in a declamatory tone, not just the particulars of the battle plan. Please listen carefully, dear Director, and if you haven't already noticed this, you will do so. I have already marked with red in the promptbook the places that are *too declamatory*. The book I *shall send you*. Please keep it to yourself because of many remarks I have made during rehearsal. Be especially careful that Teller doesn't speak too fast, and that he pays close attention to his pronunciation of "a," which always sounds like "ae."

5. At the very end of the act Nesper must show more will, as if he had every right.

6. From the sight of the ring on, where Natalie recognizes the glove, Kainz must appear blessed, must be radiant—radiant when he says, "Then will he have the fanfares sounded"—radiant, radiant in his musing, radiant when the grand duke mentions him; in short, all through this part. He should speak the last sentence not too fast and give a lift to the word "Happiness." In general, he has spoken the lines very well. But when the other gentlemen do not enter into the action, eager and intent on the battle, the scene is nothing.

7. Nissen enters into the action here, in the Berlin scene, and in the 5th act most naturally.

II Act, 1st scene

GENERAL REMARKS: Who can take over Hellmuth's [Wilhelm Hellmuth-Bräm] role in a few days? [Gustav] Kober? Speak with him, for as soon as the rainy season comes, Hellmuth's arthritis may return. Have you given him my book?

Who could take over for Nesper? I consider Richard the best—so Nissen must quickly learn the part of Hohenzollern, and Richard that of the grand duke, whom he is very much like. "Foresight is the mother . . ."—well, you know.

1. In the battle scene the gentlemen speak their various sentiments too monotonously. I have made remarks thereon in the promptbook.

2. There is *much* too much shrieking.

2d scene

1. Heinz should bind a white cloth around his forehead; the black one is not now visible against his dark hair. He speaks too softly, should speak ringingly, but in the [tone] of the mood.

2. The grand duchess prepares well for her swoon. Even as Heinz speaks his last words, she must indicate that she feels faint and she must speak the sentence, "A ring too dearly sold, I like it not," tonelessly, not pathetically, but wounded.

3. Kainz must, especially at the beginning of this scene, make more pauses and speak as if crushed by unhappiness; for example, a pause as soon as he enters before he begins to speak. He enters and sees not only Natalie, but also the grand duchess. He takes Natalie's hand *silently* and does not speak until he lays it on his heart. Then speaks in a really *mezzo voce*.

4. "I will become the executor, etc." must be said in a manly way; to me it is too timid.

5. During Kober's account Frau Berg must never for a second forget to show the quality of blessedness that the grand duke praises. Also in the description of the battle, she may not appear more anxious; she knows now that nothing has happened to her husband. For Froban's death, sorrowfully thankful, a little weeping, but certainly no sobbing. It must not be a repetition of Heinz's account; the situation is completely different. The difference between the two situations is not now marked enough in Frau Berg's acting.

6. Fräulein Pauli in her embarrassment at the end of the act makes too dark a face—she must always remain lovingly embarrassed.

7. Kainz's last words, "O, Caesar, etc." must be just as fiery as before, but not too loud.

Act III, scene 1

1. At the beginning, Kainz really unsorrowful, unembarrassed, not downcast, completely trusting. On the other hand, Richard must show himself very downcast—looks at the prince sideways, shakes head, makes pauses, etc.

2. Kainz speaks too loud here, for example, at the words, "Because I stand," and many others. There are some little remarks in the promptbook—please read them, I have not enough time to write them all out.

Scene 2

1. The grand duchess must not forget to move to the window when she says, "In uncle's cabinet, I see a light."

2. When the grand duchess puts the scarf around Natalie, she must put it under her hair—Natalie herself in this situation cannot bother with it, but it does not look good when the hair is all pressed down by the scarf.

3. Fräulein Krause should participate in the scene only with her expression and should *pay attention and listen.*

4. Kainz is too loud in this scene. Read remarks in promptbook. Kainz really sweats a great deal. Could you tell him gently and delicately that he can discreetly wipe the sweat away when he feels it?

5. Frau Berg is least effective in this scene; she says everything in the same toneless voice. This scene concerns itself with the prince's life. She is not shaken enough by his sudden surprising cowardice.

IV Act, sc. 1

1. Nesper must guard against the allure and tone of a professional lover.

2. Fräulein Pauli must make a pause before she kneels, and another after she kneels and speaks again.

3. At *all* rehearsals work on the sealing [with wax] and writing in ink with *all* props. Nothing looks worse than that poorly done—especially when the sealing is done in haste and disorder. A little drop of sealing wax, for example, is so easily smeared. As a rule, hold the wax to the candle and then let it fall from there to the paper.

4. Fräulein Pauli must take notice of *all* the poet's annotations as she reads, etc.

Scene 2

1. Procure a chair only for here—little Gravenberg must not forget to cross over the stage to the chair, which will then be no longer needed.

2. In this scene observe the poet's *directions*, something that wasn't done in the last scene.

3. Kainz in the speech, "I will to him, who stands so worthy, etc.," must be noble, honorable, calm, and resolute, not rude or angry toward the grand duke. This speech must awaken respect for the prince.

4. Pauli's admonition, "Take this kiss," should be deeply felt, not, for heaven's sake, as in the last performance with a long pause after "take."

5. At the end, going with a farewell, turning to the prince, but still going willingly.

V Act, scene 1

1. Nesper should listen once to his little soliloquy, "If I were the Bey of Tunis," spoken by Werden, who is at the rehearsal anyway and speaks it charmingly.

2. Teller must be more animated in tone and movement.

3. In this scene especially, Nesper should be very careful of his high tones, which do not fit the character of the grand duke or Nesper's impressive appearance.

4. The duke has already written you about the silent playing of the officers.[7]

5. General Pronouncements on Staging, 1894-1899

Georg made a practice of writing detailed letters to the intendant after every performance. Paul Lindau, intendant from 1894 to 1899, published a number of these letters. Max Grube points out that although Lindau was an experienced theater writer and critic, stage management was new to him; thus the duke was forced to review for him the Meininger's long-held principles. It should be remembered that these letters were written some thirty years after the duke began his reforms. Everything seems to indicate that in the early years, Georg, the baroness, and Chronegk tried things out. If they worked, they used them. Still, it is valuable to read the duke's ideas on staging in his own words.

We should take into consideration in the composition of a stage picture that the middle of the scene does not correspond with the middle of the stage. If the composition proceeds from the geometric middle, two halves result. From this the danger follows that in the arrangement of groups, disposing them to the right and left will result in a somewhat symmetrical balance. This will appear wooden, stiff, and boring.

The charm of Japanese art rests on the avoidance of all symmetry. "L'ennui naquit un jour de l'uniformité," said Boileau about artistic creation in general. In plastic art, "uniformity," which the French aesthete pointed out as the mother of tedium, is called symmetry. The exception confirms the rule. A composition with the principal figure or the principal group centered and the subordinate figure or groups standing on each side at more or less regular intervals can be justified artistically on the stage, if one aspires to present a solemnly austere—one might even say ascetic—impression. The Sistine Madonna of Raphael is an example that comes readily to mind. Such a picture always has the character of serenity. But the principal requirement of the stage is to reveal the motion and impetuous progress of the action; therefore, in general, this arrangement is to be avoided, since it is stiff and hinders the impression of movement.

It is seldom good to have anything stand in the middle of the stage. It is practical to set movable or other scenery to one of the sides, naturally at a distance from the wings so that it can be easily seen by those sitting in the auditorium.

The actor should at no time stand in the middle of the stage directly in front of the prompt box, but should instead always stand a little to the right or the left of the prompter. The middle of the stage, reckoned as about as wide as the prompt box and extending from the footlights to the perspective in the background, should serve for the actor only as a passageway from right to left, or vice versa. He has no business there for any other reason. It is also best, if possible, to avoid having two persons standing at the same exact distance from the prompt box.

More attention should be paid to a pleasing relationship between the actors' positions and the set decorations. It is a widely current misconception in directing that in the relationship of the actor to the architecture, no attention need be paid to the perspective of the painted trees, buildings, etc.

It is true that some mistakes cannot be avoided when the living forms of the actors, unchangeable in size, become proportionately too large with every step backward into the sharp perspective of the painted settings. But if they can appear to diminish in size, then the disturbing effect will disappear. For example, an actor should not approach the scenery in the upstage wings so closely that the disproportion becomes striking. He should not—as one often sees—stand immediately in front of a painted house where a door reaches only up to his hips, where without stretching, he can look into a window on the second floor, and where if he raised his hand, he could touch the chimney.

The scenic pieces toward which the actor moves must always be approximately in the same proportion to a man as real ones would be. As an example, the temple in *Iphigenia in Tauris* should be placed toward the front of the stage, so that its tall columns rise upward to the flies and tower over the human figures. It does not matter if members of the audience cannot see the top of the temple building. Indeed, it is really more pleasing if they can see part of the entablature above the columns, the supporting beams, and a portion of the dome, with the remainder of the dome hidden in the greenery of the foliage borders.

The balcony of *Romeo and Juliet* is usually placed much too low. There is one disadvantage that in a really correct placement of the balcony, Juliet stands somewhat high, but that is less important than the customary mistake—that with a balcony of moderate height, there is always one disturbing thought: even if Romeo were not a particularly good gymnast, he could with only one leap reach his "inaccessible" sweetheart and fold her in his arms.

The actors must never lean against the painted scenery (columns and the like). If the movement is vigorous, the contact will shake the painted piece and any illusion is lost. Yet if the actor uses the necessary caution not to joggle the canvas scenery with his movements, this lack of freedom restricts his actions to the point where they are offensive in their rigidity.

Scenic pieces against which an actor may lean or upon which he can support himself (such as door frames and tree trunks) must be made of sturdy materials and must be solid (as indeed is becoming the usual practice in the better theaters).

With the simultaneous use of painted and three-dimensional objects on the stage, all possible care must be taken so that the differences in these materials are not readily apparent. The shading, for example, from real or artificial flowers and leaves to those that are openly painted must be so finely achieved that the audience can scarcely distinguish the painted from the real. (It is absolutely inartistic, even absurd, if, for example, on a rose bush the one rose that is to be plucked is the only three-dimensional one among many painted ones; or if one sees on the rear elevation in the workshop of *The Violin Maker of Cremona* a half-dozen painted violins, the real one seems to be much too large, almost the size of a viola.)

The attempts to bring the human figure into harmony with the architecture at the back of the stage—for example, using children in appropriate costumes and masks as laborers on the scaffolds of the fortress of Uri in *Tell* to represent adults working at a distance—cannot be said to be successful. A boy's figure is plainly quite different from an adult's. In addition, the blending of contours and the shading of hues that nature achieves by distance, and that can be reproduced by painting, are not attained by the living figures in the background. The living form shows a more sharply etched clarity than the painted surrounding, and the eyes of the viewer do not see working adults made small by distance, but little gnomelike creatures, dwarfs, with faces painted to look old. Borders made of cut strips painted blue to represent the sky (called in stage slang "ozone rags") and running crosswise above the stage must never be used. In scenes depicting country landscapes, trees with widely extending boughs may be employed. These extended arches can usually be used for town scenes, streets, and marketplaces, too. Sometimes the action presents a place in such a way that above the streets and squares garlands or banners, flags or pennants, can be stretched. If this is impractical and the sky must appear above the scene, even then cloud borders are preferable to the painted blue linen. There is no place in the artistically decorated set for this tediously ugly blue border.

At the first rehearsal of a new play with crowd scenes and numerous personnel, the director's hair usually stands on end. He almost despairs of the possibility of enlivening and molding the stiff, inflexible mass. A great help in solving this problem is to have the scenery up permanently from the very beginning. Any change in the setting during the rehearsals, such as hanging or shifting scenery or moving furniture, slows them terribly, upsets the nerves, and wearies and unnerves the actors.

In costume plays everything should be tested as early as possible with weapons, helmets, armor, swords, etc. Then during the play the actors will not be hindered in their actions by the unfamiliarity and ponderous weight of the weapons.

In these plays it is essential even before dress rehearsal, which should differ from the opening performance only in the absence of the public, that the artists should rehearse in costume—either the proper one, or, if this is not yet ready or must be kept fresh, in one of corresponding cut. For several rehearsals before the dress rehearsal, the actors must wear headdresses, cloaks, trains, etc., either exactly like or somewhat like those to be worn on opening night. The actor should encounter nothing unforeseen or surprising at the time of performance; he should be given the opportunity to make himself at home in the unfamiliar costume of the past. The viewers should not perceive in his entrance and actions that he is wearing a costume that a wardrobe man has just put on him; they should not be reminded of a costume ball or a masquerade.

Carriage and movement are influenced by different costumes and modes. In the costume of an earlier period, from ancient times to the Renaissance, an actor cannot assume our present manner of standing with heels together, the required stance in our society for both military man and civilian. This way of standing, heel to heel, seems to have come into universal use no earlier than the dance steps of the minuet. A leader of the mercenaries would not stand like an elegant abbot of the eighteenth century or like a modern second lieutenant with feet close together. The natural, correct, and most pleasing manner of standing in any costume up to the eighteenth century is straddle-legged, with one foot ahead of the other. A general rule is this: for the most part everything parallel on the stage is to be avoided. This is especially true in costume plays.

Spears, halberds, lances, etc., should never be carried in a straight upward position as are the muskets and swords of our present-day infantry and cavalry. In the handling of old weapons, discretion must prevail: they should not be held at the same distance from each other or in exact formation. Here they should be pulled together, there spread farther apart, and held not perpendicularly, but obliquely and crosswise.

Every helmet, except the antique, must be set so low on the forehead that only the muscles above the eyebrows are visible. The popular manner, placing the helmet at the back of the head and down on the neck, is the way of the tenor, but is not suitable for the theater. Our gentlemen in costume probably fear that if they wear their helmets properly, they will disarrange their curly locks; but we're not concerned with that.

It is a real mistake to place the actors in positions parallel to one another. If it is necessary to place groups parallel to the footlights, then a direct face-to-face position is not attractive; this is especially true when two actors of the same height stand parallel to the footlights. If the actor has to move from the right to the left, he should avoid moving directly across; that is not the best way on the stage. Instead he should move unobtrusively at an angle to break the straight line.

If three or more actors in a scene are on the stage at the same time, they should avoid above all else standing in a straight line. They should always stand at an angle. The distances between the individual actors should not be equal. If they stand at equal intervals, they will become uninteresting and as lifeless as figures on a chessboard. It is always attractive if the actor can unaffectedly touch a piece of furniture or some other suitable object on the stage. This gives the appearance of life and naturalness. If the stage has different levels—steps, hilly ground with rocks, and the like—the actor can effect a harmonious line by making his movements rhythmical. He should also, for example, when ascending a flight of stairs, avoid standing on one step with both feet at the same time. If he climbs down from an elevation and has to stop to say something or to make an observation, he should place one foot a little lower than the other. By so doing, his whole body gains in freedom and attractiveness. "One leg high" is the usual command from the director in this instance.

The management of masses on the stage demands special and different attention during rehearsal. There is hardly a theater capable of casting from its own company all the extras essential for a large crowd scene. Besides the members of the chorus and the so-called house supers, whom the really skillful and experienced actors might join, workers in even greater numbers must be drawn for the *komparserie* [supers], untrained masses for whom this is just extra work and for whom each rehearsal and each performance is paid at an agreed rate. In many cases one finds available among these people, who change often and whom the director cannot know, those who can be trained, who can understand what the director says, and who are not awkward in performances. But along with such people, there are many to whom nothing can be taught and whose appearance is very comical. Often they want to play in their own manner and can cause a great deal of harm. It is the business of the director and his stage manager to discover quickly the especially capable and the especially incapable, and to separate the sheep from the goats, so that the problematical ones can do no harm.

The extras should be divided into smaller groups, each of which is separately trained. Each of these groups should be led by a skilled, thoroughly trained actor or by a clever member of the chorus, who "covers" the others, and who therefore stands conspicuously in the foreground. To some extent, this leader must carry the responsibility of seeing that the subordinates entrusted to him obey the orders he gives. He himself is responsible to the director for such subordinates and must see to it that positions, movements, etc., will be produced on cue. These leaders receive partial scripts with cues, in which the directions are often only generally given by the author as "noise," "tumult," "murmurs," "cries," "shrieks," and the like; these the director has to put into words to be committed to memory by the performers. Such insertions must naturally be presented in different forms and must not be given simultaneously by all the groups in the same manner.

The leader of a group of walk-ons does not have a simple task. It is a regrettable error and one very harmful to artistic efforts when members of the company engaged as "actors" consider these roles valueless and unworthy of real artists, and try to avoid them whenever possible; or if they are required to play such parts, they make no effort to hide their disinclination.

In Meiningen all artists without exception are required to do duty as extras. (It was this practice that achieved the amazing effect at the first appearance of the

Meininger, for the genuine interplay of the crowd contrasted remarkably with the awkward stiffness and apathy of the walk-ons to which audiences had long been accustomed.)

The lack of beauty resulting from poor placement of individual artists in relation to one another is especially disturbing in crowd scenes. The principal charm of grouping lies in a beautiful line of actors' heads. Just as uniformity of carriage is to be avoided, absolute uniformity in the height of those placed next to each other is to be avoided. Should it happen that several of the same height must be placed together, then they should stand on different levels. Depending on the situation, some might kneel, some stand, some bend over, others remain erect. It works out very well if an irregular semicircle can be built around the person or the object on which the group's gaze is fixed.

The director must also ensure that all those standing nearest the audience, and therefore most prominent in the eyes of the audience, be placed and arranged so that their shoulders are not all at the same angle to the footlights. It should be impressed on every extra that he must alter his position if he notices he is standing in exactly the same position as his neighbor. In no well-composed picture would one find many figures standing together at the same height and in the same position. This order should be repeated to the actors and extras at almost every rehearsal of the mob scenes, because they always forget it.

The extras must be forcefully instructed not to look out into the audience. It is natural that they should do this; for many, "play-acting" is new and unusual, and they cannot refrain from satisfying their curiosity by looking into the dark auditorium.

Action that is not really attractive—for example, dragging off the dead and wounded—must be "covered" and thus be hidden as much as possible from the eyes of the audience. But this should not be done in such a way that a thick and impenetrable wall of men hides the action; that is ridiculous. The masking should be somewhat spotty; the viewer should not see everything that is happening, but he should see enough so that he can surmise what the action is all about.

To give the impression that a very large crowd of people is on the stage, groups should be arranged so that those standing on the edge of the group extend into the wings. From no place in the auditorium should anyone see the edge of the crowd. To the members of the audience it should be believable that still more people are thronging farther offstage.[8]

TWO ACCOUNTS OF THE MEININGER ON TOUR

1. V. I. Nemirovich-Danchenko's Account of a Performance in St. Petersburg, 1885

When the Meininger appeared in Russia in 1885, most of the criticism, both positive and negative, centered on the new method of staging, but Vladimir Ivanovich Nemirovich-Danchenko, later co-founder of the Moscow Art Theater, attacked the interpretation of *Julius Caesar* in an open letter to the editors of the newspaper *Theater and Life*. This letter, published in a Moscow paper in March, was intended to forewarn the audiences of that city of the shortcomings of a production that was to be seen there in April.

Allow me by means of your newspaper to express several observations that may in some ways be helpful to those who wish to determine more exactly the significance of the Meiningen troupe. Certainly no one would disagree that the outward appearance of the *Julius Caesar* production by the Meiningen company is astounding in every way; yet a far more serious question arises about the way in which the inner substance of this most imposing tragedy of Shakespeare is interpreted by the troupe.

It is well known that *Julius Caesar* is sharply divided into two parts: the situation of the Roman republic at the time of Caesar's assassination and the fatal failure of the "last Romans," Cassius and Brutus, in the struggle against the antirepublican party. History separates these two events by a number of years, during which a whole series of events took place in Rome. For example, originally the Senate was benevolently restrained in the matter of Caesar's assassination.

Shakespeare was not at all interested in these events. The first part of his tragedy ends with the people stirred up by Antony's speech, and the second part begins with the meeting of the "Second Triumvirate." Obviously, it is in the omission of the intervening events that one must discover Shakespeare's view of the epoch. And really, the entire attention of the great poet is centered on the characters of Brutus and Cassius, and on their inner crisis after Caesar's murder. Somehow evil Fate rested on them. Misfortune after misfortune overtakes them, entirely senselessly and randomly. Brutus's wife, deceived by false reports, dies as a result of swallowing white hot coals; likewise Cassius stabs himself prematurely because of his receiving untrue news. The noble ideas that called forth the death of Caesar could have been easily realized, but Fate laughed as it literally demonstrated that public welfare is not to be attained through murder, no matter how noble-minded the motive behind it. That is how I understand the substance of the Shakespeare tragedy.

Well now, what does the Meininger company give us? Does it successfully draw a complete picture of the situation in Rome under the influence of passions, the settling of personal accounts, petty dissensions? I shall not speak of the first part of the tragedy, in which the Meininger—thanks to the richness of their exterior colors—have really known how to create a broad picture of Roman life. But nothing else! What this company has made of the second part, into what it has turned Shakespeare, only Allah knows! I'll begin with Mark Antony. This crafty, gifted, practical man, this characteristic representative of a pampered age, later an indolent, foul libertine, who lacks almost every ethical principle of conduct, appears in the Meiningen production as a noble-minded youth.

This is very productive for stage effectiveness. Why should an actor rummage around in the abysses of all shadings of character if idealization satisfies the desires of a superficial audience? Herr [Willy] Felix does not captivate all listeners for the fun of it. Still in regard to this noble-minded youth there arises in the third act this question: how will Herr Felix create a transition to the scene of the Triumvirate, where Antony's practical, spoiled nature reveals itself in all its nakedness and where through Shakespeare's monologue no other tone can be used? Well, how then? The Meininger get around this difficulty very easily. They calmly cut out the entire meeting of the Triumvirate, possibly a tedious scene for stage effectiveness, but one almost indispensable for the characterization of Antony.[1] They strike also the little scene of the war between Octavius and Antony at the beginning of the act. A very ingenious method, isn't it? But with Cassius and Brutus they proceed even more boldly. Everything that disturbs the idealization and everything that Shakespeare has so compassionately and with such tremendous understanding of the human heart compiled has been omitted. The great poet used his complete palette to depict the reaction that is taking place in both these men, and all these colors have been wiped out without a trace by the Meininger, and—at the same time—the meaning of the tragedy has been changed decisively.

After the quarrel between Brutus and Cassius a reconciliation takes place. Read carefully this astonishing scene as written by Shakespeare, and you will feel how insincere this reconciliation appears. Something has come between these two former friends that will no longer permit a frank relationship. This "something" swells, excites their small-minded ambition, and in the scene with the poet following the reconciliation, seeks a way out. The poet plunges into Brutus's tent and puts them to shame with his candid, honest opinion:

POET: For shame, you generals! What do you mean? / Love and be friends, as two such men should be; / For I have seen more years, I'm sure, than ye.

Since they are both dissatisfied with themselves, the rage of Cassius as well as of Brutus erupts on the poor poet:

CASSIUS: Ha, ha! How vilely does this cynic rhyme!

BRUTUS: Get you hence, sirrah! Saucy fellow, hence!

CASSIUS: Bear with him, Brutus. 'Tis his fashion.

But Brutus is more honest than Cassius, and is more powerfully struck by a feeling of dissatisfaction with himself. He cannot calm himself for a long time; and he demands wine. The Meininger have cut the entire scene with the poet, and *they have delivered the reconciliation scene as the whole truth,* so that the viewer who hardly knows *Julius Caesar* simply wonders why Shakespeare needed a quarrel between Cassius and Brutus that really dissolves into nothing. Nevertheless—I mention a trifle—they have not cut the wine, perhaps to parade an overabundance of external detail: how and from which kind of jug Brutus drinks wine in camp. In any case, this liberty necessitates having the Shakespearean Brutus demand wine without any motivation.

Furthermore, as an added proof of the pettiness of which Brutus and Cassius are capable, Shakespeare contributed the following scene: after the departure of the poet, Brutus reveals the death of his wife to Cassius, something about which he has already been informed. Immediately thereafter, Titinius and Messala enter the tent, and the latter carefully reveals the news in the belief that Brutus has not yet heard it. And now? Brutus, the always somehow strange, elegant Brutus, acts as if he is hearing the news for the first time and as if he were bearing the pain heroically. Cassius, his friend, supports him in this.

This comedy, which harshly destroys the idealization of character and is difficult to shape, the Meininger have cut. Instead, they achieve in the final scene beautiful and ingenious stage pictures. The entire tragedy is staged in this spirit. The sets, the crowds, the heathen noises, the thunder and lightning—all these are incomparable, but no single character is realized. It remains only for me to add that all newspapers have remarked on the glittering head of Caesar (another external) and recognized the omission of every imperial, energetic tone so as to subdue all around Caesar. Even Casca, that sly one, who according to Shakespeare in Act I gives himself the air of a lazy, indifferent person, and who hides the glowing spark within him until he is asked to act, is in the Meininger a brisk, jolly fellow.

If Moscow would view the offering of *Julius Caesar* by the Meininger as a remarkable, external rendering of those scenic beauties in which the tragedy is so rich, then I would not ask that my letter be printed, but Moscow is presenting this company as one interpreting Shakespeare's creation with completeness and extraordinary accuracy.[2]

2. *André Antoine's Account of Some Performances in Brussels, 1888*

In 1888 the French actor and theater manager André Antoine saw the Meininger in Brussels and in a discerning letter to the conservative critic Francisque Sarcey, he declared himself "ravished" by the crowd scenes in *Wilhelm Tell* and *The Winter's Tale*, though he did not overlook elements he considered negative.

I must tell you that I have just come from Brussels where I have spent a fortnight studying that German troupe. You know that I am going to put on *La Patrie en danger* this winter, and in connection with it I had been thinking of trying an interesting experiment with crowds. To go and see the Meininger was then a matter of course. Since I have been going to the theatre I have been annoyed with what we do with our supernumeraries. If I except *La Haine*, and the circus in *Théodora*, I have never seen anything which has given me the sensation of a multitude. Well, I did get that sensation on seeing the Meininger. They showed us things absolutely new and very instructive. Their crowds are not like ours, composed of elements picked haphazard, working-men hired for dress rehearsals, badly clothed, and unaccustomed to wearing strange and uncomfortable costumes, especially when they are exact. Immobility is almost always required of the crowds on our stage, whereas the supernumeraries of the Meininger must act and mime their characters. Don't understand by that that they force the note and that the attention is distracted from the protagonists. No, the tableau is complete, and in whatever direction you may look, you fix your eyes on a detail in the situation or character. At certain moments its power is incomparable.

The troupe of the Meininger contains about seventy actors of both sexes. All those who do not take a part are expected to figure in the play, and every evening too. If there are twenty actors occupied, the fifty others, without a single exception, even in the case of the leading players, appear on the stage in the tableaux, and each leading actor is the chief, the corporal of a group of real supernumeraries, whom he directs and watches as long as the company is under the eye of the public. This obligation is such that the wife of Hans von Bülow, one of the stars of the Meininger, having refused to perform this service, which she considered beneath her talent, was dismissed. . . . In this way they obtain ensembles that are extraordinarily true to life. Just try to apply this principle on our stage and demand even of a fifth-rate player that he occupy with his presence the salon of the Princesse de Bouillon! And so we are forced to use worthy people who have no idea of what they are doing on the stage, nor why they are there at all. I know all about it, I used to be a supernumerary at the Comédie-Française with Mévisto. Thus we used to see at close quarters the actors who had roused our enthusiasm when we were in the audience. Well, the Meininger adapt themselves to circumstances. Mlle. Lindner, their star, playing in the *Winter's Tale*, took a silent part in the tableau of the seat of justice, and mimed a woman of the people as conscientiously and as carefully as she interpreted on the following evening the important rôle of Hermione in the same piece. That is the secret of their crowds, which are absolutely superior to ours.

Why should not these new, logical, and not at all costly things eventually replace those insupportable conventions which everybody endures with us without knowing why? The word "mechanical," which M. Claretie has used, does not seem to me very just.[3] Is not everything at the Comédie-Française, where certain works are repeated month after month, arranged mechanically? The mechanics of tableaux are perfected in superior fashion in the crowds of the Meininger, that's the truth. In tableaux, the protagonist who is on the stage can make periods of silence ring true with a gesture, a cry, a movement. And if the crowd listens and looks at the actor instead of looking at the audience, or, as at the Comédie-Française, at the stars, with silent but visible deference, it will be found quite natural that a crowd of two hundred persons should be silent together, listening in rapt attention to a character who interests everybody. . . .

Why shouldn't we try to appropriate for ourselves the best elements of these interesting innovations? I am going to put a little of what I have seen in Brussels into Goncourt's *Patrie en danger* and Hennique's *Mort du duc d'Enghien*.[4]

NOTES

NOTES

The following abbreviations are used in the Notes: COL, Theatermuseum Institut für Theater-, Film-, und Fernsehwissenschaft, University of Cologne; GA, Geheimes Archiv, Meiningen State Archives; HA, Hausarchiv, Meiningen State Archives; StBBH, Handschriftenabteilung, Nachlass Georg II. von Sachsen-Meiningen, German State Library, Berlin, GDR. An StBBH citation, in the form K7 M8 B8, is to be read "carton 7, folder 8, sheet 8."

Introduction

1. Eduard Fritze, "Was man vor 50 Jahren über das Meininger Hoftheaters sagte und schrieb," *Festschrift zum 100. Geburtstage Georg II. von Sachsen-Meiningen* (Marbach, 1926), p. 21. Compare Max Grube, *The Story of the Meininger*, tr. Ann Marie Koller (Coral Gables, Fla., 1965), p. 5.

2. Fritze, p. 21.

3. Berthold Litzmann, *Das deutsche Drama in den literarischen Bewegungen der Gegenwart*, 4th ed. (Hamburg, 1897), pp. 48-49.

4. The development of the German Hoftheater is covered in detail in Eduard Devrient, *Geschichte der deutschen Schauspielkunst* (Zurich, 1929), pp. 162-67, 406-37. See also Max Martersteig, *Das deutsche Theater im neunzehnten Jahrhundert* (Leipzig, 1924), pp. 74-113.

5. Friedrich Rosenthal, *Unsterblichkeit des Theaters* (Munich, 1924), pp. 183-84.

6. See Helmut Schanze, *Drama im Bürgerlichen Realismus, 1850-1890* (Frankfurt, 1973), pp. 168-210, for a list of the plays in the repertoire of the Berlin Königliches Schauspielhaus, and pp. 211-16, for a list of those in the Frankfurt am Main repertoire, 1849-86.

7. Joseph Kainz, *Der junge Kainz*, ed. Arthur Eloesser (Berlin, 1912), p. 47. Kainz was only 18 years old at the time, but he feared that he would never have an opportunity to play the great roles. On March 3, 1876, he wrote: "The beautiful time is over, and instead of the young heroes like Kosinsky and Rudenz, etc., etc., we have Ingomars, Jasons, Montaiglins; and it will not be long before I shall have to play the Old Moor" (p. 49).

8. Cited by Martersteig, p. 312.

9. Franz Wallner, "Meine Erinnerungen an Meiningen," *Volksspielkunst* (Dresden), July 7, 1926, p. 107. On Oct. 26, 1875, Kainz wrote: "Today, the leading lady and I revolted against the director because every day we are given so many massive parts to learn. Not that they are hard, only conversation pieces, but because we simply cannot learn any more. I was absolutely stupid and could not shove another thing into my head. Yesterday we played *Durchgegangene Weiber*. I played the leading role; and she, my wife. We knew our parts so little that when the prompter began to whisper a sentence, we both began to speak it at the same time. If, at the end of the second scene, the prompter had not hissed, 'Get off!' I'd be standing there yet." (*Der junge Kainz*, p. 16.)

10. Role category and role monopoly should not be confused, although one naturally led to the other.

11. On the Fach system, see Hans Doerry, *Das Rollenfach im deutschen Theaterbetrieb des 19. Jahrhunderts* (Berlin, 1926). See also Eduard von Winterstein, *Mein Leben und meine Zeit* (Berlin, 1947), for an amusing and informative account of Winterstein's experience on the 19th-century stage at a time when the Fach system was "a wall around the possession of roles by individuals, which was broken through in only the most unusual cases; and when that did happen, it was only after the hottest of struggles."

12. That most actresses refused to admit the passing of time and did not change categories until forced to do so is shown by a little verse popular in the 19th-century theater and quoted in Doerry, p. 17: "That sly miss should be ashamed! / Relying on her youth, she's seized / All the roles for blushing maids / In which for *forty* years *I've* pleased!"

13. Grube, pp. 8-9.

14. Winterstein, p. 76.

15. This term, appearing repeatedly in letters and memoirs, seems to have covered everything one actor found objectionable in another.

16. Carl Hagemann, *Regie: Studien zur dramatischen Kunst* (Berlin, 1902), p. 71.

17. As a young actor Kainz complained constantly about the lack of direction. In 1875 he wrote: "I doubt that I acted as well as I was costumed. For I don't believe that anyone with such a large role to be studied and learned in less than two days and to be performed after one rehearsal can be successful with a public that really understands art. I must watch myself, though, not to become uncivil or arrogant, for then it would really not go well with me here. The director told me I should 'indicate' at the rehearsal, but that I can't do; it's too easy to become accustomed to it, and I'm afraid I'll do it on the night of the performance." (*Der junge Kainz*, p. 37.) Later, he wrote (p. 50): "You can't imagine how happy I'd be if I could just once hear a capable director say, 'You, That's not right! Do it this way,' or if just once I could have a week or even two weeks to learn a part." Winterstein, p. 224, says that before he went to Berlin in 1896, he never heard an actor rehearse in full voice.

18. Max Grube, *Jugenderinnerungen eines Glückskindes* (Leipzig, 1917); Alois Wohlmuth, *Ein Schauspielerleben* (Munich, 1918); and Kainz, *Der junge Kainz*, among others.

19. Adolf Winds, *Geschichte der Regie* (Berlin, 1925), p. 25.

20. Paul Lindau, "Aus der Hauptstadt," *Die Gegenwart*, 5.9 (1874): 301.

21. Ludwig Barnay, *Erinnerungen* (Berlin, 1903), p. 196; Grube, *Story of the Meininger*, p. 48; Winterstein, *Mein Leben*, p. 74.

22. Paul Heyse, letter to the editor of the *Wartburgstimmen*, March 1906; cited in *Herzog Georg II. und die Meininger Kunst: Festschrift zum 80. Geburtstage Herzog Georgs am 2. April 1906* (Hildburghausen, 1906), pp. 26-27.

23. Ellen Franz, the duke's third wife and assistant in his theater reforms, encountered such a situation in her first position, at the Gotha court theater. Prepared to play the roles of the Young Sentimental, she found that they all went to an older actress; and worse still, that the actress was the favorite of the ruling duke who, whenever she was indisposed, preferred to cancel the announced drama, rather than allow a substitute in the part.

24. Gotthold Lessing, *Hamburgische Dramaturgie* (Halle, 1895), p. 354 (350. *Stück*, Jan. 12, 1768).

25. Friedrich Haase, *Was ich erlebte, 1846-1896*, 2d ed. (Berlin, n.d.), p. 47. Winterstein, p. 142, also tells this story. Freytag, in his memoirs (*Gesammelte Werke*, Leipzig, 1906, 1:253-55), urges the actor to respect the words of the poet. He is especially vehement on the subject of the comic who adds his ideas and jokes to a play.

26. Martersteig, Devrient, Winterstein, and Grube, among others, discuss the harmful effects of relying on the star system, especially on the smaller theaters and on actors who were just learning their profession. See also Max Kurnik, *Ein Menschenalter Theater-Erinnerungen, 1845-1880* (Berlin, 1882), pp. 244-49. Haase, pp. 47ff, defends the star system and guest appearances; he calls those opposed to them "doctrinaire" and "pedantic."

27. Devrient, *Geschichte*, p. 211.

28. Robert F. Arnold, *Das moderne Drama* (Strassburg, 1912), pp. 13-14.

29. Julius Steiner, *Zur Reorganization der Theater-Verhältnisse* (Bremen, 1849), p. 19.

30. *Grenzeboten* (Leipzig), 1868, no. 1, p. 409; cited in Schanze, *Drama*, p. 6.

31. Erich Drach, *Ludwig Tiecks Bühnenreformen* (Berlin, 1909). See also Martersteig, *Das deutsche Theater*, pp. 372-78; Gerhard Wahnrau, *Berlin, Stadt der Theater* (Berlin, 1957), pp. 391-96; Heinz Kindermann, *Theatergeschichte Europas* (Salzburg, 1967), 6:14-22, 26-31.

32. Martersteig, pp. 356-63; Kindermann, 6:67-82. It is hard to overestimate the value of Immermann's reforms; they influenced nearly every theater man who succeeded him in Germany.

33. Martersteig, p. 639.

34. Quoted in Friedrich Rosenthal, *Unsterblichkeit des Theaters*, p. 126.

35. *Ibid.*, p. 135.

36. It was said that his speech master, Alexander Strakosch, drilled his actors with a baton, beating out the measure.

37. Paul Lindau, *Nur Erinnerungen* (Stuttgart, 1917), 2:213.

38. John Oxenford, tr., *Conversations of Goethe with Eckermann and Soret*, rev. ed. (London, 1898), p. 121.

39. Laube cited in Rosenthal, p. 137.

40. R. Junack, "Heinrich Laubes Entwicklung zum Reformator des deutschen Theaters," Ph.D. dissertation, University of Erlangen, 1922, pp. 8-9. Unless otherwise noted, the evaluation of Laube's work is taken from this dissertation.

41. Rudolf Tyrolt, "Laube als Regisseur," in *Aus der Theaterwelt* (Leipzig, 1879), p. 28.

42. Rosenthal, p. 78.

43. On March 15, 1852, Friedrich Hebbel wrote to his wife, after attending a

rehearsal of *Agnes Bernauer*: "Dingelstedt knows how to bring off the ensemble *like* no other" (*Briefe*, ed. R. M. Werner, Berlin, 1908, 1:384). Dingelstedt's great contribution to the German stage was his careful and continuous fostering of Hebbel's work.

44. A letter from Dingelstedt to Georg (cited in Heinz Isterheil, "Die Bühnendekorationen bei den Meiningern," Ph.D. dissertation, University of Cologne, 1938, p. 45) seems to suggest that Georg, then crown prince, was present at performances of the *Gesamtgastspiel*, but there is no documentation to support this.

45. Both critics are quoted in Rosenthal, *Unsterblichkeit des Theaters*, pp. 175-76.

46. Eugen Kilian, *Beiträge zur Geschichte des Karlsruher Hoftheaters unter Eduard Devrient* (Karlsruhe, 1893), p. 162.

47. *Ibid.*

48. Rudolf Goldschmidt, *Eduard Devrients Bühnenreform am Karlsruher Hoftheater* (Leipzig, 1921), pp. 130-45.

49. Eugen Kilian, "Eduard Devrient," in *Dramaturgische Blätter* (Munich, 1905), 1:281-99.

50. Haase, *Was ich erlebte*, p. 47.

51. Eugen Kilian, "Georg von Meiningen und seine Bühnenreform," in *Dramaturgische Blätter* (Munich, 1913), 2:287.

52. See Muriel St. Clare Byrne's vigorously argued article "Charles Kean and the Meininger Myth," *Theatre Research*, 6.3 (1964): 137-53. See also Sybil Rosenfeld, *Georgian Scene Painters and Scene Painting* (Cambridge, Eng., 1981).

53. It is now a critical commonplace to find Kean's productions excessively "antiquarian," and his place in them vain and absurd. But as J. M. D. Hardwick points out in the introduction to *Emigrant in Motley* (London, 1954), pp. xv-xvi, "His scholarship literally saved the theatre. . . . When he came to management, everything was at its lowest ebb. Everywhere plays were produced in the cheapest possible way, with skimpy scenery, patched and makeshift costumes, and the crudest effects. The plays themselves were commonplace, cliché-ridden, and full of strutting and bellowing. It was the end of an age. . . . When Macready retired in 1851, Kean found himself virtually the last of the classic tragedians. In his own lifetime the drama had sunk from a high art form to a vulgar exhibition." It was through Kean's splendid, often too-splendid, productions that Shakespeare ceased to be exclusive, and the public began to acquire a taste for the great things in English drama. "If," says Hardwick, "[Kean] was not a great actor, he was a good one; if not inspired, he was intelligent and painstaking; if not a revolutionary, he made innovations upon which others could improve. If not an immortal, he was a good man for the time when one was sorely needed."

54. Helene Richter, *Josef Lewinsky* (Vienna, 1926), p. 106.

55. Haase, pp. 163-64.

56. Shirley Allen, *Samuel Phelps at Sadler's Wells* (Middletown, Conn., 1971), pp. 201-47.

57. Frances Ann Kemble, *Records of Later Life* (New York, 1884), pp. 637-38.

58. Frances Ann Kemble, *Journal* (London, 1835), p. 96.

59. *The Athenaeum* (London), Oct. 2, 1847.

60. Ernst Gombrich, *The Story of Art*, 13th ed. (Oxford, Eng., 1978), pp. 399-402.

61. Hans Sedlmayr, *Verlust der Mitte* (Salzburg, 1948), pp. 44-47. See also

Hans Mayer, *Richard Wagner in Bayreuth*, tr. Jack Zipes (New York, 1961), pp. 19-24.

62. Sedlmayr, p. 43.

63. Robert Prölss, *Das Herzogliche-Meiningen'sche Hoftheater, seine Entwicklung, seine Bestrebungen und die Bedeutung seiner Gastspiele* (Leipzig, 1887), p. 64.

Chapter One

1. It is amusing to notice that as Georg grew older he took on many of the attitudes that he had once found objectionable in his father. He came to regard the citizens as extensions of his own family and laid down "family rules." No trader—tinker or market man—might remain in the town of Meiningen after sundown unless his home was within the town limits. Every merchant had to keep the premises in front of his business as clean as the courtyard in front of the castle. Children tumbling on the lawns or running through the park as the duke walked in it expected reproof, as if from a familiar elder, "Don't we have any paths in Meiningen?" Then there was likely to be a quizzing about lessons. A few of these children are at this writing still living in Meiningen.

2. Mary Hopkirk, *Queen Adelaide* (London, 1950), p. 190. When Adelaide, Georg's older daughter, became queen of England as the wife of William IV, she was appalled at the large number of Englishmen who could neither read nor write. She had been taught that "only by education could mob rule be averted and replaced by law-abiding democracy." Adelaide herself could read Greek, spoke French and English, and wrote better English than her niece Victoria. (*Ibid.*, pp. 191-92.)

3. Baroness von Heldburg to Adelheid, princess of Sachsen-Meiningen, Aug. 13, 1903, in Helene, Freifrau von Heldburg, *Fünfzig Jahre Glück und Leid* (Leipzig, 1926), p. 72.

4. W. Rossmann to Duke Bernhard, n.d. 1841, GA: XV LL2.

5. Max Grube says that the duke was always fascinated by "those things that make us shudder," fear in two senses of the word: that fright brought about by melodramatic action, but also the terror that Goethe characterizes by the verb *schaudern*, the result of profound awe and understanding. (Max Grube, *The Story of the Meininger*, tr. Ann Marie Koller, Coral Gables, Fla., 1965, p. 91.)

6. Josef Kainz, *Der junge Kainz* (Berlin, 1912), p. 193.

7. Hopkirk, pp. 142-43.

8. Cited in Kuno Fischer, *Erinnerungen an Moritz Seebeck* (Heidelberg, 1886), p. 48.

9. Moritz Seebeck, *Aus sonniger Kindheit* (Berlin, 1916), p. 86.

10. *Ibid.*, p. 166.

11. Georg to Gustel, June 27, 1841, in *ibid.*, p. 175.

12. After he was grown, Georg wrote to his parents saying that he was happy that his sister was allowed to attend the theater, and that his mother was more tolerant than she had been when he was a child and had declared that no child under thirteen should be allowed in the theater. "When I was that age," he wrote, "I went to the theater far less than Auguste. As a child, going to the theater gave me indescribable happiness." (StBBH: K8 M72 B27, Rome, March 3, 1856.)

13. Seebeck, pp. 76-77.

14. A second artist, the highly romantic Carl Wagner, working in the theater at the same time, seems to have had no impact on the prince. For descriptions of Georg's early artistic training, see Carl von Stein, *Die Kunst in Meiningen unter Herzog Georg II.* (Meiningen, 1909), p. 6; Volker Reissland, "Herausbildung und Grundzüge der Meininger Theaterreform im letzten Drittel des 19. Jahrhunderts als Wegbereiter für die Weiterentwicklung der Schauspielkunst im beginnenden 20. Jahrhundert" (thesis, Karl Marx University, Leipzig, 1977), p. 42; and Heinz Isterheil, "Die Bühnendekorationen bei den Meiningern" (Ph.D. dissertation, University of Cologne, 1938), pp. 38-40.

15. Marie, duchess of Meiningen, StBBH: K7 M9 B28-29, Altenstein, n.d. 1841.

16. Georg did not lose contact with Lindenschmitt after he left Meiningen. On Oct. 10, 1845, the artist wrote to Duke Bernhard while the prince was at Bonn University: "I have declared with pleasure that as soon as possible I shall paint the tournament as it has been sketched by His Highness, the crown prince" (GA: XV JJ56 B23).

17. StBBH: K27 Miscellany.

18. Seebeck, *Aus sonniger Kindheit*, p. 180.

19. *Ibid.*, p. 200.

20. *Ibid.*, pp. 201-2.

21. The people of Meiningen have always been exceedingly proud of their connection with the Bach family. See the extensive bibliography of relevant literature in Hermann Pusch, *Meiningen und die Meininger Bachsen Nebenlinien*, in *Das Thüringer Fähnlein*, vol. 4 (Jena, 1935). Thirty years after his confirmation, Georg, by then the duke, decided to honor Johann Sebastian Bach. On Dec. 25, 1873, the musician Hans von Bülow wrote from Meiningen, where he was guest conductor, to Professor Karl Hillebrand in Florence: "Next Sunday there will be a great classical concert here with double prices for the benefit of the Bach statue in Eisenach" (Hans von Bülow, *Briefe*, Leipzig, 1907, 6:123).

22. Seebeck, p. 218.

23. George Rowell, *Queen Victoria Goes to the Theatre* (London, 1978), pp. 42-43.

24. Alan S. Downer, *The Eminent Tragedian: William Charles Macready* (Cambridge, Mass., 1966), pp. 252, 352. Downer believes that Georg "derived his first notions of the possibility of a new kind of production" from seeing Macready's principles carried out in Berlin by Samuel Phelps in 1859. But the same argument holds against this assertion as against the idea that Georg was deeply influenced by Charles Kean's performance of *Richard II* in London in 1857. He was more than 30 years old. He had been attending the theater for more than 20 years and had already enunciated in writing his ideas on art and music. His taste was set.

25. Seebeck, p. 242.

26. Dahlmann (1785-1868), a liberal, had been a professor at the University of Göttingen, where his book *Quellenkunde der deutschen Geschichte* had long been considered indispensable to the study of German history. In 1837, when the reactionary King Ernest Augustus revoked the constitution of Hanover, seven professors, among them Dahlmann and the Grimm brothers, issued a protest and

were dismissed. Celebrated as the Göttingen Seven, these men became symbols as victims not only of abridged academic freedom, but of the general oppression under which the nations of Europe were becoming restive. Arndt (1769-1860) had been one of the most resolute opponents of Napoleon I. His book *Geist der Zeit* and his patriotic poetry helped arouse German opposition to Napoleon; for his activity he was forced to flee to Sweden and Russia.

27. Welcher (1784-1868), professor of classical philology and archaeology at Bonn in 1844-45, founded the Bonn Bibliothek and the Academic Art Museum. Kinckel (1815-82), art historian, poet, and publicist, taught at Bonn in the years 1842-49. Among all his academic colleagues, he was the only one who took part in the Baden-Pfalz uprising in 1849. He was condemned to life imprisonment in Spandau, but escaped to England where he became the leader of the middle-class German expatriates in London.

28. Georg to his mother, StBBH: K7 M11 B19, Bonn, Nov. 13, 1844.

29. Reissland, "Herausbildung," p. 53.

30. Georg to his mother, StBBH: K7 M8 B8, Bonn, Oct. 31, 1844.

31. *Ibid.*, M11 B11-12, B15-16, B19, B29, Bonn, Nov. 7, 11, 13, 26, 1844.

32. *Ibid.*, M12 B26, Bonn, n.d.

33. *Ibid.*, M13, 18, B13, 18, Bonn, Jan. 26, 1845.

34. Georg to his father, HA, Bonn, May 6, 1845 (unnumbered); Georg to his mother, StBBH: M8, B26, Bonn, n.d. *La Muette de Portici* was also well known under the name *Masaniello.*

35. August Wilhelm Schlegel, *Lectures on Dramatic Art and Literature*, tr. John Black (London, 1815), 2:198.

36. Fischer, *Erinnerungen an Moritz Seebeck*, p. 68. Seebeck remained in Meiningen, where Duke Bernhard appointed him vice-chancellor of the Lutheran Consistory. He remained close to the ducal family and served Meiningen importantly during the Revolution of 1848. In 1849 he represented the duchy at the Frankfurt Parliament. In 1851 he was made curator at the University of Jena, where he remained until his retirement. He never lost his interest in or his love for Georg, as his later letters show.

37. Richard Muther, *Geschichte der Malerei im 19. Jahrhundert*, 1:390; cited in Isterheil, "Die Bühnendekorationen," p. 42. It is not surprising that Georg found the Düsseldorf academic art insipid, and that he was greatly impressed by the Renaissance works. The first picture he admired while yet a small child was Raphael's *Madonna di Loretto*, the original of which hung in his mother's rooms in Castle Elisabethenburg in Meiningen. Later Lindenschmitt introduced him to the strong, linear work of Cornelius, Kaulbach, Schnorr von Karolsfeld, and Overbeck with their religious, Old-German base; from childhood he included their works in his list of the Christmas presents he wanted. For example, his 1845 list included engravings of Michelangelo's *Last Judgment*, the frescoes of Cornelius in the Ludwigskirche in Munich, Bendemann's friezes, Schnorr's frescoes on the exterior of the Munich Residence, and Kaulbach's cycle of drawings engraved by Thaeter (StBBH: K7 M21 B10; cited in Reissland, p. 45).

38. Charles Walstein, "The Court Theatre of Meiningen," *Harper's New Monthly Magazine*, 82 (1891): 6.

39. Georg to his mother, StBBH: K7 M15 B27, Paris, n.d.

40. *Ibid.*, B26, Paris, March 17, 1845.

41. *Ibid.*, B35, Paris, March 27, 1845.

42. Cited in Max Martersteig, *Das deutsche Theater im neunzehnten Jahrhundert* (Leipzig, 1904), p. 572.

43. Heinz Kindermann, *Theatergeschichte Europas* (Salzburg, 1967), 6:144-45. Ciceri (1782-1868), working at a time when the French theater was turning toward romantic realism, was one of the designers who had elevated the art of set and costume design to the same level of importance as the art of the composer and the librettist. How original his designs were is uncertain. Barry Daniels, a student of this period, writes of Ciceri: "The history of stage design during the first half of the nineteenth century has not yet been carefully enough studied for us to be certain how innovative Ciceri was. It seems to me that he was certainly influenced by the work of [Allesandro] Sanquirico [1777-1849] and [Karl Friedrich] Schinkel [1781-1841] as well as that of [Louis Jacques] Daguerre [1789-1851]. He can be credited with introducing 'romantic realism' as developed at the melodrama theatres into the major Paris theatres, the opera, and the Comédie Française." (Letter to the author, June 5, 1982.) For more details, see Daniels, "Ciceri and Daguerre," *Theater Survey*, May 1981; and Daniels, "Victor Hugo on the Boulevard," *Theater Journal*, March 1980. We can look forward to finding the answers to a number of puzzling questions concerning the genesis of many of the designs in this period when Professor Daniels's work is published in its entirety.

44. Ivor Guest, *The Romantic Ballet in Paris* (London, 1966), p. 84.

45. Georg to his mother, StBBH: K7 M15 B22, Paris, March 15, 1845.

46. Martersteig, pp. 566-68; Kindermann, 6:145-46.

47. The Paris production, first given 12 years before Georg saw it, was one of Ciceri's masterpieces; the cloister scene, a triumph. How original this was with Ciceri is questionable. According to Barry Daniels, it was certainly greatly influenced by Schinkel's sketches (letter to the author, June 5, 1982).

48. Georg to his mother, StBBH: K7 M15 B28, Paris, March 17, 1845. *Giselle ou les Wilis*, inspired by Heine's account of the old Slavonic legend of the "wilis," souls of innocent maidens, was first presented in Paris in 1841. It became enormously popular and has remained one of the best-loved ballets in the classical repertoire. In *Giselle, apothéose du ballet romantique* (Paris, 1942), Serge Lifar traces the alterations that changed the ballet from the one Georg saw to the one we see today. This and other studies of the romantic ballet are valuable to an understanding of the Meininger staging because Georg, who in his impressionable years was an avid admirer of the ballet, was struck by and made extensive use of the composition of the corps de ballet as an ensemble (crowd) supporting principal players.

49. For convenience, here is a complete list of the productions Georg mentioned seeing in Paris: *La Muette de Portici* (opera), *Wallensteins Lager, Wallensteins Tod, Maria Stuart* (opera), *La Favorita* (opera), *Robert le Diable* (opera), *Lucia di Lammermoor* (opera), *Giselle* (ballet), *Le Gendre d'un millionnaire* (Comédie Française), *George Dandin* (Comédie Française), two unnamed pieces at Porte Saint-Martin, and some sort of pageant about Napoleon at Cirque-Olympique (*L'Empire?*).

50. Georg to his mother, StBBH: K7 M20 B2, Weimar, Sept. 23, 1845; B3, Dresden, Oct. 1, 1845.

51. *Ibid.*, M21 B8, Bonn, Nov. 11, 1845.

52. Unquestionably, Georg was affected by these ideas, especially as preached by Prof. Moritz Arndt. But they did not greatly affect his theater reforms.

53. Georg to his mother, StBBH: K7 M25 B11, London, April 11, 1846.

54. For an account of Astley's Amphitheatre, which gave Georg as child and man as much pleasure as any theater he ever visited, see A. H. Saxon, *Enter Foot and Horse: A History of Hippodrama in England and France* (New Haven, Conn., 1968), especially pp. 12-15, 53-55, 141-42, 155ff. Adolphe Franconi belonged to a large old French circus family, responsible for some of the most celebrated productions of their kind. See *ibid., passim.* See also Marian Hannah Winter, *The Theatre of Marvels* (New York, 1964), pp. 183-87, for a description of *The Sacred Elephants* and its predecessor by Franconi.

55. Georg to his mother, StBBH: K7 M24 B16-17, London, March 26, 1846.

56. The other three were Marie Taglioni, Fanny Cerrito, and Carlotta Grisi.

57. Reissland, "Herausbildung," p. 61, states: "Kurnatowski in *Georg II. von Sachsen-Meiningen und Hildburghausen* and others have documented Georg's seeing the 'Histories' at this time." If they mean Shakespeare's Histories, they cannot be correct, since none was playing while Georg was in London. The only plays that might be called "historical" were Nicholas Rowe's *Jane Shore*, which Phelps and Mrs. Warner were giving at Sadler's Wells, and Edward Bulwer-Lytton's *Richelieu*, which Macready was alternating with the Tragedies at the Princess.

58. The complete list of productions Georg mentioned seeing in England is as follows: the ballets *Catarina the Bandit's Daughter* and *Éoline ou la dryade*; the operas *Nino* (*Nabucco*), followed by *Divertissement: Un Bal sous Louis XIV*, danced by Grahn and Taglioni, *Linda di Chamouni, Die Kreuzfahrer, I Puritani, Norma, The Barber of Seville, Don Giovanni,* and *La Sonnambula*; at Astley's, *The Rajah of Nagpore*; at the "French plays," *La Demoiselle à marier ou la première entrevue, Le Capitaine Roquefenêtre,* and *Jean ou le mauvais sujet*; and, at the Haymarket, *A Beggar on Horseback* (followed by *My Wife's Mother*), and *The Irish Post.* He heard two concerts of ancient music at the Hanover-Square Rooms, and there was a concert at Buckingham Palace for his birthday featuring music by Mendelssohn, Meyerbeer, von Weber, and Bellini.

59. Georg to his mother, StBBH: K7 M27 B4, Bonn, June 9, 1846.

60. *Ibid.,* M21 B1, Bonn, Jan. 11, 1846.

61. See Heinrich Eduard Jacob, *Felix Mendelssohn and His Times,* tr. Richard and Clara Winston (Englewood Cliffs, N.J., 1963), pp. 289-97.

62. Cited in Martersteig, *Das deutsche Theater,* p. 569.

63. Georg's description of his life in Leipzig is found in the letters he wrote to his mother between October 1846 and January 1847, in StBBH: K7 M29-M30. The plays he mentioned seeing are *Uriel Acosta, Wallensteins Lager, Die Piccolomini,* and *Der verwunschene Prinz.* He also mentioned three operas: *Hans Heilig, Die Hugenotten,* and *Oberon.*

64. These descriptions of Georg's reactions are drawn from the letters he wrote to his mother between April 1847 and April 1848, in StBBH: K7 M29-M36. Other productions he mentioned are as follows: the plays *Die Komödianten, Die Jüdin von Toledo, Catherine Carnaro, Christoph Columbus, Dorf und Stadt, A Midsummer Night's Dream, Antigone, Donna Diana,* and *Othello*; the operas *Zaïre* (Federici), *Iphigenia auf Tauris, Faust, Don Giovanni, Romeo and Juliet,* and *Wilhelm Tell*; and the ballet *Esmeralda.*

65. Georg to his mother, StBBH K7 M37 B3, Berlin, March 10, 1848.
66. Georg to his father, GA: XV LL, Berlin, March 13, 1848.
67. Georg to his mother, StBBH: K7 M44 (entire folder), 1849.
68. Wolfgang Prasche, *Scandinavische Dramatik in Deutschland* (Basel, 1979), pp. 32-48.
69. Georg to his mother, StBBH: K7 M6 B13, B19, Berlin, Jan. 23, 26, 1850; M7 B1-2, B10, Berlin, Feb. 2, 22, 1850.
70. Herbert Marshall and Mildred Stock, *Ira Aldridge, the Negro Tragedian* (London, 1958), pp. 181-83.
71. Georg to his mother, StBBH: K8 M61 B16-17, Potsdam, April 20, 1854.
72. Anton Bettelheim, *Leben und Wirken des Freiherrn Rochus von Liliencron* (Berlin, 1917), pp. 110-12.
73. Georg to his mother, StBBH: K7 M47 B4, Berlin, May 11, 1857.
74. *Ibid.* Georg soon replaced this glittery material with genuine chain-mail and armor. Grube, *Story of the Meininger*, p. 50, describes the armor and weapons.
75. Georg to his mother, StBBH: K8 M8 B11, London, May 24, 1857. Many theater historians ascribe Georg's notion of reforming the German stage in the image of Charles Kean to his seeing this production. See, among many others, Ernst Leopold von Stahl, "Der englische Vorläufer der Meininger," in *Beiträge zur Literatur- und Theatergeschichte*, ed. Heinrich Stümcke (Berlin, 1918); and Muriel St. Clare Byrne, "Charles Kean and the Meininger Myth," *Theatre Research*, 4.3 (1964): 137-53. In view of the multiplicity of influences from art, music, and the theater that the prince had already absorbed, it is difficult to believe that a single Kean production would be any more than one of many influences. Moreover, it is important to note that Georg found the production "*pompös*" (overly magnificent).
76. Saxon, *Enter Foot and Horse*, pp. 148-71.
77. "There is everything one can wish for a daughter. She likes him, and he seems to be fond of her," Feodora wrote Victoria. "He has shown in every way much good feeling and true kindness of heart. The Meiningen parents too are so amiable. . . . I am sure my beloved child will find a pleasant home." (Harold A. Albert, *Queen Victoria's Sister: The Life and Letters of Princess Feodora*, London, 1967, pp. 164-65, 167.)
78. *Ibid.*, p. 167.
79. Soon after, Georg succeeded his father, and Feo reveled in being a duchess. She spent the winters in Nice, where the nobility of Europe gathered for a brilliant social season, and passed much time at the Villa Carlotta. Meiningen's cold winters and damp summers were not good, she said, for her already delicate health. Georg's relations with Feo's family seem to have remained good, however. Her mother expressed none of the bitterness found in the letters of Queen Victoria and her daughter, the crown princess of Prussia, over Georg's "neglect" of Feo.
80. Georg to his mother, StBBH: K8 M61 B16-17, Potsdam, April 20, 1854.
81. Georg to his father, HA: 321, Baden, July 19, 1866. Italics Georg's.
82. Reprinted in *Herzog Georg II. und die Meininger Kunst: Festschrift zum 80. Geburtstage Herzog Georgs am 2. April 1906* (Hildburghausen, 1906). See also Erich Schmidt, "Das Verhältnis Sachsen-Meiningen zur Reichsgründung 1851-1871," Ph.D. dissertation, University of Hall-Wittenberg, 1930.

83. Cited in Reissland, "Herausbildung," p. 34.

84. Eleven years after Bernhard's abdication, Cosima Wagner wrote in her diary during a visit to Meiningen: "I am received by the Princess Marie and the Dowager Duchess, which seems extraordinary in view of the hostility between the two courts" (*Diaries*, tr. Geoffrey Skelton, New York, 1976-77, entry for March 10, 1877). But this may not be altogether fair to Bernhard, for by that time other events had contrived to deepen the split between Georg and his family.

85. The complete text of these letters is in *Herzog Georg II.*, pp. 12-13.

86. Herbert A. Frenzel, *Thüringische Schlosstheater* (Berlin, 1965), p. 17.

87. Ludwig Bechstein, *Mittheilungen aus dem Leben der Herzoge zu Sachsen-Meiningen und deren Beziehung zu Männern der Wissenschaft* (Halle, 1856), pp. 178-89.

88. Herbert Frenzel, p. 97; Grube, p. 12.

89. "Wochenschau," *Thüringische-Fränkische Illustrierte Zeitung*, Dec. 17, 1931.

90. Stein, *Die Kunst in Meiningen*, pp. 4-5.

91. Among the pieces given between 1860 and 1866 were *Emilia Galotti, Faust, Egmont, Tasso, Don Carlos, Die Räuber, Maria Stuart, Kabale und Liebe, Wallensteins Tod, Hamlet, The Taming of the Shrew, The Comedy of Errors, Twelfth Night, Henry IV, Das Käthchen von Heilbronn,* and *Griseldis*. This list, including some of the finest works of Goethe, Schiller, Shakespeare, and von Kleist, demonstrates that von Stein's repertoire was equal to that of the best German theaters. The list of operas is as impressive.

92. Among the grand operas given were *Die Hugenotten, Faust,* and *Der fliegende Holländer*. The operetta repertoire was also good.

93. Stein, p. 6.

94. Robert F. Arnold, *Das moderne Drama* (Strassburg, 1908), p. 56. The other was the creation of the Festspielhaus in Bayreuth.

95. For the full text, see Appendix B, doc. 1.

96. Wagner cited in Wilhelm Greiner, *Georg II. von Meiningen und die Freifrau* (Gotha, 1939), p. 34; Liszt cited in Stein, p. 34. There is extensive literature on the duke's love of music and the support musical endeavors received in Meiningen. Among others see, Greiner, pp. 34-39; *Herzog Georg II. und die Meininger Kunst*, pp. 29-31; Paul Lindau, "Der Herzog und die Musik," in *Nur Erinnerungen* (Stuttgart, 1917), 2:333-36; Adolf Menzel, "Der Herzog und die Musik," in *Festschrift zur Feier des 100. Geburtstages Herzog Georg II. von Sachsen-Meiningen vom 2. bis 4. April 1926* (Meiningen, 1926), pp. 12-14; and Stein, pp. 23-43.

97. Reissland, "Herausbildung," pp. 14-17.

98. Stein, p. 10.

99. The following plays were given during the first season: Shakespeare, *Hamlet, Julius Caesar, King Lear, Richard III,* and *Othello*; Schiller, *Kabale und Liebe, Don Carlos, Die Räuber,* and *Maria Stuart*; Euripides, *Medea*; Björnson, *Between the Battles*; Goethe, *Faust I, Iphigenie auf Tauris,* and *Götz von Berlichingen*; Lessing, *Emilia Galotti*; Sophocles, *Oedipus Rex, Antigone,* and *Oedipus at Colonus*. There were also comedies, dramas, and farces by Ferdinand Raimund, Karl Gutzkow, Michael Beer, Giacomo Meyerbeer, and others.

100. Bodenstedt (1819-92) came to Meiningen from Munich, where he had been part of a circle of scholars around King Maximilian II of Bavaria. Holding

themselves aloof from the social and political problems of their day, these men devoted themselves to the cult of Beautiful Ideals, which expressed itself primarily in the exotic and the strange. Raised to the peerage by Georg, Bodenstedt was permitted thereafter to use "von" in his name. He considered himself the German authority on Shakespeare.

101. Grabowsky (1805-83) was largely uneducated, but was experienced, hard working, and devoted to the duke. His offices, as listed in the Meiningen Theater Archives, are puzzling: 1839-45, stage manager (*Regisseur*), and 1845-46, intendant, Wiesbaden Hoftheater; 1847-50, no position identified, Vienna Burgtheater; 1855-58, intendant, Dessau Hoftheater; 1861, stage manager, Berlin Victoria-Theater; 1863, actor and stage manager, 1867, art director, and finally, 1867-77, intendant or director (*Intendant oder Direktor*), Meiningen Hoftheater. According to Grube, *Story of the Meininger*, p. 29, Grabowsky was never more than a stage director. It is possible that Grabowsky merely put certain positions into the curriculum vitae he submitted to Meiningen, and von Stein accepted them. Certainly he was not an intendant in Meiningen as late as 1877, when Ludwig Chronegk was in charge, unless the duke accorded him an honorary title for long service. As long as the duke was the real intendant—though not named as such—there was never the close observance of position and title on the Meiningen stage that held on larger stages. It had much the air of a family enterprise about it.

102. The Shakespeare plays were *Romeo and Juliet, Richard II, King Lear, Cymbeline, Macbeth, King John, A Midsummer Night's Dream, Henry IV, Part I,* and *Richard III*. The other productions were Goethe's *Clavigo* and *Hermann und Dorothea*; Schiller's *Fiesko* and *Don Carlos*; and Euripides' *Orestes*.

103. Stein, *Die Kunst in Meiningen*, p. 13.

104. Wilhelm Oechelhäuser, "Die Shakespeare Aufführungen in Meiningen," *Jahrbuch der deutschen Shakespeare-Gesellschaft*, 3 (1868): 383.

105. Karl Frenzel, "Wie ich zu den Meiningern kam," *Bühne und Welt*, Nov. 15, 1899, pp. 688-89.

106. Bodenstedt to Georg, Meiningen, Dec. 2, 1868, HA: 125.

107. Georg to Bodenstedt, *ibid.*

108. Georg to Bodenstedt, Dec. 31, 1868, *ibid.* In fairness to Bodenstedt, it is clear from the accounts of rehearsals given by von Possart and others that the duke did not always give him a free hand at rehearsals, but very often took over himself.

109. Ernst von Possart, *Erstrebtes und Erlebtes* (Berlin, 1916), p. 234, asserts that the duke revealed his plans to him in 1868, saying, "I must carry out my work. If the mountain won't come to the Prophet, the Prophet must go to the mountain." This is the only reference by anyone suggesting that the duke was thinking about touring his company at so early a date.

Chapter Two

1. Macmillan and Company later published her book of lyrics, *Wild Roses* (London, 1878).

2. Hans von Bülow (1830-94), pianist, conductor, and at the time Ellen began to study with him, music critic for the *Vossische Zeitung*, had left his legal studies

to devote his life to music after he heard Liszt conduct *Lohengrin* in 1850 in Weimar. Often called the "first virtuoso conductor," von Bülow was in the forefront in establishing contemporary music. He was a passionate supporter of Brahms, whom he raised to the company of Bach and Beethoven by identifying the three composers as "The Three B's of Music." He was later conductor of the Meiningen court orchestra (1880-85).

3. Max Grube, *The Story of the Meininger*, tr. Ann Marie Koller (Coral Gables, Fla., 1965), p. 24.

4. *Ibid.*

5. Helene, Freifrau von Heldburg, *Fünfzig Jahre Glück und Leid* (Leipzig, 1926), pp. 73, 74, 282.

6. For an evaluation of Marr as director and educator by such men as Friedrich Hebbel and Gustav Freytag, see Paul Alfred Merbach, "Heinrich Marr als Regisseur," in *Heinrich Marr (1797-1871)* (Leipzig, 1926), pp. 166-73.

7. Helene Richter, *Josef Lewinsky* (Vienna, 1926), pp. 32-40, describes Lewinsky's experiences with Marr.

8. Merbach, pp. 170-72, cites two instances. In Weimar Marr, "in wonderful make-up," took part in the Prisoners Chorus in *Fidelio*; the conductor, Franz Liszt, was so delighted that he embraced the old actor. On another occasion Marr, who was directing *Der fliegende Holländer*, joined the seamen "to add fire" to the crowd scenes.

9. Feodor Wehl, *Fünfzehn Jahre Stuttgarter Hoftheaterleitung* (Hamburg, 1886), p. 46.

10. Birch-Pfeiffer (1800-1868), a former actress, provided a new popular play every year from 1830 to 1860. *Die Waise von Lowood*, a sentimental retelling of Charlotte Brontë's novel, enjoyed extraordinary success and played all over Europe into the twentieth century. See *Charlotte Birch-Pfeiffer und Heinrich Laube im Briefwechel*, ed. Alexander von Weilen (Berlin, 1917). Except as noted, the information on Ellen Franz's early theatrical career is drawn from her own work: Heldburg, pp. 3-11.

11. Grube, p. 26.

12. *Ibid.*

13. *Ibid.*, p. 27.

14. Max Grube, *Jugenderinnerungen eines Glückskindes* (Leipzig, 1917), pp. 100-101.

15. Bodenstedt did not leave off attacking Georg and Ellen Franz even years after they were married. In 1877 Cosima Wagner, then visiting Meiningen with her husband, wrote in her diary: "We are told very dismal things about the poet Bodenstedt, who, while still drawing his full salary, talks derogatively about the Duke and his wife" (*Diaries*, tr. Geoffrey Skelton, New York, 1976-77, entry for March 12, 1877).

16. Alois Wohlmuth, one of Bernhard's partisans, gives the other side of the story in *Ein Schauspielerleben* (Munich, 1918), pp. 102-12.

17. Baroness von Heldburg to Eugenie Stösser, March 17, 1920, in Heldburg, *Fünfzig Jahre Glück*, pp. 234-35.

18. According to Meiningen Theater Museum records compiled by Volker Reissland, Ludwig Chronegk (1837-91) held the following titles (or at least is referred to in the records by them) as leader of the tours: 1876, *Oberregisseur*; 1877, *Stell. Intendant*; 1880, *Intendantrat*; 1882, *Hofrat*; 1884, *Intendant*.

19. Paul Lindau, *Nur Erinnerungen* (Stuttgart, 1916), 1:9-12.

20. For an account of Krolls Etablissement and its diverting history, see Gerhard Wahnrau, *Berlin, Stadt der Theater* (Berlin, 1957), pp. 428-35.

21. Meiningen Theater Museum records show him playing comic roles in Pest, Zurich, Leipzig, and Königsberg between 1861 and 1866.

22. Max Kurnik, *Ein Menschenalter Theater Erinnerungen, 1845-1880* (Berlin, 1882), p. 244. Grube, *Story of the Meininger*, p. 30, identifies the piece performed by Chronegk as "the false Cataloni."

23. He also appeared as Spiegelberg in *Die Räuber*, von Blinkopf in *Götz von Berlichingen*, and von Kalb in *Kabale und Liebe* that first season.

24. Karl Grube, *Die Meininger* (Berlin, 1904), p. 31.

25. Chronegk to Ludwig Barnay, Dec. 23, 1873, in Barnay, *Erinnerungen* (Berlin, 1903), p. 193. Apparently Bodenstedt had some such authority also, since he engaged Ellen Franz on his own.

26. Max Grube, *Story of the Meininger*, p. 30.

27. Constantin Stanislavski, *My Life in Art*, tr. J. J. Robbins (Boston, 1938), pp. 196-206. Stanislavski later recognized the duke's work. In 1906, when the Russian players were in Berlin, he arranged a celebration for the duke's 80th birthday. See Claus Just, "Stanislavski und das deutschsprachige Theater," Ph.D. dissertation, University of Erlangen, [1970?], pp. 34-37.

28. Ludwig Barnay, "Die Meininger in London," *Die Deutsche Bühne*, Dec. 1909, p. 325. In "Charles Kean and the Meininger Myth" (*Theatre Research*, 4 [1964]: 137-53), Muriel St. Clare Byrne makes a good case against the notion that English soldiers were used as extras. She suggests that Germans then living in England would be the logical persons to be so employed. But Jean Anderson, working with materials in the Victoria and Albert Theatre Museum, concludes from a review in the *London Figaro* (and other references) that the extras were English soldiers (letter to the author, July 9, 1981).

29. Karl Grube, p. 24.

30. Chronegk to Georg, Aug. 5, 1881, cited in Heinz Isterheil, "Die Bühnendekorationen bei den Meiningern," Ph.D. dissertation, University of Cologne, 1938, p. 34.

31. *Ibid.*, p. 34.

32. Telegrams, Georg to Chronegk, in Meiningen Theater Museum.

33. Dingelstedt to Georg, June 6, 1876, COL.

34. Baroness von Heldburg to Max Grube, April 23, 1899, in Heldburg, p. 63.

Chapter Three

1. Georg in Liebenstein to Paul Lindau, Oct. 23, 1879; reprinted in *Die Deutsche Bühne*, Dec. 1909, p. 323.

2. Ludwig Barnay, *Erinnerungen* (Berlin, 1903), p. 249.

3. The history of the Schiller Prize during these years demonstrates the paucity of distinguished new drama. The prize, awarded every three years for the most outstanding dramatic work written during that time, was given in 1863 to Friedrich Hebbel for *Nibelungen*, a worthy recipient. In 1866 it was given to Albert Lindner for *Brutus und Collatinus*, a poetic drama weak in conception and

execution, but showing promise as a youthful effort. In 1869 the prize went to Emanuel Geibel, the most beloved lyricist of his time, for his dramatically worthless *Sophonisbe*. In 1872 and 1875 the commission could find no recipient at all, and in 1878 the prize was given to Adolf von Wilbrandt, Ludwig Anzengruber, and Franz Nissel, not for any designated work, but in recognition of outstanding talent. Unfortunately, when the commission found a good drama in 1893 in Ludwig Fulda's *Talisman*, and in 1896 recommended Gerhart Hauptmann's *Hanneles Himmelfahrt*, the emperor refused to accept the recommendations and awarded the prize to Ernst von Wildenbruch for his now forgotten historical dramas *Heinrich* and *Heinrichs Geschlecht*.

4. Max Grube, *The Story of the Meininger*, tr. Ann Marie Koller (Coral Gables, Fla., 1965), p. 108.

5. Alfred Kruchen cites Max Grube to this effect in "Das Regie-Prinzip bei den Meiningern zur Zeit ihrer Gastspielepoche 1874-1890," Ph.D. dissertation, University of Danzig, 1933, p. 54.

6. Wolfgang Pasche, *Skandinavische Dramatik in Deutschland* (Basel, 1979), pp. 32-48.

7. Although the letters between the baroness and contemporary writers show her wide knowledge of literature and her sensitivity toward authors, at least on one occasion she allowed her partiality to overcome her judgment. In 1886 she insisted on producing Byron's *Marino Faliero* against the wishes of the translator, Arthur Fitger, who asserted that Byron had refused to have the play staged during his lifetime. On March 13, 1886, she wrote Fitger: "I have read the foreword to his collected pieces, and I find only that he says he wrote *Faliero* without any thought of staging it. . . . He spoke very disparagingly of the public, or better said, he did not wish to be stamped on by them. But such reasons don't bind us. Had he really prohibited a production, that would be quite different, but in no way did he do that." A few weeks later on April 29, she admitted she was wrong after Fitger sent her clippings: "I am ashamed that I knew so little about Byron's protests about seeing his play on stage. And to think I wrote you in such a way! . . . You should have simply answered me: 'Before you come to me again with warnings and considerations and that sort of thing, stick your nose deeper in a book.'" (Helene, Freifrau von Heldburg, *Fünfzig Jahre Glück und Leid*, Leipzig, 1926, p. 51.) By this time the Meininger were already committed to the play.

8. There are 10 undated notebooks in the Meiningen Landesarchiv with the beginnings of an adaptation of *Troilus and Cressida* by the baroness. They probably date from 1887-88, for on Nov. 27, 1887, she wrote to Fitger: "The greatest experience of the summer was my seeing *Henry VIII* and *Troilus and Cressida*, both of which I am eager to give." The method here seems to have been to copy each act of a very early reading edition into a notebook, compare it with an acting edition, and then recopy it into a notebook with changes, omissions, etc. Since neither the reading copy nor the acting copy is in the archives, it would take a textual scholar to determine just how the changes were made. The drama was never given in Meiningen, and the reworking was probably never carried beyond the place where it was left in the notebooks.

9. For a dissenting view of the duke's staging of *Julius Caesar*, see V. I. Nemirovich-Danchenko's letter, Appendix C, doc. 1.

10. Max Martersteig, *Das deutsche Theater im neunzehnten Jahrhundert* (Leipzig, 1904), pp. 515-627; Elizabeth Gilmore Holt, *From the Classicists to the*

Impressionists (Garden City, N.Y., 1966), pp. 127-414, especially pp. 343-53; Ernst H. Gombrich, *The Story of Art*, 13th ed. (New York, 1978), pp. 399-403.

11. Volker Reissland, "Herausbildung und Grundzüge der Meininger Theaterreform im letzten Drittel des 19. Jahrhunderts als Wegbereiter für die Weiterentwicklung der Schauspielkunst im beginnenden 20. Jahrhundert," thesis, Karl Marx University, Leipzig, 1977, pp. 23-66. Much of the information in the following section is from this source, pp. 51-56.

12. Georg to his mother, StBBH: K8 M72 B19-20, Meiningen, n.d. 1848. Those who professed to see nothing but externals in the staging of the Meininger were fond of comparing Georg's staging with the colorful historical paintings of the time. Ludwig Speidel, opposed to everything new in the theater, pointed out what seemed to him to be a close relationship between the Meininger staging and Piloty's declamatory style, and asserted: "Georg II hoped to bring the spirit of the drama to life by reforming the properties" (cited in Heinz Isterheil, "Die Bühnendekorationen bei den Meiningern," Ph.D. dissertation, University of Cologne, 1938, p. 43). As late as 1937 Kurt Sauer, attacking the realistic theater, wrote in *Deutsche Theaterzeitung*, no. 133, of the "unbearable plundering of the Piloty epoch." Georg's own words make it irrefutable that his intentions lay far from putting an ordered historical picture on stage. In 1861, after seeing the Exhibition of Art in Cologne, which as Reissland points out, betrayed the ideals of Cornelius and Georg's other revered masters, he commented: "The most superficial naturalism now prevails and our tasteless public allows itself to be so bluffed by the Pilotys and their associates that it no longer has any appreciation of the old genuine compositions. The much prized painting *Nero* I find shockingly ordinary and completely trivial in conception and execution. . . . This whole direction will be the ruin of art. . . . What is the purpose of art if not to elevate mankind; with the ordinary we elevate no one. . . . Nowadays in art the same tendency expresses itself as in politics and in national life—everything should become leveled." (Georg to his mother, StBBH: K8 M88 B2, Cologne, n.d. 1861.)

13. Wilhelm von Kaulbach (1805-74), whose work reflected a penchant for the dramatic and a love for the grotesque, had influenced Georg since his university days in Bonn. He is reported to have said to Georg: "Too bad you are a little prince, you might have been a great artist." In July 1846 Kaulbach gave Georg a drawing lesson on capturing movement, the gist of which he conveyed to his mother: "You see, you take a suitable cloth and throw it to and fro along the floor until you get a good curve; then you draw it" (StBBH: K7 M7 B5, Bonn, July 6, 1844).

14. The papers of the Brückners are in the Theater Museum, University of Cologne (COL).

15. Stein to Brückners, COL, Meiningen, n.d., 1866.

16. In her diary entry for June 6, 1876, Cosima Wagner notes that the Brückners, who were making sets for the opening of the Festspielhaus, put the duke's wishes above all others: "Richard is terribly worn out and annoyed by how far behind many things are, above all the decorations by the Brückner brothers, who in the meantime have painted fourteen sets for the Duke of Meiningen." Again on July 12, a month before the opening of *Das Rheingold*: "R. gets very angry with the Brückner brothers, who express themselves very clumsily (they say they could not neglect their oldest customer, the Duke of Meiningen). The word 'customer' upset R. terribly." Wagner had accosted the Brückners in a café, demanded to know why his work had not been finished, and was outraged to hear a ruling

NOTES TO PAGES 91-101

German prince called a "customer." Cosima concludes: "He regrets this and cordially begs pardon of the Brückners." (*Diaries*, tr. Geoffrey Skelton, New York, 1967, vol. 1).

17. Josef Kainz, *Der junge Kainz* (Berlin, 1912), p. 235; Aloys Prasch, "Erinnerungen eines ehemaligen Meiningers," *Bühne und Welt*, 1 (1899): 701.

18. G. Brückner to Georg, COL, Coburg, Nov. 11, 1882.

19. Georg to M. Brückner, COL, Meiningen, n.d. 1882.

20. Chronegk to Brückners, COL, Berlin, May 12, 1882.

21. Georg to M. Brückner, COL, Meiningen, Oct. 14, 1869, Bad Liebenstein, Sept. 14, 1872.

22. *Ibid.*, Jan. 29, 1875, n.d. 1885, n.d. 1894; telegram, baroness von Heldburg to M. Brückner, Meiningen Theater Museum, Meiningen, Feb. 11, 1899. Much of the material on the relationship between the Brückners and Georg that I have used was given to me by Heinz Isterheil, who got it from Prince Ernst, Georg's son.

23. Georg to M. Brückner, COL, Meiningen, n.d. 1881.

24. *Ibid.*, Jan. 19, 1886.

25. *Ibid.*, April 11, 1886.

26. Albert Lindner, "Die Meininger und ihr Kunstprinzip," *Westermanns Jahrbuch der Illustrirten Deutschen Monatshefte*, 44 (1878): 436.

27. Georg to M. Brückner, COL, Meiningen, July 21, 1876.

28. Ibsen to Georg, COL, Munich, Nov. 13, 1886. Italics Ibsen's.

29. Georg to M. Brückner, COL, Meiningen, Nov. 15, 1886.

30. Heinrich Bulthaupt, *Dramaturgie des Schauspiels* (Oldenburg-Leipzig, 1905), 1:228ff, discusses the problem of shifting on the illusionistic stage.

31. Isterheil, "Die Bühnendekorationen," p. 57.

32. Georg to M. Brückner, COL, Meiningen, n.d. 1877.

33. *Ibid.*, Nov. 3, 1880, Jan. 30, 1882, March 15, 1882.

34. Cited in Michael R. Booth, *Victorian Spectacular Theatre, 1850-1910* (Boston, 1981), p. 52. Professor Booth's admirable chapter "The Taste for Spectacle" describes the use of spectacle for its own sake on the Victorian stage.

35. Isterheil, pp. 71-72.

36. Prasch, "Erinnerungen," p. 701.

37. Ernst von Possart, *Erstrebtes und Erlebtes* (Berlin, 1916), p. 236.

38. Georg to M. Brückner, COL, Meiningen, Dec. 27, 1874.

39. *Ibid.*, July 8, 1875.

40. Georg wanted each set individualized. On the Danube sketch for *Die Räuber* (Meiningen Theater Museum), he instructed Max Brückner: "Keep the river landscape in a strong light, so that it looks German and not Italian."

41. "Bei den Meiningern hinter den Coulissen," *Heimatgarten*, Feb. 1882, pp. 378-81.

42. Georg to M. Brückner, COL, Meiningen, Jan. 3, 1872.

43. M. von Szeliski, "Aus der Hauptstadt," *Die Gegenwart*, 5.25 (1874): 398.

44. Isterheil, "Bühnendekorationen," p. 66.

45. Chronegk to Georg, Aug. 8, 1876, cited *ibid.*

46. *Ibid.*

47. Grube, *Story of the Meininger*, p. 100.

48. "Das Gastspiel des Herzoglich sachsen-meiningenschen Hoftheaters zu Berlin," *Hof- und Adel-zeitung*, June 1, 1876.

49. "Das Gastspiel der Meininger," *Kickeriki* (Vienna), Sept. 30, 1875.

233

50. *Münchner Nachrichten und Anzeiger*, July 1, 1883.

51. The spontaneous applause the lighting on the prospects elicited from the more than 200 International Federation for Theatre Research (FIRT) scholars visiting Meiningen in September 1981 seems to indicate that Georg's effects still work magic.

52. Paul Lindau, "Aus der Hauptstadt," *Die Gegenwart*, 5.22 (1874): 349.

53. Chronegk to Brückners, COL, Meiningen, Dec. 7, 1886.

54. *Düsseldorfer Volksblatt*, June 10, 1886.

55. "Bei den Meiningern," pp. 378-81.

56. *Die Neue Freie Presse* (Vienna), Nov. 1, 1883. The eerie squeaking was achieved by scraping a bow across a taut violin string.

57. Information given to the author in 1961 by W. Probst, who had worked with the original Meininger players and later became crew chief.

58. Chronegk to unnamed addressee, [Barmen], April 18, 1886; Isterheil, "Bühnendekorationen," p. 81, who was shown the letter by Prince Ernst in 1937.

59. Telegram, Georg to Chronegk, Meininger Theater Museum, Meiningen, Nov. 12, 1887.

60. Dingelstedt to Georg, COL, Vienna, June 9, 1876.

61. Otto von Kurnatowski, *Georg II. Herzog von Sachsen-Meiningen, ein Lebens- und Kulturbild* (Hildburghausen, 1914), p. 69.

62. Karl Grube, *Die Meininger* (Berlin, 1904), p. 40.

63. Kainz, *Der junge Kainz*, p. 196.

64. Prasch, "Erinnerungen," p. 702.

65. Cited in Isterheil, p. 105.

66. Max Grube, *Story of the Meininger*, p. 50.

67. Siegward Friedmann, "Das erste Gastspiel in Meiningen," *Die Deutsche Bühne*, Dec. 1909, p. 329.

68. Karl Frenzel, *Berliner Dramaturgie* (Hannover, 1877), 2:111.

69. Telegram, Georg to Chronegk, Meiningen Theater Museum, Meiningen, June 6, 1875.

70. Georg to Wardrobe Inspector Raupp, May 4, 1876; reprinted in *Bühne und Welt*, April 1906, pp. 698-99.

71. *Zweite Beilage zur Allgemeinen Zeitung* (Munich), 1883, no. 99. Not all critics were in agreement; see Nemirovich-Danchenko's letter in Appendix C.

Chapter Four

1. Josef Kainz, *Der junge Kainz* (Berlin, 1912), pp. 196-97.

2. Hans von Bülow, *Briefe* (Leipzig, 1907), 6:139. At her request he sent her some "hints" to ensure her success: "Titles (important!): the Duke: Highness. (His Highness now and then speaks somewhat rapidly, unclearly—he doesn't like it when he is not understood.) His wife: Madame." And so on through the court and theater personnel. "Remember," he warned, "that at the hotel there is one table for actors, another for officers, one for traveling businessmen. . . . As a newcomer you will be stared at." (*Ibid.*)

3. Karl Weiser, "Herzog Georg von Sachsen-Meiningen als Regisseur," *Illustrierte Zeitung*, Dec. 23, 1909.

4. This did not always work out in practice. When Kainz, who like the others

in the company was accustomed to repertory playing, was told that the run of *Die Räuber* in Berlin would be 14 nights, he asked Chronegk to alternate him with another actor in the role of Kosinsky, but Kainz was so successful with the public in the part that Chronegk was reluctant to do so. (Kainz, p. 202.)

5. Aloys Prasch, "Erinnerungen eines ehemaligen Meiningers," *Bühne und Welt*, 1 (1899): 702.

6. Karl Weiser, "Zehn Jahre Meiningen," in *Archiv für Theatergeschichte*, ed. Hans Devrient (Berlin, 1904), 1 : 121.

7. Wolfgang Drews, *Die Grossen des deutschen Schauspiels* (Berlin, 1941), pp. 174-75.

8. Josef Kainz, "Ein Brief an einen Engländer," Berlin, Aug. 27, 1891, in *Kainz, ein Brevier*, ed. Marie Mautner Kalbeck (Vienna, 1953), p. 28. At the time he wrote this letter, Kainz was barred from working in Berlin because of a contract dispute. It is interesting to note that he quotes Marr's favorite expression— that the actor should be "a well-polished stone in a beautiful mosaic."

9. Eduard von Winterstein, *Mein Leben und meine Zeit* (Berlin, 1947), 1 : 156.

10. *Ibid.*

11. Kainz, "Ein Brief," p. 28.

12. Max Grube, Karl Grube, Aloys Prasch, and Amanda Lindner, among others. Georg had no illusions that in training Kainz he was developing an artist who would remain in Meiningen; from the beginning Kainz bent every effort to obtain an engagement at the Burgtheater in Vienna, but he was to play on many stages before he reached that goal. And in far different circumstances from those in Meiningen, too. In Munich, for example, King Ludwig II, unlike Georg, expected a "personal" actor. For Kainz's years in Munich, see Felix Philippi, *Ludwig II und Josef Kainz* (Berlin, 1913), pp. 7-46.

13. Ludwig Barnay, *Erinnerungen* (Berlin, 1903), p. 261.

14. Amanda Lindner, "Erinnerungen," *Thüringen: Eine Monatsschrift für alte und neue Kultur*, 1 (1926): 20-22. Georg was interested in everything that took place in Meiningen. Hans von Bülow repeatedly complained in letters that Georg customarily attended even the separate rehearsals of the winds, strings, and other sections.

15. The table on p. 236 shows a typical season for one actor, Ludwig Chronegk, in 1869-70. He did not of course appear in every play given by the company.

16. The duke began the exacting rehearsals as soon as he took over the theater and let nothing interfere with his schedule. On Dec. 29, 1873, Hans von Bülow, then guest conducting at Meiningen, wrote: "Immediately after the midday meal, the duke and his wife had to go to a rehearsal of *Twelfth Night*, which is to be given tomorrow" (letter to Joachim Raff in von Bülow, *Briefe*, 6 : 120-21). Since the duke and the baroness took their large meal of the day in the middle-class style, at 2:00 P.M., they were in the theater by 4:00 P.M. Karl Uhlig, "Proben Erinnerungen," *Thüringen: Eine Monatsschrift für alte und neue Kultur*, 1 (1926): 27-29, says there were 25 rehearsals for *Die Jungfrau von Orleans* not counting the rehearsals of the crowd and the tutoring of the individual actors, and 30 for *The Pretenders*.

17. Paul Lindau, *Nur Erinnerungen* (Stuttgart, 1916), 2 : 344.

18. *Der junge Kainz*, p. 199.

19. Weiser, "Zehn Jahre," p. 122; Alois Wohlmuth, *Ein Schauspielerleben* (Munich, 1918), p. 104.

Table to Note 15. Ludwig Chronegk's Roles in the 1869-70 Season

Author	Play	Role
Goethe	*Faust*	Brander
Shakespeare	*Taming of the Shrew* (4x)	Grumio
Molière	*Médicin malgré lui*	Sganarelle
Jacobson	*Beckers Geschichte*	Siegfried
Shakespeare	*Julius Caesar* (4x)	Third citizen
Lederer	*Weiblichen Studenten*	Heinrich
Raupach	*Vor hundert Jahren*	Wex
Pohl	*Gold-Onkel*	Florian
Görner	*Glücklicher Familienvater*	M. Leichthin
Eschenbach	*Doktor Ritter*	Vogt
Schiller	*Wallensteins Lager*	Recrut
Shakespeare	*Twelfth Night*	Sir Andrew
Malten	*Er muss taub sein*	Timotheus
Wages	*'s Lorle*	von Stritzow
Björnson	*Sigurd the Bastard*, part 3 (2x)	K. Harald
Töpfer	*Beste Ton* (2x)	Nikolas
Kleist	*Käthchen von Heilbronn*	J. Pech
Schiller	*Kabale und Liebe*	von Kalb
Müller	*Onkel Moses*	Simon
Baumann	*Versprechen hinter'm Herd*	Arthur
Kalisch	*Einmal hunderttausend Taler*	Stullmüller
Laube/Schiller	*Demetrius*	E. von Lemberg
Braun/Suppe	*Flotte Bursche* (4x)	Fleck
Belly	*Monsieur Herkules* (2x)	Caesar
F. Moser	*Unversichtigkeit* (2x)	Samuel
Wolff/Weber	*Preciosa*	Contreras
Töpfer	*Eine Frau, die in Paris war*	Johann
Salingre	*Durch's Schlüsselloch*	Krümel
Friedrich	*Muttersegen*	Pierrot
Goldoni	*Gutherzige Polterer*	Piccard
Mosen	*Er kommpromittiert seine Frau*	von Dickelberg
Shakespeare	*Romeo and Juliet*	Peter
Ploetz	*Verwunchene Prinz*	Wilhelm
Nestroy	*Lumpacivagabundus* (2x)	Zwirn
Ludwig	*Erbförster*	Gottfried
Goethe	*Egmont*	Jetter
Shakespeare	*Merchant of Venice* (3x)	Launcelot
Scribe	*Mein Glückstern*	Paimpol
Freytag	*Journalisten* (2x)	Bellmaus
Minding	*Papst Sixtus V* (4x)	Jacopo
Schneider	*Kurmärker und die Picarden*	Schulze
Shakespeare	*King Lear*	Fool
Gründorf	*Opfer der Consulin*	Horatius
Benedix	*Hochzeitsreise*	Hahansporn
Shakespeare	*Much Ado About Nothing*	Cyprian[a]
Meyr	*Herzog Albrecht*	von Wannen
G. Moser	*Wie denken Sie über Russland*	Melzer
Shakespeare	*Midsummer Night's Dream*	Flute/Thisby

SOURCE: Compiled from the archives of the Meiningen Theater Museum by Volker Reissland, 1981.
NOTE: Except for plays that ran several times during the season (shown, e.g., as 3x), the list shows performances in the order in which they were given, from October 7 to April 18.
[a] The nature of this role is unknown; possibly a walk-on part.

20. Siegward Friedmann, "Das erste Gastspiel in Meiningen," *Die Deutsche Bühne*, Dec. 1909, p. 338.

21. Helene, Freifrau von Heldburg, *Fünfzig Jahre Glück und Leid* (Leipzig, 1926), pp. 50-51.

22. The duke's handwritten directions for *Marino Faliero* above and those following for *The Merchant of Venice* were extracted from records in the Meiningen Landesarchiv and transcribed by the former director, Friedrich Heide.

23. The duke's instructions for Acts II and III, part of which are quoted here, are instructive of his approach to arranging an acting version of Shakespeare's comedy. He used Schlegel's translation, but cut three scenes: II, viii, a street in Venice, in which Solanio and Salarino report Shylock's reaction to Jessica's elopement; III, iii, a street in Venice, with Shylock, Salarino, and the jailer present at Antonio's arrest; and III, v, in Belmont, in which Launcelot, Jessica, and Lorenzo discuss Shylock. (See *Der Kaufmann von Venedig, Schauspiel in fünf Akten von William Shakespeare. Offizielle Ausgabe, nach dem Scenarium des Herzogl. Sachsen-Meiningen'schen Hoftheaters bearbeitet*, Leipzig, n.d.) Concern for shifting dictated Georg's cutting III, iii, and III, v; reaching for dramatic effect caused him to bring the action of II, viii, on stage by having Shylock play out the scene originally reported by the two Venetians. Wolfgang Iser, in his detailed study "*Der Kaufmann von Venedig* auf der Illusionsbühne der Meininger" (*Shakespeare Jahrbuch*, 99, 1963, pp. 72-96), makes a strong case against Georg's handling of these scenes and reducing the importance of Salarino and Solanio. He contends that the two Venetians have the important function of delineating the atmosphere of historical Venice, that reducing them to hardly more than walkons completely alters their scenes, and that what the duke put on the stage to please the eye did not compensate the audience for what was lost to the ear and mind.

24. Karl Uhlig, who played this part originally, says the duke saw this person in Venice, quickly sketched him, and had the make-up and costume copied in Meiningen ("Proben Enrinnerungen," p. 27). Max Grube found the figure of the old man an unnecessary touch.

25. The duke wanted his actors to begin to get into their characterization from the first day and impressed on them that they must have the words of the dramatist well in mind to do that. In 1906 Kainz wrote to a young actor: "A classical role should be learned quickly, by the second time through" (*Kainz, ein Brevier*, p. 80).

26. Weiser, "Herzog Georg."

27. Ludwig Barnay, "Mein Debut in Meiningen," *Bühne und Welt*, April-May 1906, p. 584.

28. Eight such notebooks, not all complete, remain in the Meiningen Landesarchiv and were transcribed for me by the former director, Friedrich Heide.

29. Franz Wallner, "Meine Erinnerungen an Meiningen," *Volksspielkunst*, 7 (1926): 107-9.

30. During the 26 years that Goethe was the administrator of the Weimar court theater, two of the actors he coached, Pius Alexander Wolff and Karl Franz Grüner, kept a record of his instructions; in 1824 these were organized and printed with Goethe's permission as a sort of primer of acting. According to these so-called Rules for Actors, an actor was always to remember that he was acting for the audience (which is to say, Goethe's Weimar audience, a social and cultural

elite). Rules 35-89, dealing with the movement of the body on stage, "must be considered as a valiant attempt to stem the tide of realism and to defend the sacred precinct of poetic drama." (A. M. Nagler, "Weimar Classicism," in *A Source Book in Theatrical History*, New York, 1952, pp. 425-33.)

31. Weiser, "Zehn Jahre," p. 124.

32. Telegram, Georg to Chronegk (in Berlin), Meiningen Theater Museum, Meiningen, May 16, 1878.

33. Baroness von Heldburg to Chronegk, *ibid.*

34. Prasch, "Erinnerungen," p. 700.

35. The former actors gathered for gala occasions: the silver wedding anniversary of the duke and the baroness in 1898; the duke's 80th birthday in 1906; the opening of the new theater in 1909; the 100th anniversary of the duke's birth in 1926.

36. Adele Sandrock, *Mein Leben* (Berlin, 1940), pp. 38-39.

37. Kainz's mother to Kainz, Vienna, May 21, 1878, in *Kainz, ein Brevier*, p. 16. How justified the complaints were is questionable, as Kainz himself realized years later, when he looked back ruefully on this period of his life. In 1888 he wrote in his diary: "Yesterday I read all my old letters to my parents. . . . In general, a completely false judgment and false perception of all that was happening! Why? Because the 18-year-old Pepi placed himself in the center of the world and everything revolved around him. He related everything directly or indirectly to his really unimportant self. If a director made a harmless remark, he saw it as a carefully calculated attack on himself. . . . The blockhead was not wrong about his talent; he was only enraged that the world did not give him proper recognition and disagreed with his opinion of himself. . . . He also loved. Indeed he loved with all the fervor of his wounded spirit. . . . Too bad his willfulness was stronger than his love! Otherwise he would have become a man (*Mensch*) sooner." (*Ibid.*, p. 17.)

38. Sandrock, pp. 39-40.

39. Weiser, Max Grube, and others report this favorite saying of the duke's.

40. Weiser, "Herzog Georg."

41. Heldburg, *Fünfzig Jahre*, p. 183.

42. See, for example, G. Romberg, *Allegemeine Theater Chronik* (Vienna), 7.42 (Oct. 20, 1883). Romberg discusses at length the hazards of introducing realism into the classics.

43. Albert Lindner, "Die Meininger und ihr Kunstprinzip," *Westermanns Jahrbuch der Illustrirten Deutschen Monatshefte*, 44 (July 1878): 463-42.

44. See Dieter Hoffmeier, "Die Meininger—Historismus als Tageswirkung," *Material zum Theater*, 16.54 (1974): 40-42.

45. Serge Diaghilev, in defending the Moscow Art Theater's production of *Julius Caesar* against the criticism that the company should not have tried the play when it had no tragic actors, stated: "Think of the sarcasms heaped on the Meininger players when they appeared in countries educated in the tradition of psychopathic enthusiasm for all sorts of art tricks from Tamberlic's *contre ut dieze* to Komisarkevska's sour tears. All this 'straight from the heart' business, these 'moments of inspiration,' this bestial pursuit of 'the soul,' which seems impossible to throw off, have greatly harmed our art. Just as a portrait is no good 'unless it comes out of the frame,' so we refuse to accept our classical theater unless it contains at least 'one tragic actor.' Any flabby seventy-year-old Othello—

say Salvini—will make all . . . lie on their backs: that is the charming custom we have inherited." (*The World of Art*, 1902, cited in Serge Lifar, *Serge Diaghilev: His Life, His Work, His Legend*, New York, 1940, p. 80.)

Tamberlic was an Italian tenor of great international fame in the 1850-60 period. Like all great singers of his time and school, he attached, as did his public, an exaggerated importance to the highest note of his register, C, C-sharp (*contre ut dieze*), and sometimes even D. When one of these was due in a part, everyone on both sides of the footlights stopped and prepared to listen to the marvelous sound produced by the singer, with extreme deliberation and absolute contempt for the dramatic situation or even the musical sense of the moment. The post-Wagnerian style condemned this practice as inartistic and senseless; the ordinary listener still raved about it.

46. Wohlmuth, *Ein Schauspielerleben*, pp. 104-12. Wohlmuth, an oldtime virtuoso of the second rank, considered the time he spent in Meiningen wasted. He believed that ensemble playing ruined the individuality of the actor, and that the natural style of acting was no style at all.

47. Charles Waldstein, "The Court Theater of Meiningen," *Harper's New Monthly Magazine*, April 1881, pp. 743-58.

48. Karl Frenzel, "Berliner Chronik," *Deutsche Rundschau*, 3 (1876): 151-55.

49. C. Halford Hawkins, "The Meininger Court Theater," *Macmillan's Magazine*, April 1877.

50. Max Martersteig, *Das deutsche Theater im neunzehnten Jahrhundert* (Leipzig, 1904), p. 643.

51. Prasch, "Erinnerungen."

52. After the Oriental Pavilion at the Paris World's Fair of 1867 offered an exhibition of Japanese art, the taste for all things Japanese became the fashion. Georg owned a number of books on Japan and Japanese art. Max Grube recalled seeing such a volume with the duke's marginal notes; but since the books are no longer in the Meiningen library, we can only assess their influence on him by observing what he did on the stage.

53. "Bei den Meiningern hinter den Coulissen," *Heimatgarten*, 6.5 (Feb. 1882): 381.

54. Max Grube, *The Story of the Meininger*, tr. Ann Marie Koller (Coral Gables, Fla., 1965), p. 65.

55. Prasch, p. 701.

56. *Ibid.*

57. Bülow, *Briefe*, 6:513.

58. Georg noted the cutting of the scene and the changing of the set in a letter to Max Brückner, COL, Meiningen, Dec. 27, 1874.

59. "Die Meininger im Gärtnerplatztheater," *Münchner Neueste Nachrichten*, July 28, 1883.

60. Constantin Stanislavski, *My Life in Art*, tr. J. J. Robbins (New York, 1956), p. 198.

61. "Theater am Gärtnerplatz," *Zweite Beilage zur Allgemeinen Zeitung* (Munich), July 6, 1887, pp. 1-2.

62. Prasch, "Erinnerungen," pp. 695-96.

63. Paul Lindau, "Papst Sixtus V," *Die Gegenwart*, 5.21 (1874): 331-33.

64. Ludwig Speidel, *Schauspieler*, vol. 4 of *Ludwig Speidels Schriften* (Berlin, 1911), pp. 47ff.

65. "Die Meininger in München," *Münchner Neueste Nachrichten*, July 7, 1887, p. 4.
66. Alfred Skene, "Die Hermannsschlacht," *Deutsche Zeitung* (Vienna), Oct. 17, 1875.
67. Wohlmuth, *Ein Schauspielerleben*, p. 104.

Chapter Five

1. Max Grube, *The Story of the Meininger*, tr. Ann Marie Koller (Coral Gables, Fla., 1965), pp. 58-77, describes the first Berlin appearance from the point of view of the actor.
2. Cosima Wagner, *Diaries*, tr. Geoffrey Skelton (New York, 1976), 1:442-43 (entry for March 21, 1874).
3. Ludwig Barnay, *Erinnerungen* (Berlin, 1903), pp. 200-201.
4. Telegram, Georg to Chronegk, Meiningen Theater Museum, Meiningen, May 1, 1874. Pfutz, an extra, had devised such an agonizing death scene for himself that the duke feared he might get guffaws from the audience.
5. Max Grube's statement that the sets for *Julius Caesar* had to be done over gives the false impression that the Brückners had to repaint their own sets. Over the years, Georg changed some details as new archaeological discoveries were made, but when the sets were redone for the English tour of 1881, they were substantially the same as the sets for 1874.
6. For an assessment of the historical accuracy of Georg's staging of *Julius Caesar*, see Inge Krengel-Strudthoff, "Das Antike Rom auf der Bühne und der Übergang vom Gemalten zum Plastischen Bühnenbild. Anmerkungen zu den *Caesar*-Dekorationen Georgs von Meiningen," in *Bühnenformen-Bühnenräume Bühnendekorationen* (Berlin, 1973), pp. 160-75. Unless otherwise noted, the information on details of set decoration in this and the following section is drawn from Heinz Isterheil, "Die Bühnendekorationen bei den Meiningern," Ph.D. dissertation, University of Cologne, 1938.
7. Letter in possession of Prince Ernst in 1937, cited in Isterheil, p. 98.
8. The weapons had been made according to the originals, which Napoleon had collected in the museum at St. Germain for his studies for *The History of Julius Caesar* (Carl, Freiherr von Stein, *Die Kunst in Meiningen unter Herzog Georg II*, Meiningen, 1909, p. 11).
9. Georg to M. Brückner, COL, Meiningen, Sept. 2, 1880.
10. The Roman original of this statue was in marble, but because of the expense, Georg had the stage piece made of papier-mâché (Georg to M. Brückner, COL, Meiningen, March 8, 1881).
11. To show Max Brückner how the stone in the columns should look, Georg sent him some samples of red porphyry and Nubian serpentine from Rome and Tivoli (*ibid.*, Jan. 21, 1881).
12. Heinrich Bulthaupt, *Dramaturgie des Schauspiels* (Oldenburg-Leipzig, 1920), 2:231.
13. For a dissenting view on the value of this scene, see Nemirovich-Danchenko's letter, Appendix C, doc. 1.
14. Karl Frenzel, *Berliner Dramaturgie* (Erfurt, 1877), 2:106.
15. Grube, *Story of the Meininger*, p. 5.
16. Ernst von Possart, *Erstrebtes und Erlebtes* (Berlin, 1916), p. 238.

17. Hans Hopfen, "Die Meininger in Berlin," *Die Neue Freie Presse* (Vienna), May 30, 1874.

18. Hans Hopfen, *Streitfragen und Erinnerungen* (Stuttgart, 1876), pp. 331-33.

19. *Zeite Beilage zur Allgemeinen Zeitung* (Munich), Aug. 2, 1883. Max Grube found the comic scenes among the best staged by the Meininger. He describes the garden scene, praised by nearly everyone who saw the comedy, in detail on pp. 62-64.

20. Although Lindner's Roman tragedy *Brutus und Collatinus*, which had won the Schiller prize in 1866, had not justified the award, his *Bluthochzeit* in 1871, despite poorly motivated characters, showed great progress. Especially because of the passionate energy of the speech and the dramatic power of the individual scenes, great hopes were placed on him as a new writer. *Bluthochzeit* was to remain his most famous work, for like Julius Minding, author of *Papst Sixtus V*, he led an unhappy life and died early. Minding committed suicide. Lindner died in a charity hospital for the insane in 1888.

21. Paul Lindau, *Dramaturgische Blätter* (Breslau, 1879), 1:79ff.

22. Karl Frenzel in *National Zeitung* (Berlin), June 8, 1874.

23. Theodor Fontane, *Plaudereien über Theater* (Berlin, 1905), p. 527. Reprint of his 1874 review in *Vossische Zeitung*.

24. Georg to M. Brückner, COL, Meiningen, Jan. 20, 1870.

25. Wolfgang Iser, "*Der Kaufmann von Venedig* auf der Illusionsbühne der Meininger," *Shakespeare Jahrbuch*, 99 (1963): 72-94. The concerns that Iser investigates in this article are common to all Shakespearean productions on the illusionistic stage.

26. Moritz Ehrlich, *Das Gastspiel der Meininger oder die Grenzen der Bühnenausstattung* (Berlin, 1874), pp. 28-29.

27. Grube, *Story of the Meininger*, p. 68. For a discussion of the strengths and weaknesses of the Meininger company during the years 1874-76, see Robert Prölss, *Das Herzoglich Meiningen'sche Hoftheater und die Bühnenreform* (Erfurt, 1876), pp. 40-51.

28. Genée discusses the Meininger principles at length in "Das Gastspiel der Meininger in Berlin," *Deutsche Rundschau*, 1 (1875): 457-63.

29. *Allgemeine Zeitung* (Augsburg), May 25, 1874.

30. The material on this letter and the ensuing controversy is from Barnay, *Erinnerungen*, pp. 201-2; and the two newspapers as cited in the text.

31. "Illustrirte Rückblicke," *Kladderadatsch*, June 30, 1874.

Chapter Six

1. Much of the material in this chapter is based on Max Grube, *The Story of the Meininger*, tr. Ann Marie Koller (Coral Gables, Fla., 1965), pp. 69-77.

2. Paul Lindau, *Dramaturgische Blätter* (Breslau, 1879), 2:26.

3. Heinz Isterheil, "Die Bühnendekorationen bei den Meiningern," Ph.D. dissertation, University of Cologne, 1938, p. 80.

4. Robert F. Arnold, *Das moderne Drama* (Strassburg, 1908), p. 14.

5. Ludwig Speidel, *Schauspieler*, vol. 4 of *Ludwig Speidels Schriften* (Berlin, 1911), pp. 47ff.

6. "The Meiningen Dramatic Troupe," *The Academy*, April 27, 1876.

7. Karl Frenzel, "Das Gastspiel der Meininger," *Deutsche Rundschau*, March 1878, p. 152.

8. Grube, p. 79.

9. Georg to Brückner, COL, Meiningen, Jan. 20, 1870.

10. Hans Melde, "Zur Schillerinterpretation bei den Meiningern," *Material zum Theater*, 54.16: 52-55.

11. Speidel, pp. 95ff.

12. Isterheil, p. 137.

13. Ann Marie Koller, "Ibsen and the Meininger," *Educational Theatre Journal*, 17.2 (May 1965): 101-3.

14. *Macbeth* is the only play not printed in the official Meininger editions and so must be reconstructed from Isterheil's study ("Die Bühnendekorationen," p. 104) and reviews (Karl Frenzel, *Berliner Dramaturgie*, Erfurt, 1877, 2:156; Max Kurnik, *Ein Menschenalter Theater-Erinnerungen, 1845-1880*, Berlin, 1882, pp. 330-32). Although Kurnik says that "not one scene transposition, combination, or shortening detracted from the power of the poetry," Frenzel objected to some of the changes, particularly the cutting of the murder of Banquo. The arrangement was this: Act I, i-iv and v-vii played as two scenes; Act II, iii (after the porter's monologue) and iv were cut; Act III, i (Banquo's murder) and vi (the meeting of Lennox and another lord) were cut; Act IV, i, Hecate's lines were cut. Act V was played as in the original. An examination of these cuts will indicate the sacrifices Georg thought he had to make if Shakespeare's rapid shifting was to be staged on the illusionistic stage without endless scene curtains. But he achieved unity at a cost that many in the audience did not care for.

15. Ernst Leopold von Stahl, *Shakespeare und das deutsche Theater* (Stuttgart, 1947), p. 454.

16. Gerhart Hauptmann, "Aus den Jugenderinnerungen," *Berliner Börsen-Courier*, Nov. 13, 1932.

17. Felix A. Voight and Walter A. Reichart, *Hauptmann und Shakespeare* (Goslar, 1947).

18. Eugen Kilian, "Schillers Massenszenen," in *Dramaturgische Blätter* (Munich, 1914), 2:190.

19. Theodor Fontane, *Plaudereien über Theater* (Berlin, 1926), reprint of review of May 3, 1878.

20. Karl Frenzel, "Das Gastspiel der Gesellschaft des Meiningen'schen Hoftheaters," *Deutsche Rundschau*, June 11, 1878, p. 145.

21. Both quotes are on a sketch in the Meiningen Theater Museum.

22. Georg to M. Brückner, COL, Meiningen, Feb. 12, 1881.

23. Speidel, "Zweites Gastspiel in Wien," in *Schauspieler* (reprinted from his 1879 review); *Die Neue Freie Presse* (Vienna), Nov. 15, 1879.

24. Stahl, p. 458.

25. André Antoine to Francisque Sarcey (see Appendix C); Constantin Stanislavski, *My Life in Art*, tr. J. J. Robbins (Boston, 1938), pp. 196-97.

26. Josef Kainz, *Der junge Kainz* (Berlin, 1912), pp. 232-33.

27. Helen Richter, *Josef Lewinsky* (Vienna, 1926), p. 147.

28. Frenzel, "Die *Faust*-Aufführungen in Weimar, Mai 6-7, 1876," in *Berliner Dramaturgie*, 2:159-86.

29. Hans von Bülow, *Briefe* (Leipzig, 1907), 6:40. This letter is written in English.

30. Augustus Harris, manager of the Drury Lane Theatre since 1879, carried on all arrangements for the Meininger's London visit. Unfortunately, the theater's account books for 1881 are lost, so we are not at all certain what the conditions on either side called for. See Muriel St. Clare Byrne, "Charles Kean and the Meininger Myth," *Theatre Research*, 4 (1964): 143-44.

31. Sarah Bernhardt appeared in London at the same time as the Meininger. The contrast between a poor French company supporting a brilliant star and brilliant Meininger ensemble with few outstanding talents raised a controversy in the English newspapers.

32. For a full appraisal of the Meiningen company in London, see Muriel St. Clare Byrne, "What We Said About the Meiningers in 1881," *Essays and Studies* (London, 1965), pp. 45-72.

33. W. A. S. Benson, cited in J. C. Trewin, *Benson and the Bensonians* (London, 1960), p. 215.

34. Lawrence Irving, *Henry Irving, the Actor and His World* (New York, 1952), pp. 471-72. Irving, says his grandson, prepared a "confection of lyrical melodrama and infernal pageantry with none of the feelings of a conscious vandal, but with all the zest of an ambitious actor and producer, who knew he was on to a good thing." He further notes that his grandfather applied to stage effects Gounod's principle—"When literature interferes with music, it blunders." The idea that literature could interfere with staging was incomprehensible to Georg.

35. Robert Speaight, *William Poel and the Elizabethan Revival* (London, 1954), pp. 103, 218-19.

36. J. T. Grein, "The Meiningers: The Last Meet on May-day," in *Premieres of the Year* (New York, 1900), pp. 22-26.

37. There are no surviving sketches for this production.

38. Ludwig Ganghofer (1855-1920) and his Bavarian countryman, Hermann Teodor von Schmid (1815-80), may be credited with bringing the Peasant Drama into popularity. That genre, when taken over by Ludwig Anzengruber (1839-99) and brought to the north, was much admired by proponents of the naturalistic movement. (Max Martersteig, *Das deutsche Theater im neunzehnten Jahrhundert*, Leipzig, 1904, p. 649.)

39. This set is on permanent display in the restored great hall of the Meininger Theater Museum.

40. *Beilage zur Nr. 345* of the *Pester Lloyd*, Dec. 16, 1889.

41. Fontane, *Plaudereien über Theater*, p. 10.

42. Helene, Freifrau von Heldburg, *Fünfzig Jahre Glück und Leid* (Leipzig, 1926), pp. 60-61.

43. Karl Frenzel to baroness von Heldburg, Dec. 6, 1886, cited in Volker Reissland, "Herausbildung und Grundzüge der Meininger Theaterreform im letzten Drittel des 19. Jahrhunderts als Wegbereiter für Weiterentwicklung der Schauspielkunst im beginnenden 20. Jahrhundert," thesis, Karl Marx University, Leipzig, 1977, p. 93.

44. Koller, "Ibsen," pp. 101-10, describes in detail the production of *Ghosts* in Meiningen, as well as a private performance mounted by a circle of young enthusiasts and billed as a "dress rehearsal," which played on April 14, 1886, in Augsburg.

45. Richard Voss, *Aus einem phantastischen Leben* (Stuttgart, 1922), p. 178.

46. Eight years earlier, Georg had not been pleased when Bernhard wished to

marry Charlotte, daughter of Crown Prince Friedrich, since her mother, Victoria, had been one of the people most opposed to his marrying Ellen Franz. ("Georg expects so much attention to be paid to her," the crown princess had written her mother, Queen Victoria, on May 28, 1877, after Georg and the baroness visited the Prussian court, "much more than he can fairly ask.") When the officers stationed in Meiningen refused to salute a former actress, Georg appealed to the emperor, who despite the objections of the crown princess, ordered them to do so. Charlotte, if we can believe the unflattering portrait of her by her not entirely unbiased cousin Marie, queen of Rumania (*The Story of My Life*, New York, 1934, pp. 344-47), was a schemer who got what she wanted. In any case, she got around the duke, an indulgent father, and she and Bernhard were married on Feb. 18, 1878. Her mother wrote Queen Victoria: "The Duke of Meiningen has quite softened and has become very amiable, and delighted with Charlotte, who is quite taken with his goodness, while Bernhard's kind heart has quite melted towards his papa" (*Letters of the Empress Frederick*, ed. Sir Frederick Ponsonby, London, 1929, pp. 82-83). As long as the duke lived, Charlotte behaved correctly toward the baroness, but after his death, she was as indifferent to her as she was cruel to her own mother.

47. John Osborne, *The Naturalistic Drama in Germany* (Manchester, Eng., 1971), pp. 23-35.

48. On Dec. 19, 1887, the critic of the *Dresdener Nachrichten* praised the production but declared that dramas "such as *Ghosts* should be kept from our stages."

49. Although Chronegk's health was important in the breaking down of negotiations for the U.S. tour, there were other difficulties. Georg was not satisfied with the American agents, no guarantees had been advanced by the promoters, and unfavorable publicity for the company resulted from disputes about tickets. Steven DeHart, *The Meininger Theater: 1776-1926*, Ann Arbor, Mich., 1981, pp. 44-52, gives an account of the negotiations. See also Carl Niessen, "Weshalb die Meininger nicht in Amerika gastierten," *Theater der Welt. Zeitschrift für die gesamte Theaterkultur*, 1 (1937): 596-602.

50. Grube, *Story of the Meininger*, pp. 105-8, gives a full description of this production.

51. Stanislavski, *My Life in Art*, p. 198; *Dresdener Nachrichten*, Nov. 17, 1887.

52. Heldburg, *Fünfzig Jahre*, p. 61.

53. The extraordinary amount of Russian critical literature, both positive and negative, on the Meininger attests to the interest the company aroused. Unfortunately for the non-Russian reader, very little has been translated into one of the Western languages.

54. Heldburg, pp. 54-55.

55. Chronegk to Georg, July 22, 1890; cited in Reissland, "Herausbildung," p. 95.

56. Cited in Reissland, p. 98. Reissland believes that the plans for a farewell tour were dropped because no suitable theater could be found in Berlin. The ducal couple were not enthusiastic about a farewell tour.

57. Paul Richard, *Chronik sämmtlicher Gastspiele des Herzoglich Sachsen-Meiningen'schen Hoftheaters während der Jahre 1874-1890* (Leipzig, 1891).

58. Reissland, p. 97.

59. Cited in *ibid.*, p. 30.

60. Walter Lohmeyer, *Die Dramaturgie der Massen* (Berlin, 1912), p. 251.

61. "The Meiningen players developed a technique of dramatic production which included everything which was necessary to give their particular audience complete satisfaction. That audience consisted of a *bourgeoisie* which was rationalistic in spirit. They had great respect for historical and scientific authenticity." (Georg Fuchs, *Revolution in the Theatre*, tr. Constance Connor Kuhn, Ithaca, N.Y., 1959, p. 44.)

62. Stanislavski, *My Life in Art*, p. 201.

Epilogue

1. Baroness von Heldburg to Max Grube, Aug. 27, 1890, in Helene, Freifrau von Heldburg, *Fünfzig Jahre Glück und Leid* (Leipzig, 1926), p. 61.

2. There are two accounts of where these properties were sold. According to Kurt Vieweg (the Meiningen Theater librarian), "Bilder-Beilage," *Meininger Tageblatt*, Sept. 5, 1934, the sets for *Die Ahnfrau, Nathan der Weise, Othello, Hamlet, Des Meeres und die liebe Wellen,* and *Caesar and Cleopatra* stayed in Meiningen (as did the sets that were rebuilt after the fire of 1908 for *Jenseits von Gut und Böse, Makkabäer, Wilhelm Tell,* and *Hermannsschlacht*). The sets for *Maria Stuart* and *Die Jungfrau* went to the Königlisches Schauspielhaus in Berlin; those for *Julius Caesar* and (the original) *Hermannsschlacht* went to unnamed theaters in the U.S.; and the one for *Bluthochzeit* went to the Stadttheater in Strassburg.

According to a later article in the same paper ("Mit den Meiningern kreuz und quer durch Europa," *Meininger Tageblatt*, Dec. 22, 1934), the sets for *Julius Caesar* and *Die Hermannsschlacht* did indeed go to the U.S.; those for *Die Ahnfrau, Fiesko,* and *Bluthochzeit* went to Strassburg; some, including *Die Jungfrau,* went to the Schauspielhaus in Berlin; and the *Wallenstein* sets went to an unnamed theater in Weimar.

Volker Reissland states that there are no actual bills of sale to substantiate either of these accounts, but the materials in the Meiningen State Archives concerning the sales have not been thoroughly studied. In a letter to Max Grube dated Oct. 3, 1890, the baroness indicates that the Berlin Schauspielhaus was going to buy most of the sets and costumes (Heldburg, p. 62). Aloys Prasch states that in January 1891, when he was intendant at the Mannheim Stadttheater, he was invited to Meiningen to bid on sets and costumes. He considered those for *Fiesko, Bluthochzeit,* and *Die Ahnfrau,* but he does not say whether or not he bought any. ("Erinnerungen eines ehemaligen Meiningers," *Bühne und Welt,* 1, 1899, p. 696.) Recent finds in Meiningen indicate that perhaps not so much was sold as has been thought. For example, the front curtain painted by Arthur Fitger, believed sold or lost, has been discovered and is now being restored ("Der Fitgervorhang ist da!," *Meininger Schüler-Rundbrief,* 40, 1982).

3. The authorship of *Rabbi David* is uncertain, but the baroness believed it to be the work of Josef Victor Widman, a Swiss poet who died in 1911 (Heldburg, p. 63).

4. *Ibid.*, p. 49.

5. Kainz to Lindau, Nov. 8, 1897, in *Kainz, ein Brevier* (Vienna, 1953), p. 36.

Appendix B

1. Georg to von Stein, in Max Grube, *The Story of the Meininger*, tr. Ann Marie Koller (Coral Gables, Fla., 1965), pp. 16-18.

2. Pietro Ercole Visconti (1751-1818), Italian archaeologist and director of the Vatican Collection, whose sketches were used for the sets of *Julius Caesar*.

3. Here Max Grube, the source from which this letter is taken, says in parentheses: "At this point there are some remarks about the clever use of space between columns."

4. Grube, pp. 18-20.

5. Ludwig Barnay, *Erinnerungen* (Berlin, 1903), pp. 250-51.

6. Georg to M. Brückner, COL, Meiningen, Dec. 22, 1874.

7. Meiningen State Archives. Unfortunately, the promptbooks of which the baroness speaks are no longer to be found; Friedrich Heide, the former curator, made a thorough search for them in 1964.

8. Originally printed in *Die Deutsche Bühne*; cited in Grube, pp. 41-48.

Appendix C

1. Karl Frenzel wrote of this scene, which was originally in the production, that it could be "passed over as superfluous" (*Berliner Dramaturgie*, Erfurt, 1874, 2:105).

2. V. I. Nemirovich-Danchenko, *Selected Letters* (Moscow, 1954), pp. 45-48, as translated from the Russian and edited by Dieter Hoffmeier, "Die Meininger—Historismus als Tageswirkung," *Material zum Theater*, 54.16 (1974): 40-42.

3. Jules Claretie, "Les Meiningers et leur mise en scène," *Le Temps*, July 13, 1888.

4. Translation of letter as published in *Le Temps* from Samuel Montefiore Waxman, *Antoine and the Théâtre Libre* (Cambridge, Mass., 1926), pp. 95-96.

INDEX

INDEX